DATE DUE

DEC 20 '10	
DEC 27 '10	
DEC 29 '10	
JAN 28 2011	
MAR 18 2011	
APR 02 2011	
AUG 5 2011	
SEP 8 2011	
SEP 26 2011	
MAR 06 2012	
OCT 30 2012	
AUG 11 2016	

BRODART, CO.   Cat. No. 23-221

EATING LOCAL

EATING LOCAL

The Cookbook Inspired by America's Farmers

SUR LA TABLE

with Janet Fletcher

Foreword by
ALICE WATERS

Photography by
SARA REMINGTON

Andrews McMeel
Publishing, LLC
Kansas City • Sydney • London

10 11 12 13 14 SDB 10 9 8 7 6 5 4 3 2 1

ISBN-13: 978-0-7407-9144-4
ISBN-10: 0-7407-9144-3

Library of Congress Control Number:
2009942964

Photography: Sara Remington
Design: Jennifer Barry Design, Fairfax, CA
Production Assistance: Kristen Hall
Food Stylist: Kim Kissling
Assistant Food Stylist: Sarah Fairhurst
Prop Stylist: Kerrie Sherrell Walsh
Assistant Prop Stylist: Lori Engels

www.andrewsmcmeel.com
www.surlatable.com

Mixed Sources
Product group from well-managed
forests, controlled sources and
recycled wood or fiber
www.fsc.org Cert no. SCS-COC-000648
© 1996 Forest Stewardship Council
FSC

*To America's hardworking farmers,
who make eating locally possible.*

CONTENTS

FOREWORD by Alice Waters

It is almost forty years since we opened the doors of our restaurant, Chez Panisse. After returning from studying abroad in France I dreamt of re-creating the kinds of restaurants I had so enjoyed there. Simple, beautiful places, where all would feel welcome, a place that would not only serve perfect, flavorful food but be connected with its community. Chez Panisse has always had this mission at its heart and we continue to strive daily for that on Shattuck Avenue in Berkeley.

It has always been my belief that delicious food is a powerful way to inspire people, to bind them and to build community. When we first opened, we found it was nearly impossible to find produce that was truly flavorful. We set about finding producers who were growing quality, diverse fruits and vegetables. Fishermen and foragers that were capturing the peaks of the season and ranchers that let their animals happily roam. As we unearthed more and more local producers to supply the restaurant, they in turn became a crucial part of the Chez Panisse community. With our daily menu we celebrate their work, creating dishes where the ripest, freshest, plumpest produce is always the hero.

In the beginning this idea was radical. It is now with great pleasure that I see people all over the country rediscovering real food by shopping in farmers' markets, belonging to a CSA, or being involved in the establishment of school gardens. Real food is good for the environment, supports local economies, nourishes our communities, and, quite simply, tastes delicious.

Sur La Table's *Eating Local* cookbook celebrates real food and beautifully demonstrates the relationship between a producer's raw materials and the cook's kitchen. Janet Fletcher, formerly of Chez Panisse, has written a collection of recipes that is simple, approachable, and, crucially, lets the ingredients speak for themselves.

Introduction

In home kitchens across the country, cooks are making a change you can taste. Parents concerned about what they are feeding their children, young people with a sustainability bent, and others who simply prize freshness are seeking out foods that are locally grown. In communities from Portland, Oregon, to Portland, Maine, diners are sitting down to meals made with ingredients that did not travel far: maybe chops from pigs pasture-raised on a nearby farm, green beans picked the day before, or applesauce prepared with fruit from a neighboring county.

The locavore movement has taken root in America and is destined to spread, nurtured by farmers' markets—which have doubled in number in a dozen years to an estimated forty-eight hundred—and a boom in community-supported agriculture, or CSA.

No phenomenon better demonstrates the nation's appetite for local food than the astonishing growth of CSA. A farm that participates in CSA grows some or all of its produce for "shareholders," people who pay up front (usually in spring) for a portion of the farm's future harvest. On most CSA farms, shareholders—some farms call them members or subscribers—participate in both the booms and the busts. If the farm has a banner melon harvest, shareholders reap the bounty; if a virus devastates the tomatoes, shareholders may get none. On other farms, CSA members receive only a part of the harvest, with the remainder sold at farmers' markets or to wholesalers.

The benefits accrue to both sides—a win for all. Farmers receive cash in time to help pay for operations, and they share the risk of crop failure with members. Shareholders receive produce—and sometimes eggs, pork, chicken, lamb, or rabbit—that couldn't be fresher unless they grew it themselves. Many CSA farms host preserving workshops, volunteer workdays, or harvest parties with

instructions to take, perhaps, one bunch of beets, one pound of fingerling potatoes, two pounds of tomatoes, and all the basil they want.

For proof that the CSA movement has hit its stride, just look at the history. The first two community-supported farms debuted in the United States in the mid-1980s, inspired by the ideas of Rudolf Steiner, the Austrian philosopher credited with articulating the principles of biodynamic agriculture. Both of these pioneering farms—Indian Line Farm in Massachusetts and Temple-Wilton Community Farm in New Hampshire—are still in business, and their example has spawned hundreds more. Although no government agency keeps an official count, Local Harvest, an online resource that maintains a directory of CSA farms, had more than twenty-five hundred

kids' activities so that urban youngsters can learn about life on the farm and shareholders can feel like family.

Typically, members receive a share once a week, fetching it at an urban drop site or sometimes at the farm itself. Red Fire Farm, in western Massachusetts, sends a truck to Boston several times a week to accommodate its large CSA membership there. Gigi Nauer of Nitty Gritty Dirt Farm drops shareholder boxes at the music studio near Minneapolis where she teaches and at the church where her partner, Robin, preaches. Many farms pack each share separately in a box or bag, but some, like Green Gate Farms in Austin and Dancing Roots Farm near Portland, Oregon, display the week's harvest farm-stand style and members help themselves, following

farms in its database in 2009. That's up from sixty in 1990 and a 50 percent increase from 2004.

The ten CSA farms profiled in this book are a representative cross section of the movement. They operate in states from Oregon to Massachusetts. They are as small as Green Gate Farms, with its seventy-five shareholders, and as large as Northern California's Full Belly Farm, a two hundred–acre enterprise with fifteen hundred CSA members. They reflect the diversity of what America grows, from avocados, kumquats, and macadamia nuts (Southern California's Morning Song Farm) to cider apples (Red Fire Farm) and quinoa greens (Dancing Roots Farm). Some of them, like Nitty Gritty Dirt Farm, raise livestock, too, and offer meat or egg shares to CSA members; others, like Amy's Garden, near

Richmond, Virginia, are locally famous for cut flowers. Most are family farms, but one, the nonprofit DeLaney Community Farm, on the outskirts of Denver, provides a stirring example of community service.

Thanks in part to the dependable revenue from CSA, these farmers have a business model that works. Many rely on interns for some or all of their labor needs—not to save money, as you might think, but because they believe in mentoring the next generation. One hopeful sign for the future of America's small farms is the number of young people vying for these modestly paid positions. Most farms turn away many applicants.

If you join a CSA, embrace the experience with a spirit of adventure. The week's share may include produce that you have never cooked before, or even

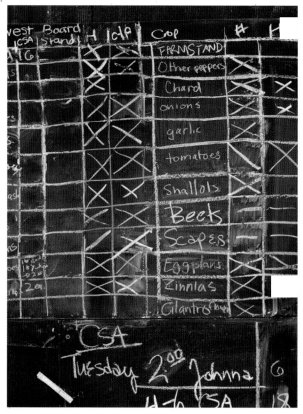

items that you thought you didn't like. And when the kale harvest is in, you may receive enough for three meals that week. Learning to prepare produce in multiple ways—to use that kale in risotto, a soup, and a stir-fry—will enable you to eat locally and seasonally with great satisfaction.

The mission of this book is to encourage you to celebrate the food grown in your community. If you don't have a CSA option, or aren't comfortable with the subscription concept, then shop at a farmers' market. Your support will help preserve family farms and farmland, especially on the urban edge where development pressure is highest. In return, you will enjoy ingredients that are fresher, more nutritious, more varied, better tasting, and often grown more sustainably than most supermarket produce.

HOW TO USE THIS BOOK

To be most useful to readers who shop at farmers' markets or subscribe to a CSA, the recipes in *Eating Local* are organized not by type (soup, salad, dessert) but by the dominant ingredient. Thus, if your CSA box contains a lot of beets one week, you can easily find recipes that use them. A separate chapter, Poultry, Meat, and Eggs, addresses the needs of readers who may lack ideas for using the pasture-raised pork or farm eggs they are buying locally.

Of course, many of these recipes contain more than one fruit or vegetable, necessitating a decision about appropriate placement. Should a peach and rhubarb crisp reside under "Peaches" or under "Rhubarb"? To make sure you don't overlook a recipe, turn to the indexes in the back. The Recipe Index by Category will help you find all the soups or salads. The main Recipe Index will guide you to all the recipes using rhubarb, fennel, or pork.

For readers who want to take localism a step further and grow or raise food at home, the final chapter on urban homesteading offers numerous resources. Even apartment dwellers can participate in the rhythms of the growing season by cultivating chives, tarragon, and lettuces on a deck or windowsill. The chapter also provides leads for the more ambitious locavore who wants to plant a vegetable garden, keep bees, or raise chickens.

A Note About Language

Although CSA stands for community-supported agriculture, the acronym has come to be used as a shorthand for the farm subscription program that characterizes the movement. So it's common to hear people say, "I belong to a CSA" or "I get a CSA box"—not strictly grammatical, but their meaning is clear. In keeping with common usage, this book utilizes CSA in the multiple ways that supporters of the movement do.

Technique Notes

The following techniques are used repeatedly in the recipes.

Toasting walnuts and pecans: Preheat the oven to 350°F. Spread the walnuts on a baking sheet and toast until fragrant and lightly colored, about 10 minutes. Let cool.

Toasting pine nuts: Preheat the oven to 325°F. Spread the pine nuts on a baking sheet and toast until fragrant and lightly colored, 8 to 10 minutes. Let cool.

Toasting almonds: Preheat the oven to 350°F. Spread the almonds on a baking sheet and toast until fragrant and golden brown inside, about 8 minutes for sliced almonds, 12 to 15 minutes for whole almonds. (Break one open to check.) Let cool.

Toasting cumin seed: Put the whole cumin seed in a small, dry skillet over moderate heat. Cook, swirling the pan frequently, until the cumin begins to darken and the toasty fragrance becomes apparent. Let cool.

Grating plum (Roma type) tomatoes: Cut the tomatoes in half lengthwise. Discard the seeds if the recipe directs. Grate the tomato flesh on the coarse holes of a box grater until only the tomato skin remains in your hand. Discard the skin.

Preparing a grill for indirect grilling: Some foods, especially those that cook quickly, can be grilled directly over a bed of charcoal or a gas flame. Other foods, such as fatty meats that might cause flare-ups or dense vegetables like carrots, cook better when grilled more slowly, by indirect heat—that is, not directly over the charcoal or flame. And some recipes call for both approaches—perhaps an initial searing or final crisping directly over the coals or flame, but with the rest of the cooking over indirect heat.

When a recipe calls for indirect grilling, or a combination of direct and indirect methods, prepare an area on the grill rack that is not directly over the heat source. With a charcoal grill, you can bank the coals under one-half of the grill rack, or make a ring of coals with bare space in the center. With a gas grill, you can light only one or two of the burners, leaving one burner unlit.

VEGETABLES

One of the benefits of joining a CSA or shopping at a farmers' market is access to produce that conventional supermarkets don't sell. Even CSA farmers who grow only "the basics"—broccoli, carrots, cauliflower, spinach—can choose varieties for their flavor, not their shippability, uniformity, or shelf life. But many growers who sell via farmers' markets or CSAs take advantage of their direct relationship with customers to grow more unusual crops, such as golden beets, Tuscan kale, or lemon cucumbers. Thanks to these farmers, adventurous eaters are encountering new tastes with every season and expanding their vegetable universe. In the pages that follow, you will find fresh ideas for familiar vegetables— grilled "steaks" made from cauliflower (page 59), carrot soup scented with lemongrass (page 57), grilled romaine lettuce (page 100)—as well as recipes for vegetables you may not have cooked often before. If you have hesitated to purchase kohlrabi, parsnips, Jerusalem artichokes, or broccoli rabe, you will find all the inspiration you need in this chapter.

Stuffed Artichokes with Pine Nuts and Currants

Serves 4

With their leaves spread to embrace the filling, these hefty artichokes resemble pompom chrysanthemums—a reminder that they are in fact flower buds. Stuffed with garlicky focaccia crumbs, a single one makes a satisfying lunch.

Ingredients

3 tablespoons dried currants

½ cup hot water

2 lemons

4 large artichokes

4 cups plain focaccia crumbs, from about ½ pound day-old focaccia

½ cup freshly grated pecorino cheese

2 tablespoons minced fresh Italian parsley

1 tablespoon dried oregano

1 large plum (Roma type) tomato, grated (page xiv)

2 cloves garlic, minced

¼ cup extra virgin olive oil

¼ cup pine nuts, toasted (page xiv)

Scant 1 teaspoon kosher or sea salt

Freshly ground black pepper

1 Put the currants in a small bowl, add the hot water, and let soften for 20 minutes. Drain.

2 Preheat the oven to 375°F. Fill a large bowl with cold water and add the juice of 1 lemon. Cut the other lemon in half.

3 Working with 1 artichoke at a time, cut off the stem flush with the base. Rub the base with a lemon half to prevent browning. With a serrated knife, slice off the top 1 inch of the artichoke; rub the exposed surface with lemon. With scissors, snip off the pointed tips of the remaining leaves. With your fingers, carefully pry open the center of the artichoke to reveal the pale, prickly inner leaves and fuzzy choke, taking care not to break any leaves. Pull out the innermost prickly leaves, then use a small spoon or melon baller to scrape the hairy choke from the artichoke bottom. Squeeze some lemon juice into the cavity, and drop the trimmed artichoke into the lemon water. If necessary, invert a plate over the artichoke to keep it submerged. Repeat with the remaining 3 artichokes.

4 In a large bowl, combine the focaccia crumbs, cheese, parsley, and dried oregano, crumbling the dried herb between your fingers. Add the tomato, garlic, olive oil, pine nuts, currants, salt, and several grinds of pepper. Mix well with your hands. Measure the volume of the filling so that you can put one-quarter of the volume in each artichoke.

5 Remove the artichokes from the lemon water and invert on paper towels briefly to drain excess water. With your fingers, fill the center cavities with some of the stuffing, then tuck more stuffing between the leaves. The inner leaves are too close together to separate without breaking them, but pack stuffing between leaves where you can.

6 Set a rack inside a deep baking dish large enough to hold the artichokes. Stand the artichokes upright on the rack, then add boiling water to a depth of ½ inch to the dish. Cover the artichokes with a sheet of parchment paper, then cover the baking dish tightly with a lid or aluminum foil.

7 Bake until you can pull a leaf out easily, 1 to 1¼ hours. Taste the leaf and make sure the base is tender. Let cool for at least 20 minutes before serving. The artichokes are best when warm, not hot.

Sicilian Spring Vegetable Stew

Serves 4

In Sicily, this well-cooked braise of artichokes, fava beans, and peas is sometimes used as a pasta sauce. Consider making a double batch so you have enough to toss with spaghetti the following day.

Ingredients

1 lemon, halved

16 to 20 baby artichokes, about 1½ ounces each

¼ cup extra virgin olive oil

1 small yellow onion or spring onion, minced

4 cloves garlic, minced

¼ teaspoon hot red pepper flakes

Kosher or sea salt and freshly ground black pepper

1½ cups water

2 pounds fresh fava beans, shelled (to yield about 2 cups shelled, unpeeled beans)

1 pound English peas, shelled

¼ cup chopped fresh basil

1 Fill a large bowl with cold water and add the juice of ½ lemon. Working with 1 artichoke at a time, peel back the tough outer leaves until they break at the base. Keep removing leaves until you reach the paler yellow-green inner leaves, which are more tender. Cut across the top of this artichoke "heart" to remove the sharp leaf tips. If the stem is still attached, trim it down to ½ inch, then pare the stem and base with a small knife, removing any dark green or brown parts. Cut each heart lengthwise into 6 wedges and place immediately in the lemon water to prevent browning. Repeat with the remaining artichokes.

2 Heat the olive oil in a large skillet over moderately low heat. Add the onion and sauté until softened, about 10 minutes. Add the garlic and hot pepper flakes and sauté for about 1 minute to release the garlic fragrance. Drain the artichokes and add them to the skillet. Season with salt and pepper and add 1 cup of the water. Bring to a simmer, cover, and adjust the heat to maintain a gentle simmer. Cook for 10 minutes, then add the fava beans, the peas, and the remaining ½ cup water. Re-cover and simmer until all the vegetables are tender, about 10 minutes. Add a little more water if needed to keep the mixture from cooking dry.

3 Stir in the basil and season with salt and pepper. Remove from the heat. Let rest for about 15 minutes before serving to allow the flavors to meld. Serve warm, not hot.

GRILLED PIZZA WITH MOZZARELLA, ARUGULA, AND CHILE OIL

Makes 1 pizza; serves 2 to 4

Wispy leaves of young arugula are used like an herb in this recipe, sprinkled on the sizzling pizza just as it comes off the grill. Note the long, slow rise on the dough—a total of six hours—which produces a particularly light, chewy, and flavorful crust.

INGREDIENTS

DOUGH

¾ cup warm (105° to 115°F) water

1½ teaspoons active dry yeast

1 tablespoon olive oil, plus more for the bowl

1 teaspoon kosher or sea salt

About 1¾ cups unbleached all-purpose flour

CHILE OIL

2 tablespoons extra virgin olive oil

1 large clove garlic, finely minced

¼ teaspoon hot red pepper flakes

Pinch of kosher or sea salt

½ teaspoon dried oregano

Cornmeal, for dusting the pizza peel

½ pound low-moisture whole-milk mozzarella
  cheese, grated on the large holes of a box grater

Large handful of baby arugula

1 To make the dough, put the warm water in a bowl and sprinkle the surface with the yeast. Let stand for 2 minutes to soften, then whisk with a fork to blend. Let stand until bubbly, about 10 minutes. Whisk in the olive oil and salt, then begin adding 1½ cups of the flour gradually, beating with a wooden spoon until fully incorporated. The dough will be very moist and sticky.

2 Turn the dough out on a lightly floured work surface and knead with floured hands until smooth and elastic, about 5 minutes, incorporating as much of the remaining ¼ cup flour as needed to keep the dough from clinging to your hands or the work surface. The dough will remain moist and a little tacky but should not be sticky. Shape into a ball. Oil a bowl, transfer the dough to it, and turn the dough to coat it with oil. Cover the bowl with plastic wrap and let the dough rise at room temperature for 2 hours.

3 Punch the dough down. Reshape into a ball, re-cover the bowl, and let the dough rise again for 4 hours.

4 If using a charcoal grill, prepare a moderate fire. When the coals are ready, arrange them in an even layer on one-half of the grill bed.

5 If using a gas grill, preheat all burners to high. About 15 minutes before grilling, put a baking stone on the grill rack. The internal temperature of the grill should be 575° to 600°F.

6 Punch the dough down, turn it out onto a lightly floured work surface, and shape into a ball. Dust the surface of the dough with flour, cover with a dish towel, and let rest for 30 minutes.

continued next page

GRILLED PIZZA WITH MOZZARELLA, ARUGULA, AND CHILE OIL **continued**

7 To make the chile oil, in a small bowl, whisk together the olive oil, garlic, hot pepper flakes, and salt. Add the oregano, crumbling it between your fingers as you do, and whisk again. Let stand for 30 minutes to blend the flavors.

8 If you are using a round kettle grill with charcoal, you will need to shape the dough into a rectangle so that you can cook the crust first directly over the bed of coals, then flip it and finish cooking it over indirect heat. If you are using a gas grill with a baking stone, you can shape the dough into a circle because you will not need to flip it.

9 Dust a pizza peel or rimless baking sheet generously with cornmeal. To prepare the dough for topping, you can stretch it with a rolling pin or your hands. Lightly flour a work surface. To use a pin, roll out the dough on the floured surface into a 13- to 14-inch circle or into a roughly 16- by 10-inch rectangle, depending on your grill. Transfer to the prepared peel. To work by hand, flatten the dough into a round, then drape the round over the back of your two flour-dusted hands. Form your hands into fists and rotate the dough on your fists. The dough is supple enough that it will stretch with little effort on your part. Stretch into a 13- to 14-inch circle or into a roughly 16- by 10-inch rectangle, depending on your grill. Transfer to the prepared pizza peel.

10 **If you are grilling the pizza over charcoal**, slide the dough off onto the grill rack, directly over the coals. Cook uncovered until the dough begins to puff and blister and the bottom becomes nicely browned or even lightly charred in spots, 1 to 2 minutes. With tongs or your hands, flip the dough over onto the half of the grill with no coals. Working quickly, top with the cheese, spreading it evenly but leaving a ¾-inch rim uncovered. Brush the rim with the chile oil, then drizzle more of the oil, including the garlic and herbs, over the pizza, reserving a little oil for brushing the pizza rim after grilling. Cover the grill and cook until the pizza rim is well browned and the cheese is melted and

bubbling, about 5 minutes. Transfer the pizza to a cutting board, scatter the arugula over the cheese, and brush the rim with the remaining chile oil. Cut into wedges and serve immediately.

If you are grilling the pizza in a gas grill on a preheated baking stone, top the round of dough with the cheese, spreading it evenly but leaving a ¾-inch rim uncovered. Work quickly so the dough does not stick to the peel. Brush the rim with the chile oil, then drizzle more of the oil, including the garlic and herbs, over the pizza, reserving a little oil for brushing the pizza rim after grilling. Raising the lid of the grill as little as possible to avoid loss of heat, slide the pizza onto the baking stone and quickly close the grill. Cook until the crust smells well browned, even a little charred, 5 to 6 minutes; resist the urge to open the grill beforehand or you will release too much heat. Transfer the pizza to a cutting board, scatter the arugula over the cheese, and brush the rim with the remaining chile oil. Cut into wedges and serve immediately.

SPAGHETTI WITH ARUGULA, TUNA, AND TOMATO

Serves 4 to 6

When farmers are growing for local customers, they can plant the super-flavorful, thin-skinned cherry tomatoes that don't stand up to long shipping, varieties like Sun Gold and Sweet 100. When you have more of these little gems than you can eat out of hand, use them in this ten-minute pasta sauce.

INGREDIENTS

1 (7-ounce) can olive oil–packed tuna, drained
6 tablespoons extra virgin olive oil
4 cloves garlic, minced
1 small fresh red chile, thinly sliced (remove seeds for less heat), or large pinch of hot red pepper flakes
1 pound cherry tomatoes, halved
Kosher or sea salt
1 pound spaghetti
¾ pound arugula, thick stems removed

1 Bring a large pot of salted water to a boil over high heat. Put the tuna in a bowl and break it up with a fork until finely shredded.

2 Heat the olive oil in a large skillet over moderate heat. Add the garlic and chile and sauté until the garlic is fragrant and beginning to color, about 1 minute. Add the cherry tomatoes and season with salt. Cook, stirring, until the cherry tomatoes begin to soften and release their juices; do not let them fully collapse.

3 Add the tuna to the skillet and stir to coat with the seasonings. Reduce the heat to low.

4 Add the spaghetti to the boiling water and cook, stirring often with tongs, until al dente. Set aside 1 cup of the boiling water, then drain the pasta in a sieve or colander and return it to the hot pot over moderate heat. Add the contents of the skillet and the arugula and, using tongs, toss the pasta with the sauce just until the arugula wilts, adding some of the reserved hot water as needed to moisten the pasta. Serve immediately.

GRILLED ASPARAGUS WITH CITRUS OIL

Serves 3 as a first course, or 4 as a side dish

Many specialty stores and well-stocked supermarkets now carry aromatic oils made by pressing olives together with lemons, blood oranges, limes, or other citrus. Just a drizzle of one of these highly perfumed oils can make grilled vegetables seem dressed up for company. Serve as a first course or an accompaniment to fish, roast chicken, or a steak.

INGREDIENTS

1 pound asparagus

2 teaspoons extra virgin olive oil

Kosher or sea salt

1 tablespoon citrus oil (see introduction), such as
  Meyer lemon or blood orange oil

1 Prepare a moderate charcoal fire for indirect grilling (page xiv) or preheat a gas grill to medium (375°F), leaving one burner unlit.

2 To trim the asparagus, hold each spear horizontally between both hands and bend it. It will snap naturally at the point at which the spear becomes tough. Discard the tough end.

3 Put the trimmed asparagus spears on a platter and toss with the olive oil, which should just coat them lightly. Sprinkle with salt and toss again.

4 Place the spears over indirect heat, taking care to place them perpendicular to the bars of the grill rack so they do not fall through. Cover the grill and cook, turning the spears once halfway through, until almost tender, 4 to 5 minutes total. For the final minute or so of cooking, move the spears directly over the coals or gas flame and cook uncovered to char them slightly.

5 Transfer the spears to a serving platter and drizzle with the citrus oil. Toss to coat them evenly. Taste for salt. Serve immediately.

ASPARAGUS WITH A FRIED FARM EGG AND TRUFFLE SALT

Serves 2

Asparagus and eggs are a compatible duo that can meet in many ways: scrambled eggs with asparagus tips, an asparagus omelet or frittata, or grilled asparagus with a soft-boiled egg. In this variation on the theme, the asparagus are boiled—steam them if you prefer—then topped with a fried farm egg "over easy" and a sprinkle of aromatic truffle salt. The runny yolk creates an instant sauce, and the truffle salt makes the dish restaurant caliber. Provide bread for sponging up the buttery puddles.

INGREDIENTS

1½ pounds asparagus of any thickness
2 large eggs
2 tablespoons unsalted butter
Black truffle salt (see Note) or fleur de sel
Freshly ground black pepper

1 To trim the asparagus, hold each spear horizontally between both hands and bend it. It will snap naturally at the point at which the spear becomes tough. Discard the tough end.

2 Crack each egg into a small custard cup or bowl.

3 Bring a large pot of salted water to a boil over high heat. Add the asparagus and boil until crisp-tender, about 3 minutes for medium asparagus. Lift the spears out with tongs and drain on a double thickness of paper towels or on a kitchen towel. Working quickly so the spears stay hot, pat them thoroughly dry and divide them between 2 salad plates. Put 1 teaspoon of butter on each portion and toss with your hands until the butter melts and glosses the spears. Season with truffle salt.

4 Heat a large nonstick skillet over moderate heat. Add the remaining 4 teaspoons butter and swirl to coat the skillet as it melts. When it begins to sizzle and foam, carefully slide the eggs, one at a time, into the skillet, and reduce the heat to moderately low. Cook until the whites are set but the yolks remain runny, about 2 minutes. Adjust the heat so the butter browns lightly but does not burn.

5 With a nonstick offset spatula (pancake turner), flip the eggs over, browned side up, onto the asparagus. Spoon any butter from the skillet over the eggs. Season the eggs with truffle salt and several grinds of pepper. Serve immediately.

NOTE: Black truffle salt is available from some fine-food stores, online merchants, and specialty cookware shops.

Avocado, Frisée, and Fennel Salad

Serves 6

Avocado's smooth, buttery texture plays well against crisp salad elements like frisée and crunchy fennel. That trio makes an inviting winter salad that you can serve as a course on its own or as an accompaniment to a roast chicken, grilled fish, or lamb chops. Navel orange or grapefruit segments would be an appealing addition.

INGREDIENTS

DRESSING

¼ cup extra virgin olive oil, or more if needed

2 tablespoons fresh lemon juice, or more if needed

1 tablespoon plus 1 teaspoon capers, preferably salt packed, rinsed and finely minced

1 teaspoon fish sauce (see Note)

1 large shallot, finely minced

Kosher or sea salt and freshly ground black pepper

2 small heads frisée (about 2 quarts trimmed greens)

1 fennel bulb, halved lengthwise, very thinly sliced crosswise

⅓ cup minced fresh Italian parsley

1 large, ripe but firm avocado

1 To make the dressing, in a small bowl, whisk together the olive oil, lemon juice, capers, fish sauce, and shallot. Season with salt and pepper and adjust the oil-lemon balance to your taste.

2 Tear the frisée into bite-size pieces and put in a salad bowl. Add the fennel and parsley and toss to mix. Add enough of the dressing to coat the greens lightly; you may not need it all.

3 Cut the avocado in half lengthwise and remove the pit. With a large spoon, scoop out the avocado halves from their skin, and put them, cut side down, on a cutting board. Slice thinly crosswise.

4 Add the avocado slices to the salad bowl and toss gently so as not to break them up. Add a little more dressing if necessary. Taste, adjust the seasoning, and serve immediately.

NOTE: Fish sauce is a clear, amber liquid made from salted and fermented anchovies or other small fish. In Vietnamese and Thai cooking, it is almost as ubiquitous as salt. Used with restraint, it adds depth and a highly savory note to many Western dishes, such as salad dressings. The widely available Three Crabs brand is excellent.

Troutdale, Oregon

DANCING ROOTS FARM

The ten-acre parcel that Shari Sirkin and Bryan Dickerson purchased in 2002 might not have looked to others like a wise investment. The wild blackberries were taller than they were, and the ninety-year-old farmhouse was uninhabitable. "Ohmigod," thought Shari, surveying the long-neglected residence after the sale went through. "This is where we live."

But the site had a few promising features: a scenic setting in Troutdale, Oregon, at the gateway to the Columbia River Gorge; a history as a farm; and an enthusiastic, eco-conscious audience for local food in Portland, eighteen miles to the west. Convinced that crops would respond happily to the attention they planned to give this unkempt property, they christened their plot Dancing Roots Farm—a moniker that also alluded to Bryan's career as a saxophonist and former member of the Glenn Miller Orchestra.

Yet it was Shari who wanted to farm. After years of trying and rejecting careers—as a legislative aide, a school teacher, a community organizer, and, ironically, a career coach—Shari had finally found work that engaged her.

Running a CSA farm met all her criteria: for an outdoor job that was physically vigorous and cause oriented, and that presented opportunities to teach.

"I wanted to be *for* something," says Shari. "This farm is our activism."

With Bryan in charge of infrastructure—farm machinery, irrigation, outbuildings, and purchasing—Shari oversees the crew. She decides what to plant, when, and where; and when to harvest. She is the farm's trend spotter, the one who sits down with Portland chefs in the winter to learn what up-and-coming produce they would like her to grow—puntarelle? quinoa greens? anisse hyssop? And she is typically the one who accompanies the CSA produce to the Portland drop-off, staying until the last of 120-plus shareholders shows.

Those 2½ hours at the pickup site—a shareholder's garage in Northwest Portland—provide the week's sweetest moments. Parents arrive clutching the hands of toddlers, who call out to "Farmer Shari." She knows their names, too, especially the ones she refers to as "Dancing Roots babies"

because they have grown up on her produce. As members line up to weigh their allotted tomatoes and potatoes, Shari works the queue, offering samples of fresh coriander seed, handing out Bryan's recipe for yellow Romano beans, and beaming when a customer thanks her for the "yummy stuff" in the share.

Some of these members come to the farm for its monthly work parties, to help beat back the blackberries or plant garlic, and to expose their youngsters to rural life. Others get introduced to Dancing Roots at the annual Plate & Pitchfork dinners, al fresco events designed to raise awareness of small Portland-area farms. Shari and Bryan use the occasion to appeal for donations to their scholarship fund, which enables them to offer reduced-price shares to the needy.

On harvest days, Shari patrols the farm with a two-way radio and a tiny spiral

At a Glance

Favorite crops: Purple Peacock broccoli, Little Gem lettuce, Sylvetta arugula, Diva cucumber, Collective Farm Woman melon, Gold of Bacau pole bean. "I'm a sucker for catalog descriptions, I admit it," says Shari. "They make it sound like you can't live without it."

Inspiration: Oregon plant breeder Frank Morton of Wild Garden Seed, breeder of Purple Peacock broccoli and other gems.

Passionate about: Mentoring. The farm always has an apprentice, and Shari and Bryan take their training roles seriously. "We like to think that in addition to growing vegetables, we're growing farmers," says Shari.

Insight: "Your trials are only as good as your records," says Nellie McAdams, a farm apprentice. Shari keeps detailed records of the many varieties she tries—planting dates, watering, harvest dates, yields—to know what's worth planting again.

Strictly local: Shari turns away potential CSA members who live too far from the drop site or the farm, where they can also pick up. "I think our vegetables are golden but not worth driving 25 minutes in traffic for," says the farmer. "It defeats the purpose."

notebook, where she has recorded the day's critical numbers: how many pounds of eggplant, basil, melons, and salad greens her crew needs to cut for the afternoon delivery. All day long, just-picked cucumbers, lettuces, peppers, chard, and zucchini arrive at the small hilltop packing shed—known affectionately as the barnita—to be rinsed of their field dirt in a giant bathtub and packed in recycled cardboard boxes.

Using compost, cover crops, and other organic farming techniques, Shari and Bryan say they have noticeably improved the soil on this long-fallow farm. Yet they have never sought organic certification. It takes money and time, says Shari, who claims that her own practices are even more rigorous than organic code requires. Why should she give shareholder money to a third party to certify her farm when she has a personal relationship with customers?

"People tell us that they thank us at their evening grace," says Shari. "How can I not keep doing this? To me, it's one of the highest compliments when people introduce me and say, 'This is my farmer.'"

PICKLED YELLOW WAX BEANS WITH FRESH DILL

Makes 1 quart

Winters are long in Minnesota, making a well-stocked pantry all the more valuable. At the Nitty Gritty Dirt Farm in the tiny Minnesota town of Harris, Robin Raudabaugh transforms her slender yellow wax beans into what old-timers call "dilly beans," pickling them with garlic, red chile, and clusters of flowering dill. The neatly packed jars are stockpiled in a crawl space under the house until time works its magic, mellowing the vinegary brine. The crisp beans, served with a sandwich, bring memories of summer to a winter lunch.

INGREDIENTS

1 pound yellow wax beans, as straight as possible

1 cluster fresh dill flower heads

1 large clove garlic, halved lengthwise

1 small dried red chile

1½ cups white wine vinegar

1½ cups water

1 tablespoon kosher or sea salt

1 Fill a canning kettle with enough water to cover the top of a widemouthed quart canning jar resting on the preserving rack. Bring to a boil over high heat. Wash the jar with hot, soapy water; rinse well, and keep upside down on a clean dish towel until you are ready to fill it. Put a new lid (never reuse lids) in a heatproof bowl and cover with boiling water.

2 Remove the tips of the beans and, if necessary, trim the beans so they will fit upright in the jar. Fill the jar with the beans, dill, garlic, and chile, packing the beans in tightly but neatly.

3 Put the vinegar, water, and salt in a small saucepan and bring just to a boil, stirring to dissolve the salt. Remove from the heat and ladle the hot liquid into the jar, leaving ½ inch of headspace. Wipe the jar rim clean with a damp paper towel. Top with the lid and then a screw band. Close tightly.

4 Place the jar on the preserving rack and lower the rack into the canning kettle. If the water doesn't cover the jar, add boiling water from a tea kettle. Cover the canning kettle. After the water returns to a boil, boil for 10 minutes. With a jar lifter, transfer the jar to a rack to cool completely. Do not touch the jar again until you hear the pop that indicates that the lid has sealed. You can confirm that the lid has sealed by pressing the center with your finger. If it gives, it has not sealed and the contents should be refrigerated and used within a week. Store the sealed jar in a cool, dark place for at least 1 month before using. It will keep for up to 1 year. Refrigerate after opening.

WARM SHELLING BEAN SALAD WITH GRILLED SHRIMP

Serves 6

Farmers routinely say that shelling beans are among the most underappreciated crops they grow. That's surely because they must be shelled before cooking, and many people won't take the time. But if you can engage a friend or child to help you, the beans will be shelled before you know it. Even solo cooks can enjoy the mental downtime that such mindless kitchen tasks demand. The result—a warm and herbaceous bean salad topped with lemony grilled shrimp—will make you eager to tackle shelling beans again.

INGREDIENTS

2 pounds fresh cranberry beans, cannellini beans, black-eyed peas, crowder peas, or other shelling beans

½ yellow onion

3 cloves garlic, halved lengthwise, plus 1 large clove, finely minced

4 thyme sprigs

1½ quarts water

Kosher or sea salt and freshly ground black pepper

4 tablespoons extra virgin olive oil, plus more for drizzling

½ large red onion, halved again through the stem end, then very thinly sliced

¼ cup minced fresh Italian parsley

12 fresh basil leaves, torn into smaller pieces

2 innermost celery ribs, thinly sliced

1½ cups halved cherry tomatoes, preferably red and gold types

Red wine vinegar

18 large shrimp (about ¾ pound total), peeled and deveined

1 lemon

1 Remove the beans from their pods; you should have 3 to 3½ cups. Put them in a saucepan with the yellow onion half, garlic halves, thyme sprigs, and water. Bring to a simmer over moderate heat, then cover partially and adjust the heat to maintain a gentle simmer. Cook until the beans are tender, 30 minutes to 1 hour, depending on their maturity. Season with salt and let cool in the liquid. The beans will be even tastier if prepared to this point 1 day ahead and refrigerated in their cooking liquid.

2 Prepare a hot charcoal fire or preheat a gas grill to high (450° to 500°F).

3 Remove the onion, garlic, and thyme sprigs from the beans. Reheat the beans gently, just until they are warm. Drain them (reserve the cooking liquid for soup, if desired), and transfer them to a bowl. Add 3 tablespoons of the olive oil, the red onion, minced garlic, parsley, basil, and celery. Toss well. Add the cherry tomatoes and toss again gently. Season to taste with salt, black pepper, and a splash of wine vinegar.

4 Toss the shrimp with the remaining 1 tablespoon olive oil and season with salt. Grill directly over the coals or gas flame, turning once, until cooked through, about 2 minutes per side. Transfer them to a bowl, grate a little lemon zest over them, and toss gently.

5 Divide the bean salad evenly among salad plates. Top each portion with 3 shrimp. Drizzle with olive oil and serve immediately.

Yard-Long Beans with Sesame Seeds and Sesame Oil

Serves 4

Although the name suggests that these floppy beans reach a full three feet in length, they are more typically a mere eighteen to twenty-four inches—still, a lot of vegetable to work with compared to the familiar Kentucky Wonder. They resemble super-long pole beans but are closer to black-eyed peas botanically. Yard-long beans, cut into shorter lengths, stand up well to slow braising, and Asian cooks often stir-fry them with strong seasonings like bean paste. Here, they are briefly blanched, then rewarmed with peanut oil, toasted sesame seeds, fragrant sesame oil, and cilantro.

Ingredients

1 pound yard-long beans, ends trimmed and
   cut into 4-inch lengths

1 generous tablespoon sesame seeds

1 tablespoon peanut oil

Kosher or sea salt

2 tablespoons coarsely chopped fresh cilantro

1½ teaspoons toasted sesame oil

1. Bring a large pot of well-salted water to a boil over high heat. Add the beans and boil just until they lose their raw taste and soften slightly, 2 to 3 minutes. Do not let them become limp. Drain in a sieve or colander and immediately run under cold running water until cool. Drain again and pat thoroughly dry.

2. Toast the sesame seeds in a small, dry skillet over moderately low heat, stirring frequently, until golden brown and fragrant, about 5 minutes. Let cool.

3. Heat the peanut oil in a large skillet over moderately high heat. Add the beans and season generously with salt. (Beans need a lot of salt.) Toss to coat with the oil and cook until the beans are hot throughout. Stir in the cilantro, then remove from the heat and stir in the sesame oil and sesame seeds. Serve hot.

HARICOTS VERTS WITH ARUGULA, WALNUTS, AND RICOTTA SALATA

Serves 4

Many growers can't be bothered with haricots verts because harvesting these slender French green beans is so labor-intensive. Reward the farmers who do bring them to market by investing in a pound or two—they are never inexpensive—and preparing this green-on-green salad. The chalk white shavings of ricotta salata supply visual contrast and a salty accent, while the toasted walnuts provide crunch.

INGREDIENTS

3 tablespoons extra virgin olive oil

1½ tablespoons fresh lemon juice

2 tablespoons finely minced shallots

Kosher or sea salt and freshly ground black pepper

1 pound haricots verts, ends trimmed

¾ cup walnut halves, toasted (page xiv) and coarsely chopped

½ pound young arugula, thick stems removed

¼ pound ricotta salata cheese

1 In a small bowl, whisk together the olive oil, lemon juice, shallots, and salt and pepper to taste.

2 Bring a large pot of salted water to a boil over high heat. Add the haricots verts and boil until they have lost their crispness but are still firm, about 5 minutes. Drain in a sieve or colander and immediately run under cold running water until cool. Drain again and pat thoroughly dry.

3 Put the haricots verts, walnuts, and arugula in a salad bowl. Add enough dressing to coat the greens lightly and toss; you may not need it all. With a cheese plane or vegetable peeler, shave the ricotta salata over the salad and toss again. Taste and adjust the seasoning. Serve immediately.

Braised Romano Beans with Tomatoes, Potatoes, Chiles, and Oregano

Serves 4

In many Italian American households, the meaty, flat-podded romano (or Roma) beans are the green beans of choice. They can be boiled and served as a cool salad, with sliced red onion and a vinaigrette, or braised with tomatoes and Italian seasonings and served warm. Like many vegetable braises, this one is even better the second day.

Ingredients

3 tablespoons extra virgin olive oil

½ red or yellow onion, minced

3 cloves garlic, minced

½ pound plum tomatoes, grated (page xiv), with juices

2 teaspoons dried oregano

Hot red pepper flakes

1 pound romano beans, ends trimmed and cut into 2-inch lengths

1½ cups water

Kosher or sea salt

½ pound fingerling potatoes, peeled and cut into 1-inch chunks

1 Heat the olive oil in a large pot over moderately low heat. Add the onion and garlic and sauté until the onion is soft and sweet, about 10 minutes. Add the tomatoes, oregano (crumbling it between your fingers as you add it), and a generous pinch of hot pepper flakes. Raise the heat to moderately high and cook, stirring, until the tomatoes soften and form a sauce.

2 Add the beans and water and season highly with salt. Bring to a simmer, then cover and adjust the heat to maintain a gentle simmer. Cook until the beans begin to soften, about 20 minutes. Add the potatoes, re-cover, and continue cooking, stirring occasionally, until both the beans and potatoes are tender, about 30 minutes longer.

3 Taste and adjust the salt. If time allows, let cool to room temperature, then reheat to serve. The flavor improves when the dish is cooled and reheated.

Fava Bean and Corn Succotash

Serves 6

Moist fava beans can substitute for lima beans in an old-fashioned succotash, although the window of opportunity is brief. Fava beans typically leave the stage just when corn is coming on, in early summer, so reach for this recipe during those few weeks when they overlap. Nuggets of crisp, smoky bacon keep the succotash from being too sweet. Serve with pork ribs or chops, grilled salmon, or grilled flank steak.

Ingredients

4 thick slices apple wood–smoked bacon, cut into
   1-inch pieces
3 pounds fresh fava beans
2 ears corn
3 tablespoons unsalted butter
4 green onions, white and pale green parts only,
   coarsely chopped
Kosher or sea salt and freshly ground black pepper
½ cup water

1 Put the bacon in a large cold skillet and set over moderately low heat. Cook, turning the bacon often with tongs, until the pieces are crisp, about 8 minutes. Using a slotted spoon, transfer to paper towels. Discard the fat, rinse the pan, and set aside.

2 Remove the fava beans from their pods. Bring a large pot of water to a boil over high heat. Prepare a bowl of ice water. Add the fava beans to the boiling water and boil for 1 minute, or a little longer if the beans are large. Drain in a sieve or colander, then transfer to the ice water to stop the cooking. When the beans are cool, drain them again. To peel them, pierce the skin with your fingernail; the inner bean should slip out easily.

3 Husk the corn and cut the kernels away from the cobs with a large knife.

4 Return the skillet to moderate heat and melt the butter. Add the green onions and cook, stirring, until softened, about 1 minute. Add the fava beans and corn, season with salt, and stir to mix. Add the water and bring to a simmer. Cover, adjust the heat to maintain a simmer, and cook until the fava beans and corn are tender, 5 to 7 minutes. Add a little more water if necessary to keep the mixture juicy.

5 Uncover, stir in the bacon, and add several grinds of pepper. Cook, stirring, until the bacon is hot. Add a touch more water if needed, or raise the heat to concentrate the juices if necessary. The succotash should be moist but not soupy. Serve immediately.

Grilled Bruschetta with Fava Bean Puree and Pecorino

Serves 6

At a spring dinner party, pass these irresistible toasts with the evening's first glass of white wine. The fava bean spread is moist and sweet and a fresh spring green, with pale grated pecorino as its salty counterpoint.

Ingredients

2 to 2½ pounds fresh fava beans (to yield 2 cups shelled, unpeeled beans)

2 tablespoons extra virgin olive oil, plus more for garnish

1 large clove garlic, minced

9 fresh basil leaves

Kosher or sea salt and freshly ground black pepper

6 slices Italian country bread, about ½ inch thick and 3 inches long

Aged sheep's milk cheese (such as pecorino toscano, Manchego, or ricotta salata)

1 Prepare a moderate charcoal fire or preheat a gas grill to medium.

2 Remove the fava beans from their pods. Bring a pot of water to a boil over high heat. Prepare a bowl of ice water. Add the fava beans to the boiling water and boil for 1½ minutes, or a little longer if the beans are large. Drain in a sieve or colander, then transfer to the ice water to stop the cooking. When the beans are cool, drain them again. To peel them, pierce the skin with your fingernail; the inner bean should slip out easily.

3 Heat 1 tablespoon of the olive oil in a small skillet over moderate heat. Add the garlic and sauté until fragrant, about 1 minute. Remove from the heat.

4 Put the peeled fava beans, the sautéed garlic and all the oil in the skillet, 3 of the basil leaves, and the remaining 1 tablespoon olive oil in a small food processor. Pulse until nearly but not completely smooth; leave the spread slightly coarse. Transfer to a bowl and stir in salt and pepper to taste.

5 Grill the bread on both sides directly over the coals or gas flame until golden brown. Top each toast with some of the fava spread, dividing it evenly. Drizzle with some olive oil. Shave or grate some cheese over each toast. Garnish with a basil leaf. Serve immediately.

WARM BEET GREENS AND BEET STEMS WITH WHIPPED FETA

Serves 4 to 6

Many people discard the beet stems when preparing beets or beet greens, but the stems can be quite tasty. Boil them separately from the greens, then dress them with garlic, fruity olive oil, and lemon juice. Serve as a first course alongside the cooked greens and some garlicky whipped feta seasoned with mint. Pass warm pita bread and a bowl of Kalamata olives.

INGREDIENTS

1 pound beet greens (from about 3 bunches beets)
4 tablespoons extra virgin olive oil
2 tablespoons minced garlic
Kosher or sea salt
1 lemon

WHIPPED FETA

½ pound Greek, French, Bulgarian, or Israeli feta
    cheese
½ teaspoon minced garlic
Pinch of hot red pepper flakes or coarsely ground
    medium-hot red pepper such as Syrian Aleppo or
    Turkish Mara (see Note)
¼ teaspoon dried Turkish mint (see Note), or
    1 teaspoon finely minced fresh mint
1 to 2 tablespoons extra virgin olive oil

1 Separate the beet leaves from the stems. Cut the stems into 1-inch lengths.

2 Bring a large pot of salted water to a boil over high heat. Add the beet greens and boil until tender, about 3 minutes. Transfer them with tongs to a sieve or colander and run under cold running water to stop the cooking. Drain and squeeze dry. Chop coarsely.

3 Add the beet stems to the boiling water and cook until tender, 3 to 5 minutes. Drain in the sieve or colander and run under cold running water to stop the cooking. Drain again and pat dry on paper towels.

4 Heat 2 tablespoons of the olive oil in a medium skillet over moderate heat. Add 1 tablespoon of the garlic and sauté until fragrant, about 1 minute. Add the beet greens, season with salt, and cook, stirring, until hot throughout. Transfer to a bowl. Add lemon juice to taste and let cool until warm.

5 In the same skillet, heat the remaining 2 tablespoons olive oil over moderate heat. Add the remaining 1 tablespoon garlic and sauté until fragrant, about 1 minute. Add the beet stems, season with salt, and cook, stirring, until hot throughout. Transfer to a bowl. Add lemon juice to taste and let cool until warm.

6 To make the whipped feta, put the feta, garlic, hot pepper flakes, mint, and 1 tablespoon olive oil in a small food processor and puree until smooth, adding up to 1 tablespoon more oil if necessary to achieve a smooth consistency.

7 Arrange the beet greens on one end of a serving platter. Put the beet stems on the other end and the whipped feta in the middle. Serve immediately.

NOTE: Syrian Aleppo and Turkish Mara peppers and dried Turkish mint are available from good spice stores or by mail order from Kalustyan's (www.kalustyans.com).

GOLDEN BEET AND BUTTERMILK SOUP   Serves 4

This is one of the easiest soups imaginable and so inviting on a hot day. Made with golden beets, it is the color of lemon custard. Made with red beets, it is shocking pink, like borscht. The soup can be made up to a couple of days ahead.

INGREDIENTS

1 pound golden beets (weight without greens, about 3 medium beets)

1 large clove garlic, sliced

3 cups buttermilk

¼ cup chopped fresh chives, or 2 tablespoons chopped fresh dill, plus more finely chopped for garnish

1 tablespoon sherry vinegar or white wine vinegar, or more to taste

Kosher or sea salt

1 Preheat the oven to 375°F. If the beet greens are attached, remove all but ½ inch of the stem. Reserve the greens and stems for another use (page 31). Put the beets in a baking dish, and add water to a depth of ¼ inch. Cover tightly and bake until a knife pierces them easily, 45 to 55 minutes. When cool enough to handle, peel the beets.

2 Cut the beets into quarters. Put the beets, garlic, and 1½ cups of the buttermilk in a blender and puree until smooth. (You can use a food processor but the results will not be as smooth.) Add the remaining 1½ cups buttermilk, the dill, and the vinegar and puree again. Season to taste with salt. Transfer to a covered container and chill well.

3 Taste before serving and adjust the seasoning. Serve in cups or bowls, garnishing each portion with a sprinkle of the chives.

CREAMY BEET AND TAHINI DIP

Makes about 2½ cups

Anissa Helou, a Lebanese-born food writer living in London, makes this luscious dip for dinner parties. You can make it a day ahead, although you will probably need to adjust the lemon and salt before serving.

INGREDIENTS

1 pound red beets (weight without greens, about
   3 medium beets)

1 clove garlic, sliced

¼ cup tahini, stirred well to blend

3 to 4 tablespoons fresh lemon juice, or to taste

Kosher or sea salt

Toasted pita wedges, Belgian endive spears, fennel
   wedges, or romaine hearts for dipping

1 Preheat the oven to 375°F. If the beet greens are attached, remove all but ½ inch of the stem. Reserve the greens and stems for another use (page 31). Put the beets in a baking dish, and add water to a depth of ¼ inch. Cover tightly and bake until a knife pierces them easily, 45 to 55 minutes. When cool enough to handle, peel the beets and cut into quarters.

2 Put the beets and garlic in a food processor and puree until smooth. Transfer to a bowl and stir in the tahini. Add the lemon juice gradually. You may not need it all, or you may want a little more. The tahini requires a lot of lemon for balance. Season with salt.

3 Serve the dip with pita wedges or vegetables for dipping. It will keep, refrigerated, for up to one week.

Golden Beet and Blood Orange Salad Serves 4

Put this vivid salad on a buffet and heads will turn. Slices of beet the color of a summer sunset alternate with ruby slices of blood orange, a pairing to turn to when you're serving grilled swordfish, ham, or pork tenderloin. The salad is just as refreshing, if not quite as surprising, made with red beets and navel oranges.

Ingredients

4 medium golden beets

VINAIGRETTE

3 tablespoons extra virgin olive oil

1 tablespoon Champagne vinegar or white wine vinegar

Kosher or sea salt and freshly ground black pepper

2 large or 3 small blood oranges

¼ small red onion, very thinly sliced or shaved on a vegetable slicer

1 heaping tablespoon thinly sliced fresh mint

1 Preheat the oven to 375°F. If the beet greens are attached, remove all but ½ inch of the stem. Reserve the greens and stems for another use (page 31). Put the beets in a baking dish, and add water to a depth of ¼ inch. Cover tightly and bake until a knife pierces the beets easily, 45 to 55 minutes. When cool enough to handle, peel the beets and slice into thin rounds.

2 To make the vinaigrette, in a small bowl, whisk together the olive oil, vinegar, and salt and pepper to taste.

3 Cut a slice off the top and bottom of each orange. Working with 1 orange at a time, set the fruit on a cutting board, one cut side down. Using a chef's knife, slice away the peel from top to bottom, following the contour of the fruit and removing all the white pith. Slice the orange thinly crosswise. Repeat with the remaining orange(s).

4 To assemble the salad, alternate slices of beet and orange on a platter. Scatter the onion evenly over all. Whisk the dressing briefly and spoon it over the salad. Sprinkle with the mint and serve immediately.

Polenta with Chopped Broccoli and Pecorino

Serves 4 as a side dish, or 2 or 3 as a vegetarian main course

Many people are accustomed to using polenta as a foundation, with a meat or tomato sauce spooned over the top. But in this preparation, the polenta is the star attraction, cooked with chopped broccoli until the vegetable all but melts. By the time the polenta loses its graininess, it will be almost as green as spinach pasta, thanks to the softened florets. You can serve it directly from the pot, as an accompaniment to roast pork or chicken, or you can pour it onto a board and let it firm up before slicing into wedges.

Ingredients

1 pound broccoli
1 cup polenta
2 tablespoons extra virgin olive oil, plus more for drizzling
Handful of freshly grated pecorino cheese, plus more for serving
Kosher or sea salt

1 Bring a large pot of lightly salted water to a boil over high heat. Cut across the broccoli to separate the crown of florets, preferably in one piece, from the stalk. Discard all but the upper 2 inches of stalk. With a small knife, pare the stalks, removing the thick, tough skin.

2 Add the crown of florets and the pared stalks to the boiling water and cook until barely tender, about 3 minutes for the florets and 5 minutes for the stalks. With a wire-mesh skimmer, transfer the florets and stalks to a sieve or colander, leaving the water in the pot, and run under cold running water to stop the cooking. Drain well. Chop the florets and stalks coarsely.

3 Measure out 5 cups of the water used to cook the broccoli and put it in a medium pot. Bring to a simmer over high heat. Add the polenta gradually, whisking constantly. When the mixture thickens, reduce the heat to maintain a steady but not too vigorous bubble and switch to a wooden spoon. Cook, stirring often, for 20 minutes, then stir in the chopped broccoli florets and stalks. Continue cooking, stirring often and scraping the sides of the pan with a heatproof rubber spatula, until the polenta is no longer grainy and the broccoli florets have all but dissolved, about 30 minutes longer. Stir in the olive oil and pecorino. Season with salt.

4 Pour the polenta out onto a large serving platter, spreading evenly, and let stand for about 10 minutes to firm. Drizzle the surface with additional olive oil and shower it with more pecorino. Serve warm.

STEAMED CLAMS WITH CHINESE BROCCOLI

Serves 4

You can tell from its deep green color that Chinese broccoli—gai lan in Cantonese— is loaded with nutrients. It's a great source of vitamins A and C, with a flavor similar to Western broccoli but more intense. Steamed with clams, green onions, and sausage, it makes a speedy one-dish meal. Serve with steamed rice to soak up the juices.

INGREDIENTS

1 pound Chinese broccoli

2 tablespoons peanut oil

¼ pound bulk pork sausage

1 bunch green onions, halved lengthwise and white and green parts cut into 2-inch lengths

4 cloves garlic, minced

4 slices fresh ginger, ¼ inch thick, peeled and smacked with the side of a cleaver or chef's knife

2 small fresh red chiles, halved lengthwise, then thinly sliced crosswise

2 pounds small clams, well scrubbed

⅓ cup dry sherry

1 tablespoon toasted sesame oil

Kosher or sea salt, if needed

1 To trim the broccoli, separate the large leaves from their stalks, but leave the small inner leaves attached to their stalks. If the leaves have a tough rib, remove it. Tear the larger leaves in half. Trim the stalks so they are no longer than 3 inches. Pare them with a vegetable peeler, then slit with a paring knife so they will cook more quickly.

2 Heat 1 tablespoon of the peanut oil in a wok over high heat. Add the sausage, breaking it up into small clumps as you add it, and stir-fry until it loses most of its pink color. Transfer the sausage to a plate.

3 Add the remaining 1 tablespoon peanut oil to the wok over high heat. When it is hot, add the green onions, garlic, ginger, and chiles and stir-fry until fragrant, about 1 minute. Add the clams and stir-fry until the shells just begin to open, about 3 minutes. Add the sherry and bring to a boil, then scatter the broccoli on top. Cover and cook until the clams open fully and the broccoli is tender, about 3 minutes.

4 Return the sausage to the wok, add the sesame oil, and toss well. Taste the broccoli and add salt if needed. Clams are salty, so you may not need more. If the juices in the wok seem too thin, use a wire-mesh skimmer or slotted spoon to transfer the clams, broccoli, sausage, and aromatics to a serving platter, leaving the juices behind. Discard any clams that fail to open. Reduce the juices over high heat to the desired thickness, then pour the juices over the dish. Serve immediately.

BROCCOLI RABE AND TURNIP GREENS WITH HOT PEPPER VINEGAR

Serves 6

You can use this recipe as a template for cooking almost any greens, such as mustard, chard, and kale. And as the results demonstrate, greens are almost always tastier in combination. Sturdy greens such as kale and collards take relatively long to cook, so either give them a head start if you are pairing them with more tender greens, or cook the different types in shifts. You can omit the hot pepper vinegar and instead add a pinch of hot red pepper flakes to the oil with the garlic.

INGREDIENTS

1 pound broccoli rabe
1 pound turnip or mustard greens
⅓ cup extra virgin olive oil
3 cloves garlic, minced
Kosher or sea salt
Hot pepper vinegar, homemade (page 124) or
   store-bought

1 To trim the broccoli rabe, remove any stems that feel woody, dry, or tough. (With broccoli rabe, thick stems are often more tender than thin ones.) Trim any dry stem ends, then slit any stems that are thicker than a pencil to speed the cooking. To trim the turnip or mustard greens, remove any tough stems or thick ribs. You should have about 5 quarts mixed greens after trimming.

2 Bring a large pot of well-salted water to a boil over high heat. Unless you have a very large pot, you will probably find it necessary to boil the greens in two batches. Add half the greens to the boiling water and poke them down with tongs or a wooden spoon so they stay submerged and cook evenly. When they are tender, after 2 to 3 minutes, lift them out with a wire-mesh skimmer or tongs into a sieve or colander and run under cold running water to stop the cooking. When cool enough to handle, squeeze to remove excess moisture and chop coarsely. Repeat with the remaining greens.

3 Heat the olive oil in a large skillet over moderate heat. Add the garlic and sauté until fragrant and lightly colored, about 1 minute. Add the greens and stir to coat with the oil. Cook until hot throughout, stirring to blend the greens well. Season with salt. Transfer to a serving bowl and serve immediately, accompanied by the hot pepper vinegar.

WHOLE-WHEAT LINGUINE WITH BROCCOLI RABE AND GARLIC-CHILE OIL

Serves 6

This speedy weeknight pasta dish gets a crowning condiment of warm olive oil with crunchy bits of toasted garlic and red chiles. New Mexico chiles are mild; if you prefer a spicier dish, add a little dried hot red chile, such as cayenne.

INGREDIENTS

2 pounds broccoli rabe

1 pound whole-wheat linguine

½ cup extra virgin olive oil

6 cloves garlic, minced

Kosher or sea salt

3 tablespoons coarsely chopped dried mild to
medium-hot red chiles such as New Mexico chiles

Handful of freshly grated pecorino cheese, plus
more for the table

1 To trim the broccoli rabe, remove any stems that feel woody, dry, or tough. (Sometimes the thick stems are more tender than the spindly ones.) Trim any dry stem ends, then slit any stems that are thicker than a pencil so they cook more quickly.

2 Bring a large pot of salted water to a boil over high heat. Add the broccoli rabe and cook until the stems feel tender, 2 to 3 minutes. With a wire-mesh skimmer or tongs, transfer the broccoli rabe to a sieve or colander, reserving the boiling water for cooking the pasta, and immediately run under cold running water to stop the cooking. When cool enough to handle, squeeze to remove excess moisture and chop coarsely.

3 Add the pasta to the boiling water and cook, stirring often with tongs, until al dente.

4 While the pasta cooks, heat ¼ cup of the olive oil in a large skillet over moderately low heat. Add one-third of the minced garlic and cook, stirring, until fragrant, about 1 minute. Add the broccoli rabe and season with salt. Stir to coat with the oil and garlic and cook until hot throughout. Keep warm.

5 In a small skillet, heat the remaining ¼ cup olive oil over moderate heat. Add the remaining garlic and the chiles and cook, swirling the pan occasionally, until the garlic just begins to color and the chiles become crisp. Set aside.

6 When the pasta is al dente, set aside 1 cup of the boiling water, then drain the pasta in a sieve or colander and return it to the hot pot over moderate heat. Add the broccoli rabe and toss well with tongs, adding some of the reserved hot water as needed to moisten the pasta. Add the garlic-chile oil and pecorino and toss again. Serve immediately and pass additional pecorino at the table.

St. Anne, Illinois

GENESIS GROWERS

Vicki Westerhoff runs her twenty-acre farm with the impulses of a backyard gardener. She stoops to yank weeds when she spots them, hand-harvests pesky beetles at dusk, and says her favorite crop is the looseleaf lettuces because they look like flowers. But then, her farm really is just a garden that grew, a project she undertook in the mid-1990s in an effort to heal herself of a mysterious ailment.

Vicki's doctor had told her that he had no cure for her chronic fatigue, a symptom that had persisted for six years. After researching alternative therapies, she thought a more natural diet might help, but she couldn't find any organic produce. So she decided to return to her parents' rural property around St. Anne, Illinois. In this speck of a burg about an hour south of Chicago, surrounded by vast tracts of soybeans and potatoes, she would grow her own wholesome food.

"I had a rototiller and a pitchfork, and that's how I started," says Vicki, a former medical technician.

Today this lush, productive farm is the picture of health, and its owner is, too. For nine months a year, the land provides purple peppers, blue potatoes, red-ribbed celery, Tuscan kale, and numerous other organic crops for a four-hundred-member CSA and two Chicago farmers' markets. Toads hop among the squash vines and swallowtail butterflies flit through the hedgerows, repatriating after a long absence.

"When we were teenagers, you could barely step out of the house without seeing the hoppy toads," recalls Vicki. "But when I took over the one acre to garden, I thought, 'Where are the toads? Where are the worms?' I wasn't hearing birds. That was the first wake-up call: nothing is here that should be here."

Organic methods have restored the web of life on this farm, nurturing the soil microorganisms that nourish the lower forms of life. As fungi and bacteria returned to the soil, the earthworms returned, then the birds, the butterflies, and the toads. A big turtle has even turned up in the creek that edges the farm, another sign that the landscape is healing.

Now long rows of purple basil, fennel, cipolline onions, and peas blanket the regenerated soil. A business partner farms another twenty-acre property nearby, allowing Vicki to offer customers more variety. In a shed, big mesh bags used for washing baby lettuces dangle from hooks. "We look like a fishing village," jokes Vicki. The rinsed lettuces go into a washing machine on the spin cycle to dry, a makeshift but effective replacement for a costly commercial dryer.

Vicki's son, Jon, helps on the farm during summer breaks from college, driving a tractor with country music blaring from his radio. But Vicki wears all the other hats, from crew boss to sales, a situation that makes her an oddity in this male-dominated farming community.

At the local diner, "they were taking bets on how long it would take me to fail," says Vicki. "I don't know if anybody got the kitty, because I'm still here."

And thriving. Farm life and a natural-food diet has restored Vicki's energy. In the throes of her illness, she could sleep eighteen hours a day. Now she can work that long, fueled in part by a drive to educate city folks about farming.

"I want them to come see the weeds and the horizon and the big blue sky," says Vicki, who named her business after the Greek word for birth or beginning. "This farm was a new beginning for me, and a new beginning for the land."

At a Glance

Philosophy: "We have twenty acres, a drop in the bucket, but I can be a good steward of what we have."

Favorite crops: Purple Beauty bell pepper, Tropea red onion ("my A1 best-selling onion; I've yet to grow enough"), Pitta di Bergamo red cipolline onion, Rokyo honeydew melon, New Red Fire looseleaf lettuce, Paul Robeson tomato.

Reality check: "Everybody wants organic, but they sure don't want to see a worm. Folks, with corn you can't have it both ways."

Kitchen tips: Boil blue or purple potatoes with a splash of vinegar to keep their color. Think of bok choy ribs as a celery substitute, or as low-calorie dippers in place of chips for guacamole.

What customers don't get: "People don't understand the cycles of nature. How could they? They have a grocery store mentality. When it rains three inches in the city, the next day they get on with things; I have mud and sick crops."

A produce rap: (as performed by Vicki on the phone with a buyer) *Chard we have. / No, not yet. / Collards we have. / No, not yet. / Kale we have. / No, not yet. / Nope, that's fall . . .*

Brussels Sprouts with Caraway and Lemon Zest

Serves 4

The citrus fragrance of grated lemon zest freshens Brussels sprouts, but caraway is the real surprise here. The sprouts love its aniselike scent, as do other cabbage relatives. If you have a mortar, pound the caraway lightly to release more of its perfume.

Ingredients

1 pound small Brussels sprouts
1½ tablespoons unsalted butter, or more if desired
1 teaspoon freshly grated lemon zest
1 teaspoon caraway seed
Kosher or sea salt and freshly ground black pepper

1 To trim the Brussels sprouts, peel off any loose or discolored outer leaves from each sprout and slice across the base to remove any dried or browned flesh. Cut a ¼-inch deep slit in the base so the sprout cooks more quickly.

2 Bring a large pot of well-salted water to a boil over high heat. Add the Brussels sprouts and cook until they are tender when pierced, 8 to 10 minutes. (Remove one and cut in half to be sure.) Drain in a sieve or colander, then return to the hot pot. Place the pot over moderate heat and shake until the sprouts are completely dry.

3 Add the butter, lemon zest, and caraway. Season highly with salt—Brussels sprouts need a lot—and pepper. Stir until the butter melts, then serve immediately.

SHAVED BRUSSELS SPROUTS WITH PANCETTA AND FENNEL SEED

Serves 4

When sliced thin, Brussels sprouts cook quickly and retain their sweet, nutty taste. You could substitute cumin seed or caraway seed for the fennel seed, if you like, and you can use the same method to cook thinly sliced green cabbage. Serve as a side dish with pork chops or roast chicken.

Every towering stalk of Brussels sprouts holds both large and small sprouts—the large ones near the top, the smaller ones toward the base. If you purchase the sprouts loose, choose the smaller ones, which tend to be sweeter. If you purchase them on the stalk, farmer Vicki Westerhoff of Genesis Growers recommends leaving them on the stalk if your refrigerator can accommodate its length.

INGREDIENTS

1½ tablespoons extra virgin olive oil

2 ounces pancetta, minced

1 large clove garlic, minced

1 pound Brussels sprouts, halved through the stem, then very thinly sliced lengthwise

½ teaspoon fennel seed, crushed in a mortar or spice grinder

Kosher or sea salt and freshly ground black pepper

½ cup chicken or vegetable broth (if canned, use equal parts broth and water)

1 Put the olive oil and pancetta in a 12-inch skillet over moderate heat. Cook, stirring occasionally, until the pancetta renders some of its fat and begins to crisp, about 3 minutes. Add the garlic and cook, stirring, for about 1 minute to release its fragrance. Add the Brussels sprouts and fennel seed, season with salt and pepper, and stir to coat with the seasonings. Add the broth and bring to a simmer. Cover and adjust the heat to maintain a brisk simmer. Cook until the Brussels sprouts are tender but not mushy, about 10 minutes, uncovering to stir occasionally and make sure they are not in danger of scorching.

2 If there is excess liquid in the skillet, uncover, raise the heat to moderately high, and cook, stirring, to evaporate the liquid. Taste and adjust the seasoning. Serve immediately.

Braised Red Cabbage with Pancetta and Balsamic Vinegar

Serves 6

Long, slow cooking transforms red cabbage, rendering it soft and sweet. Pancetta adds meaty depth and balsamic vinegar supplies a mellow note. You can add a grated pear or a couple of grated raw red beets to this braise at the beginning; they will melt into the cabbage as it cooks. Serve with pork chops, grilled sausages, duck, or game. The flavor is even better the second day.

Ingredients

1 small head red cabbage, about 1½ pounds

1 tablespoon extra virgin olive oil

3 ounces pancetta, in small dice

1 yellow onion, halved and thinly sliced

2 cloves garlic, minced

½ cup dry red wine

1 bay leaf

Kosher or sea salt and freshly ground black pepper

3 tablespoons balsamic vinegar

1 Quarter and core the cabbage, then slice each quarter thinly crosswise.

2 Heat the olive oil in a large pot over moderate heat. Add the pancetta and sauté for about 3 minutes to render some of its fat. Add the onion and sauté, stirring often, until it is softened and lightly colored, 7 to 8 minutes. Stir in the garlic and sauté for 1 minute to release its fragrance. Add the cabbage, wine, and bay leaf. Season with salt and stir to coat the cabbage with the oil and seasonings. Bring to a simmer, cover, and adjust the heat so the cabbage cooks steadily but gently. Stir occasionally and lower the heat if the pot threatens to cook dry. After 30 minutes, stir in the vinegar. Re-cover and continue cooking until the cabbage is very tender, about 30 minutes longer.

3 Uncover and remove the bay leaf. If there is any liquid in the bottom of the pot, raise the heat to moderately high and cook, stirring, to evaporate the liquid. Taste for salt and add several grinds of black pepper. Serve immediately, or let cool to room temperature and reheat to serve.

SAVOY CABBAGE AND FARRO SOUP

Serves 6

This rustic soup tastes like it originated in an Italian farm kitchen. It would make a satisfying Sunday supper in cold weather, served with crusty bread and a hearty red wine. Look for farro—an ancient variety of whole wheat—in well-stocked supermarkets, Italian markets, and specialty-food stores.

INGREDIENTS

3 tablespoons extra virgin olive oil

¼ pound pancetta, chopped

1 small yellow onion, minced

4 cloves garlic, minced

2 tablespoons minced fresh Italian parsley,
    plus more for garnish

2 teaspoons minced fresh rosemary

1 cup farro

½ pound Savoy cabbage, cored and coarsely chopped

1 large or 2 small carrots, peeled and coarsely chopped

2 quarts chicken broth (if canned, use equal parts
    broth and water)

Kosher or sea salt and freshly ground black pepper

Freshly grated pecorino or Parmigiano Reggiano cheese

1 Heat the olive oil and pancetta in a large pot over moderately low heat. Cook, stirring occasionally, for about 5 minutes to render some of the fat from the pancetta, but do not let the pancetta crisp. Add the onion, garlic, parsley, and rosemary and cook, stirring often, until the onion softens and just begins to color, 5 to 10 minutes.

2 Add the farro, cabbage, carrot, and broth and season with salt and pepper. Bring to a simmer, then adjust the heat to maintain a gentle simmer. Cook uncovered, stirring occasionally, until the farro is tender, about 40 minutes. Cover and set aside for 10 minutes.

3 Taste and adjust the seasoning. Divide the soup among warmed bowls. Garnish each portion with some grated cheese and a sprinkle of parsley. Serve immediately.

Nitty Gritty Dirt Farm's Slaw

Serves 6

When the interns and owners of Minnesota's Nitty Gritty Dirt Farm gather for a summer lunch, this crunchy cabbage-based slaw might be on the table. Farmer Robin Raudabaugh makes it without a recipe, incorporating raw vegetables from the day's harvest, all chopped fine and dressed with a vinaigrette lightly sweetened with the farm's honey. Adapt it as you like, adding raw sweet peppers, carrots, kohlrabi, daikon, cucumbers, or turnips.

Ingredients

½ pound napa cabbage, cored

½ pound green cabbage, cored

1 bunch red radishes (about 12 medium to large), trimmed

½ pound broccoli, florets separated from stalks

½ bunch green onions, pale and green parts, sliced ¼ inch thick

½ pound green beans, ends trimmed and sliced ¼ inch thick

DRESSING

⅓ cup extra virgin olive oil

2½ tablespoons cider vinegar, or more to taste

1 tablespoon honey

¼ teaspoon ground ginger

Kosher or sea salt and freshly ground black pepper

1 Chop the napa cabbage, green cabbage, radishes, and broccoli florets into small pieces roughly ¼ to ⅓ inch. The vegetables do not need to be precisely diced but should be about the same size. With a paring knife or vegetable peeler, pare the tough outer layer of the broccoli stalks to reveal the pale core. Chop the cores the same size as the other vegetables.

2 Put all the chopped vegetables in a large bowl and add the green onions and green beans. Toss to mix.

3 To make the dressing, in a bowl, whisk together the olive oil, vinegar, honey, ginger, and salt and pepper to taste. Taste and adjust the balance of sweet and tart. Add the dressing to the slaw, using only as much as you need to coat the vegetables nicely; you may not need it all. Toss well, taste, and adjust the seasoning. Let rest at room temperature for about an hour before serving, or cover and refrigerate if serving later. The slaw will remain crunchy for at least 8 hours.

Indian-Style Green Cabbage with Chiles, Mustard Seed, and Coconut

Serves 6

Green cabbage becomes a thoroughly seductive side dish when transformed with the seasonings of southern India: mustard seed, cumin seed, turmeric, chiles, and coconut. In the kitchens of Kerala, India's southernmost state, coconuts are grated fresh every day for quick stir-fries like this one. Frozen unsweetened coconut, available in markets that cater to a Southeast Asian or Indian clientele, is perfectly adequate.

Ingredients

1 pound green cabbage
2 tablespoons peanut or canola oil
½ teaspoon black mustard seed
½ teaspoon cumin seed
3 shallots, thinly sliced
2 cloves garlic, thinly sliced lengthwise
1 serrano chile, halved lengthwise
¼ teaspoon ground turmeric
½ cup frozen unsweetened grated coconut, thawed
⅓ cup water
Kosher or sea salt
2 tablespoons minced fresh cilantro
¼ cup salted roasted peanuts

1 Core the cabbage and cut into pieces that will fit in the feed tube of a food processor. Fit the processor with the grating disk and grate the cabbage.

2 Heat the peanut oil in a wok or large skillet over moderate heat. Add the mustard seed and cumin seed and cook until the mustard seed pops and the cumin seed darkens. Add the shallots, garlic, and chile and stir-fry until the shallots soften and the garlic releases its fragrance, about 2 minutes. Then add the turmeric, cabbage, coconut, and water and season with salt. Stir-fry until the cabbage softens and loses its raw crunch, 5 to 8 minutes, adding another tablespoon or two of water if necessary to keep the cabbage from sticking. The cabbage should still have a touch of firmness; don't let it become limp.

3 Add the cilantro and peanuts and toss briefly to mix. Taste for seasoning, then serve immediately.

SESAME NOODLES WITH BABY BOK CHOY AND ROAST CHICKEN

Serves 4

One of the most popular vegetables in the Chinese kitchen, bok choy resembles swiss chard, with wide white ribs and large, dark green leaves. A petite variety of bok choy with spoon-shaped leaves, marketed as baby bok choy, can be cut in half lengthwise and braised. Its flavor is mild and sweet, like a young Savoy cabbage. In this recipe, chopped and braised baby bok choy is tossed with Chinese noodles, peanuts, and chicken to make a dish worthy of an Asian noodle house.

INGREDIENTS

1 pound baby bok choy (about 8)

⅓ cup peanut oil

Kosher or sea salt

1 pound fresh Chinese egg noodles or dried udon (Japanese wheat noodles)

2 tablespoons fish sauce (see Note, page 13)

2 teaspoons Chinese chile oil, or to taste

1 cup thinly sliced green onions (white and green parts)

1 cup coarsely chopped fresh cilantro

½ cup coarsely chopped dry-roasted peanuts

1 tablespoon toasted sesame oil

2 cups hand-shredded roast chicken or duck, with or without skin

1 Separate the bok choy leaves, with ribs intact, from the central core. Discard the core. With a paring knife, separate the leaves from their ribs. (You can leave the smallest inner leaves with ribs whole.) Tear large leaves in half lengthwise. Cut the ribs crosswise into 1-inch pieces. Pat the leaves and ribs dry.

2 Bring a large pot of salted water to a boil over high heat.

3 Heat the peanut oil in a large skillet over moderate heat. Add the bok choy, season with salt, then stir to coat with the oil. Cover and cook until just tender, about 3 minutes.

4 Meanwhile, add the noodles to the boiling water and cook, stirring occasionally with tongs, until al dente. In a small bowl, stir together the fish sauce and the chile oil.

5 Drain the noodles in a sieve or colander and return them to the hot pot. Add the bok choy, green onions, cilantro, peanuts, sesame oil, chicken, and fish sauce–chile oil mixture. Toss well with tongs and serve immediately.

STIR-FRIED BOK CHOY WITH SHRIMP AND OYSTER SAUCE

Serves 2 to 4

This preparation works well with medium to large bok choy, the type with broad white ribs and dark green leaves. But you can use the recipe as a template for stir-frying other green vegetables, such as broccoli, asparagus, or mustard greens. The key to stir-frying vegetables successfully is to dry them thoroughly after washing so they sear, rather than steam, in the wok. The dish will serve two as a one-pot meal, or four with other dishes.

INGREDIENTS

1 pound bok choy

2 tablespoons chicken broth

1 tablespoon oyster sauce

1½ teaspoons soy sauce

1½ teaspoons cornstarch

1 teaspoon toasted sesame oil

1 teaspoon Chinese rice wine or dry sherry

1 tablespoon plus 1 teaspoon peanut oil

½ pound medium shrimp (21 to 25 count), peeled, deveined, and patted dry

Kosher or sea salt

2 slices fresh ginger, ¼ inch thick, peeled and smacked with a cleaver or the side of a chef's knife

1 large clove garlic, sliced

½ fresh red chile, sliced (optional)

1 Separate the bok choy leaves from the white ribs. Tear each leaf into 2 or 3 pieces. Halve the ribs lengthwise, then cut crosswise into 2-inch pieces.

2 In a small bowl, whisk together the broth, oyster sauce, soy sauce, cornstarch, sesame oil, and rice wine.

3 Heat a large wok over high heat until a drop of water sizzles on contact. Add 1 teaspoon of the peanut oil and spread the oil around the bottom of the wok with a spatula. Add the shrimp, season with salt, and stir-fry until they turn pink but are not completely cooked through, 1 to 2 minutes. Transfer to a plate.

4 Add the remaining 1 tablespoon peanut oil to the wok and spread the oil with the spatula. Add the ginger and cook for about 30 seconds to release its fragrance, then add the bok choy stems, garlic, and chile. Stir-fry, adjusting the heat to prevent scorching, until the bok choy begins to soften, 2 to 3 minutes. If the stems are quite thick, you may need to add a tablespoon or two of water and cover the wok briefly to complete the cooking, but do not overcook; the stems should remain firm to the tooth.

5 Stir the oyster sauce mixture to recombine and add to the wok along with the bok choy leaves. Stir-fry until the leaves begin to wilt, less than a minute, then add the shrimp and stir-fry until they are fully cooked. Transfer to a warmed platter and serve immediately.

CARROT-ZUCCHINI BREAD WITH CANDIED GINGER

Makes two 8-inch loaves

When summer delivers too many zucchini, many people reach for a zucchini bread recipe. Here's one with a difference: wisps of grated carrot for color and nuggets of moist candied ginger for spice. The idea for jazzing up a quick bread this way comes from Annie Baker, a respected pastry chef in California's Napa Valley. Wrap and freeze the second loaf if you don't plan to eat it within a day or two.

INGREDIENTS

Nonstick cooking spray, for preparing the pan

3 cups sifted unbleached all-purpose flour

1½ teaspoons ground ginger

1½ teaspoons ground cinnamon

1 teaspoon baking soda

¼ teaspoon baking powder

1 teaspoon kosher or sea salt

½ cup minced candied ginger

3 large eggs

1 cup canola oil

1¾ cups sugar

2 teaspoons vanilla extract

1 cup carrots, peeled and grated on the large holes of a box grater

1 cup zucchini, grated on the large holes of a box grater

1 Preheat the oven to 325°F. Coat two 8½ by 4½ by 2¾-inch loaf pans with nonstick cooking spray.

2 Sift together the sifted flour, ginger, cinnamon, baking soda, and baking powder into a medium bowl. Stir in the salt and candied ginger.

3 In a large bowl, whisk the eggs until light and foamy. Add the canola oil, sugar, and vanilla, whisking vigorously until the sugar dissolves. Whisk in the carrots and zucchini.

4 Add the dry ingredients to the egg mixture all at once and stir with a wooden spoon just until blended. Divide the batter evenly between the 2 prepared pans.

5 Bake until the breads are well risen and firm to the touch, and a toothpick inserted in the center comes out clean, about 1 hour. Let cool in the pans on a rack for 10 minutes, then invert and finish cooling right side up on the rack.

GRILLED CARROTS WITH FRESH THYME

Serves 4

Who knew that carrots responded so happily to grilling? The dry heat of the grill concentrates their flavor, so they taste almost like a sweet potato. Serve these supersweet carrots with a pork roast or add to a platter of grilled vegetables.

INGREDIENTS

1 pound slender carrots (about 6), well scrubbed but not peeled
1 tablespoon extra virgin olive oil
2 teaspoons finely minced fresh thyme
Kosher or sea salt

1. Prepare a moderate charcoal fire for indirect grilling (page xiv) or preheat a gas grill to medium (375°F), leaving one burner unlit.

2. If the carrots are uniformly slender, leave them whole. If they are considerably thicker at the top than at the bottom, cut them crosswise into 3- to 4-inch lengths and halve the thick ends to make pieces of about the same size.

3. Put the carrots on a platter, drizzle with the olive oil, and then roll the carrots to coat them lightly and evenly. Season with thyme and salt.

4. Place the carrots over indirect heat, cover the grill, and cook, turning occasionally, until the carrots have softened, about 20 minutes. For the final minute or so of cooking, uncover and move the carrots directly over the coals or gas flame to char them slightly. Serve hot.

CARROT SOUP WITH LEMONGRASS

Serves 6 to 8

With an aroma that fuses lemon, ginger, and mint, lemongrass lurks in the background here. Tasters may not identify the fragrance, but they know the carrots are getting an assist. Because the carrot flavor is delicate, make sure your broth is not too intense. A tip from Vicki Westerhoff of Genesis Growers: "When our carrots are coming in fresh with awesome greens, I always make carrot top soup. You can also use the greens sparingly in juicing and in salads."

INGREDIENTS

3 lemongrass stalks

3 tablespoons unsalted butter

¾ cup thinly sliced shallots

2 pounds carrots, peeled and sliced ½ inch thick

1½ quarts chicken or vegetable broth (if canned, use equal parts broth and water), plus more if needed

Kosher or sea salt

Thinly sliced fresh chives, for garnish

1 To trim the lemongrass, cut off the fibrous, leafy tops and the hard base from each stalk. Cut the trimmed stalks into 3-inch lengths. With the side of a cleaver or a rolling pin, smash the stalks firmly enough to break the fibers.

2 Melt the butter in a large pot over moderate heat. Add the shallots and sauté until softened, about 3 minutes. Add the carrots, broth, and 6 pieces of the lemongrass and bring to a simmer. Taste and add more lemongrass if you don't perceive a subtle lemony-gingery taste. When you are satisfied that you have added enough lemongrass, partially cover the pot and simmer gently until the carrots are cooked, about 25 minutes.

3 Remove the lemongrass pieces with tongs and let the soup cool slightly. Puree in a blender or food processor until smooth, in batches in necessary. Return the soup to a large, clean pot and thin, if desired, with more broth or with water. Season with salt. Reheat to serve and divide among warmed soup bowls. Garnish each portion with the chives.

Grilled Cauliflower Steaks with Tahini Sauce

Serves 4

From each head of cauliflower, you can cut two thick "steaks," slicing from top to bottom near the center to yield a pair of slices each held together by the core. This might seem wasteful if it weren't for the many uses for the remaining florets, such as Cream of Cauliflower and Fennel Soup (page 60). The resulting "steaks," seared on the grill, make a head-turning presentation with a creamy tahini sauce. Use any leftover sauce on grilled vegetables, fish, or roasted beets.

Ingredients

TAHINI SAUCE

¼ cup tahini, stirred well to blend
¼ cup water
2 to 3 tablespoons fresh lemon juice
1 large clove garlic, minced
1 tablespoon minced fresh cilantro
Kosher or sea salt

2 medium cauliflowers
Extra virgin olive oil
Kosher or sea salt and freshly ground black pepper
Chopped fresh cilantro, for garnish

1 Prepare a moderate charcoal fire for indirect grilling (page xiv) or preheat a gas grill to medium (375°F), leaving one burner unlit.

2 To make the tahini sauce, in a small bowl, whisk together the tahini, ¼ cup water, and 2 tablespoons lemon juice until smooth. Whisk in the garlic, cilantro, and salt to taste. Taste and adjust with more lemon juice, if desired.

3 Trim each cauliflower, removing any leaves and cutting the stem flush with the base. Set a cauliflower, cut side down, on a cutting board. With a chef's knife, cut 2 "steaks," each about ¾ inch thick, from the center of the cauliflower, so that the core holds each slice together. Repeat with the second cauliflower. Reserve the remaining cauliflower for another use (see introduction).

4 Put the 4 cauliflower steaks on a tray and brush one side with the olive oil. Season with salt and pepper. Turn the steaks over, brush the second side, and season with salt and pepper.

5 Place the steaks over indirect heat, cover the grill, and cook, turning once, until tender when pierced, about 15 minutes total. For the final minute or so of cooking, uncover the grill and move the cauliflower directly over the coals or flame to char it slightly.

6 Transfer the steaks to a platter and drizzle with the tahini sauce; you may not need it all. Garnish with cilantro and serve hot or warm.

CREAMY CAULIFLOWER AND FENNEL SOUP   Serves 6

Both cauliflower and fennel peak in quality in cool weather, before hot sun damages the former's pale florets and makes the fennel more fibrous. This puree takes advantage of their complementary flavors, fusing them so that neither one dominates. If you like your soup on the thin side, you will use most of the tasty cooking broth to thin the puree; if you prefer a thicker soup, you can reserve any extra liquid for braising vegetables or thinning pasta sauce, or simply enjoy the nutritious broth the next day.

INGREDIENTS

3 tablespoons unsalted butter, plus more for serving

½ large yellow onion, thinly sliced

1 small fennel bulb, halved lengthwise, then thinly sliced crosswise (okay to include the core)

½ large cauliflower, cut into florets (about 3 cups or ¾ pound after trimming)

4 thyme sprigs

5 cups chicken or vegetable broth (if canned, use equal parts broth and water)

¼ teaspoon fennel seed, crushed in a mortar or spice grinder

Kosher or sea salt and freshly ground black pepper

Freshly grated Parmigiano Reggiano cheese, for garnish

1 Melt the butter in a large pot over moderate heat. Add the onion and sauté until it softens and just begins to color, 5 to 10 minutes. Add the sliced fennel, cauliflower, and thyme and stir to coat with the butter. Add the broth and bring to a simmer. Cover and adjust the heat to maintain a gentle simmer. Cook until the vegetables are tender, about 20 minutes.

2 Remove the thyme sprigs. With a slotted spoon, transfer the vegetables to a blender or food processor and process until smooth, working in batches as needed. Add just enough of the cooking liquid to make a puree. Return to a clean pot and stir in the remaining cooking liquid, adding just enough to make soup of a consistency that you like. You may not need it all. Stir in the fennel seed and season to taste with salt and pepper.

3 Reheat to serve and divide among warmed soup bowls. Garnish each portion with a sliver of butter and a sprinkle of cheese.

CELERY ROOT AND MUSHROOM SOUP

Serves 6

French grandmothers have built reputations off of soups such as this one, using whatever leftovers lurked in the vegetable bin, simmered in good broth, then pureed. Pale button mushrooms yield a prettier soup than the dark-skinned crimini mushrooms. To splurge, top the soup with a few drops of truffle oil.

INGREDIENTS

2 tablespoons unsalted butter

1 cup thinly sliced leeks, white and pale green parts only

½ pound celery root, peeled and cut into ¾-inch dice

½ pound white mushrooms, quartered

½ pound Yukon Gold potatoes, peeled and cut into
   ¾-inch dice

6 thyme sprigs

4 cups chicken or vegetable broth (if canned, use equal
   parts broth and water), plus more if needed

Kosher or sea salt and freshly ground black pepper

Crème fraîche or sour cream, whisked to thin, for garnish

Minced fresh Italian parsley or thinly sliced fresh chives,
   for garnish

1 Melt the butter in a large pot over moderate heat. Add the leeks and sauté until softened, about 4 minutes. Add the celery root, mushrooms, potatoes, thyme, and broth and bring to a simmer. Cover and adjust the heat to maintain a gentle simmer. Cook until the vegetables are tender, about 20 minutes.

2 Remove the thyme sprigs. Let cool slightly, then puree the soup in a blender or food processor until smooth, in batches if necessary. Return the soup to a clean pot and reheat to serve, thinning to the desired consistency with additional broth. Season with salt and pepper.

3 Divide among warmed soup bowls, garnishing each portion with a drizzle of crème fraîche and a sprinkle of parsley.

Celery Root Rémoulade with Tarragon

Serves 6 to 8

Order a platter of crudités (raw vegetable salads) in a Paris bistro, and celery root rémoulade will almost certainly be on it. Although some cooks prefer raw celery root for this salad, a brief blanching mellows its flavor and helps it absorb the creamy mustard dressing. Serve celery root rémoulade with cold roast chicken, smoked ham, or grilled sausages. You can also spoon a little onto a ham or tomato sandwich for crunch.

Ingredients

½ cup homemade mayonnaise, or ⅓ cup
   store-bought mayonnaise
3 tablespoons extra virgin olive oil, if using
   store-bought mayonnaise
2 tablespoons Dijon mustard, or more if needed
3 tablespoons white wine vinegar, or more if needed
2 tablespoons minced fresh Italian parsley
1 tablespoon minced fresh tarragon
2 quarts water
1 lemon
1 large celery root, about 1½ pounds without
   greens attached
Kosher or sea salt and freshly ground black pepper

1 Put the mayonnaise in a small bowl. If using store-bought mayonnaise, whisk in the olive oil to improve its flavor. Whisk in the mustard, vinegar, parsley, and tarragon.

2 Bring a large pot of salted water to a boil over high heat. Pour the water into a large bowl and add the juice of the lemon.

3 Peel the celery root and quarter lengthwise. Drop 3 of the quarters into the lemon water to prevent browning. Cut the remaining quarter into ⅛-inch julienne (matchsticks) about 2 inches long. You can do this by hand with a chef's knife, but a manual vegetable slicer with a julienne attachment makes the task much easier. Put the julienned celery root into the lemon water and repeat with the remaining quarters.

4 Drain the julienned celery root and blanch in the boiling salted water just long enough to remove the raw taste and soften it slightly, about 45 seconds. It should still be firm to the tooth. Drain in a sieve or colander and run under cold running water until cool. Drain well.

5 Put the blanched celery root in a large bowl and add as much of the dressing as needed to coat it lightly; you may not use it all. Season with salt and pepper and toss well. Taste for mustard and vinegar and add more if needed; the salad should have a tart edge. Serve immediately, or cover and refrigerate for up to 2 days.

WARM CHARD RIBS WITH YOGURT, TOASTED WALNUTS, AND DILL

Serves 4

Chard ribs take longer to cook than the tender leaves do, so it's a good idea to cut the ribs away and cook them separately. Hold the whole leaf upside down over a work surface and slice along the ribs with a chef's knife. Boiled until tender, then tossed while warm with creamy yogurt and toasty walnuts, they take on a Turkish flavor. Serve with lamb chops or leg of lamb. Look for chard with wide, meaty ribs for this dish. White-ribbed chard tends to have broader, sweeter ribs than other varieties.

INGREDIENTS

3 cups Swiss chard ribs, in ½-inch pieces
  (see headnote)
1 tablespoon unsalted butter
1 large clove garlic, minced
Kosher or sea salt and freshly ground black pepper
½ cup plain whole-milk yogurt, preferably Greek style
2 teaspoons minced fresh dill
⅓ cup coarsely chopped toasted walnuts (page xiv)

1 Bring a large pot of salted water to a boil over high heat. Add the chard ribs and boil until tender, 5 to 8 minutes, depending on their thickness. Drain in a sieve or colander and immediately run under cold running water to stop the cooking. Drain again and pat dry.

2 Melt the butter in a skillet over moderate heat. Add the garlic and sauté for about 1 minute to release its fragrance. Add the chard ribs, season with salt and pepper, and stir to coat with the butter. Cook, stirring, just until the chard is hot throughout.

3 Remove from the heat and stir in the yogurt, dill, and walnuts. Taste again for salt and pepper. Serve warm, not hot.

Braised Chard with Chickpeas

Serves 4

Vegetable dishes with legumes such as this one reflect the wisdom of the Mediterranean diet, a way of eating that elevates beans and greens and casts meat in a minor role. Here, chard leaves become deeply savory when braised with chickpeas and their broth, the latter flavored with a nugget of sausage. Reserve the chard ribs for another use, such as Warm Chard Ribs with Yogurt, Toasted Walnuts, and Dill (page 63).

Ingredients

¾ cup dried chickpeas

1 quart water

2-ounce chunk linguiça or Spanish-style chorizo

½ small yellow onion

1 bay leaf

1 rosemary sprig, 4 inches long

3 tablespoons extra virgin olive oil

2 large cloves garlic, minced

1 small dried red chile, torn in half

2 quarts coarsely chopped Swiss chard leaves (no ribs)

Kosher or sea salt

1 Put the chickpeas in a medium bowl, add water to cover generously, and soak overnight. Drain and rinse, then place in a medium pot with the 1 quart water. Bring to a simmer over moderate heat, skimming any foam. Add the sausage, onion, bay leaf, and rosemary, cover, and adjust the heat to maintain a gentle simmer. Cook until the chickpeas are tender, 1 to 1½ hours.

2 Let the chickpeas cool in the cooking liquid. When cool, drain the chickpeas, reserving the liquid and the sausage; discard the onion, bay leaf, and rosemary sprig.

3 Heat 2 tablespoons of the olive oil in a large skillet over moderately low heat. Add the garlic and chile and sauté for about 1 minute to release the garlic fragrance. Add the chard and season with salt. Cook, stirring, for about 2 minutes to coat the chard with the oil and wilt it slightly. Add the chickpeas and ½ cup of the cooking liquid. Cut the sausage into 4 slices and add them to the skillet as well. Cover and cook, stirring occasionally, until the chard is tender, about 20 minutes. Taste for salt.

4 Just before serving, stir in the remaining 1 tablespoon olive oil. Divide evenly among 4 plates or bowls, making sure that every diner gets a piece of sausage.

GRILLED MOZZARELLA AND ANCHOVIES IN CHARD LEAVES

Serves 4

The big, floppy leaves of Swiss chard make flexible wrappers for grilled foods—in this case, a slice of mozzarella, a pinch of oregano, and an anchovy fillet. Warmed over the fire, the chard crisps and the cheese melts. Set the seared package on a thick piece of toast and serve it as a knife-and-fork first course.

INGREDIENTS

4 large Swiss chard leaves

6 ounces fresh whole-milk mozzarella cheese, in 4 equal slices

4 anchovy fillets

1 teaspoon dried oregano

Hot red pepper flakes

Pinch of kosher or sea salt

Extra virgin olive oil

4 slices Italian country bread, about ½ inch thick and 4 inches long

1 Prepare a moderate charcoal fire for indirect grilling (page xiv) or preheat a gas grill to medium (375°F), leaving one burner unlit.

2 Separate the chard leaves from the ribs by cutting along the ribs with a sharp knife. Try to damage the leaves as little as possible.

3 Put the leaves in a large heatproof bowl and cover with boiling water. Let stand for 2 minutes. Drain in a sieve or colander and immediately run under cold running water until cool. Drain again and gently squeeze to remove excess moisture. Unfurl the chard leaves on a kitchen towel, shiny side down, and pat dry.

4 Put a slice of mozzarella in the center of each leaf. Top each slice with an anchovy fillet, ¼ teaspoon dried oregano (crumble it between your fingers as you add it), and a pinch each of hot pepper flakes and salt. Fold the bottom of each leaf over the cheese, fold in the sides, and then roll to form a neat package. Brush each package lightly all over with olive oil and sprinkle all over with salt.

5 Put the Swiss chard packets on the grill over indirect heat. Cook uncovered, turning once, until the packages feel squishy, indicating that the cheese inside has warmed enough to melt, 5 to 8 minutes total. While the chard cooks, brush the bread slices on both sides with olive oil. Place the bread on the grill directly over the coals or gas flame and toast on both sides.

6 Put a piece of toast on each plate. Top each toast with a Swiss chard bundle. Serve immediately.

CREAMY GRITS WITH SWEET CORN

Serves 6

Cut fresh corn kernels off the cob and stir them into grits for the final few minutes of cooking to impart some summery sweetness. Serve as a side dish for grilled sausages or pork chops, or as a vegetarian companion for Grilled Tomatoes with Pesto (page 165) or Slow-Roasted Tomatoes with Oregano and Feta (page 172). If you have access to a household grain mill, such as the grain mill attachment for a stand mixer, you can grind your own grits from the dried white corn (maíz blanco) sold in Mexican markets.

INGREDIENTS

2 cups corn grits (not instant), preferably
  stone-ground (see Note)
1½ quarts plus about 3 cups water
2 large or 3 small ears corn
6 tablespoons unsalted butter
Kosher or sea salt and freshly ground black pepper

1 Put the grits and the 1½ quarts water in a bowl and soak overnight. The next day, skim off any papery hulls floating on the surface.

2 In a small saucepan or a tea kettle, bring the 3 cups water to a boil, then adjust the heat to keep just below the boil. Put the grits and their soaking water in another medium saucepan and bring to a simmer over moderately high heat, stirring constantly with a wooden spoon. When the grits thicken, after about 5 minutes, cover and reduce the heat to low. Cook, stirring occasionally and adding hot water as needed to thin, until the grits are creamy and no longer gritty, about 1 hour.

3 While the grits are cooking, husk the corn and cut the kernels away from the cobs with a large knife. You should have about 3 cups.

4 When the grits are ready, stir in the corn kernels, cover, and continue cooking until the corn is tender, about 15 minutes, adding more hot water if needed to maintain a creamy consistency.

5 Add the butter and stir vigorously until it melts. Season with salt and pepper. Serve immediately.

NOTE: Stone-ground grits are available at well-stocked grocery stores and from mail-order sources, such as Anson Mills (www.ansonmills.com).

GRILLED CORN WITH
CHIPOTLE BUTTER AND CILANTRO

Serves 4

Boiling corn leaves some of its natural sweetness behind in the water, while grilling corn intensifies its flavor. Grill the ears in the husk to steam the kernels, then peel back the husks and slather the ears with a spicy, smoky chipotle butter.

INGREDIENTS

4 ears corn

4 tablespoons unsalted butter, softened

2 teaspoons finely minced canned chipotle chile in adobo sauce, or more to taste

Kosher or sea salt

2 tablespoons chopped fresh cilantro

1 Prepare a moderately hot charcoal fire or preheat a gas grill to medium-high (375° to 400°F). Carefully peel back the corn husks without removing them, then pull out and discard the threadlike silk. Replace the corn husks and tie the tips closed with kitchen twine. Soak the ears in a sinkful of cold water for 20 minutes.

2 Put the butter in a small bowl. Add the chile and a large pinch of salt and stir to blend. Taste and add more salt or chile, if desired.

3 Place the corn directly over the coals or gas flame and cover the grill. Cook for about 15 minutes, giving the ears a quarter turn every 3 to 4 minutes as the husks brown.

4 Transfer the corn to a platter. Snip the ends of the husks to remove the twine tie. Remove and discard the husks. While the corn is hot, slather it with the chipotle butter, then sprinkle with the cilantro. Serve immediately.

Bulgur Salad with Cucumbers, Radishes, and Green Onions

Serves 6

Inspired by the spicy Turkish bulgur salad called kisir, which includes hot red pepper paste, this milder interpretation puts the accent on the herbs. Fine bulgur is plumped in boiling water, then tossed with crunchy raw vegetables and coarsely chopped herbs to make a lemony summer salad or meze. Offer hearts of butter lettuce so diners can wrap up the salad, taco style, and eat it with their fingers. Or serve it with grilled lamb chops or shrimp and thick yogurt.

Ingredients

- 1 cup fine bulgur (#1 size)
- ¾ cup boiling water
- ¾ pound cucumbers, peeled and cut into ¼-inch dice
- 1 cup thinly sliced green onions, white and pale green parts only
- ¾ cup thinly sliced radishes
- 1 cup coarsely chopped fresh Italian parsley
- ½ cup coarsely chopped fresh mint
- ⅓ cup coarsely chopped fresh dill
- 1 green Anaheim chile or other moderately hot green chile, halved and thinly sliced crosswise
- ⅓ cup extra virgin olive oil
- ¼ cup fresh lemon juice, or more to taste
- 1 large clove garlic, minced to a paste
- 1½ teaspoons kosher or sea salt
- Coarsely ground medium-hot red pepper, such as Syrian Aleppo or Turkish Mara (see page 31), or freshly ground black pepper
- Hearts of butter lettuce, for wrapping (optional)

1 Put the bulgur in a large heatproof bowl and add the boiling water. Cover the bowl with a dish towel and let stand for 10 minutes for the grains to swell. Fluff the grains with a fork.

2 Add the cucumbers, green onions, radishes, parsley, mint, dill, and green chile. Toss to mix. In a small bowl, whisk together the olive oil, lemon juice, garlic, salt, and red pepper to taste. Pour over the salad and toss gently. Taste and adjust the seasoning. The salad should be lemony. Serve immediately, with hearts of butter lettuce for wrapping the salad "taco style."

GRILLED TUNA NIÇOISE WITH ANCHOVY VINAIGRETTE

Serves 8

salade niçoise exists for those days when you are inundated with summer vegetables. Replace the usual canned tuna with grilled fresh ahi, open a bottle of chilled rosé, and toast the farmers whose hard work enables this feast.

INGREDIENTS

ANCHOVY VINAIGRETTE

1 cup extra virgin olive oil

⅓ cup red wine vinegar, plus more if needed

12 anchovy fillets, minced to a paste

2 large cloves garlic, finely minced

2 tablespoons capers, preferably salt packed, rinsed and finely minced

1½ tablespoons chopped fresh tarragon

1½ tablespoons fish sauce (see Note, page 13)

Kosher or sea salt

8 small or 4 medium beets

1½ pounds waxy potatoes such as fingerlings, unpeeled

1 pound slender green beans such as haricots verts, ends trimmed

4 large eggs

1¾ to 2 pounds ahi tuna steaks, about ¾ inch thick

Extra virgin olive oil

1½ teaspoons fennel seed, crushed in a mortar or spice grinder

1 heart of butter lettuce, separated into leaves (reserve outer leaves for another use)

4 large tomatoes, cut into wedges

1 pound cucumbers, peeled and cut into small chunks

16 radishes, trimmed

¾ cup unpitted Niçoise olives

1. To make the anchovy vinaigrette, in a small bowl, whisk together the olive oil, vinegar, anchovies, garlic, capers, tarragon, and fish sauce. Season to taste with salt.

2. Preheat the oven to 375°F. If the beet greens are attached, remove all but ½ inch of the stem. Reserve the greens and stems for another use (page 31). Put the beets in a large baking dish, and add water to a depth of ¼ inch. Cover and bake until a knife pierces them easily, 45 minutes or longer, depending on their size. When cool enough to handle, peel the beets and cut into wedges.

continued next page

GRILLED TUNA NIÇOISE WITH ANCHOVY VINAIGRETTE   continued

3 Put the potatoes in a large pot and add salted water to cover by 1 inch. Bring to a boil over high heat, then reduce the heat to maintain a simmer and cook until tender when pierced, 15 to 20 minutes. Drain. When cool enough to handle, peel the potatoes and slice thickly.

4 Bring a large pot of salted water to a boil over high heat. Add the green beans and boil until they have lost their crispness but are still firm, about 5 minutes. Drain in a sieve or colander and immediately run under cold running water until cool. Drain again and pat thoroughly dry.

5 Put the eggs in a small saucepan with water to cover by 1 inch. Bring to a boil over high heat, then immediately cover and remove from the heat. Let stand for 6 minutes exactly. Drain and quickly run under cold running water until cool, then peel.

6 Prepare a moderate charcoal fire or preheat a gas grill to medium (375ºF). Coat the tuna with olive oil, then season with salt and the fennel. Grill directly over the coals or gas flame, turning once, until the tuna is just cooked through, 4 to 5 minutes per side. Let cool to room temperature.

7 At serving time, line a large platter—or 2 platters if necessary—with the lettuce. By hand, break the tuna up into smaller pieces. Put it in a bowl and toss with enough of the vinaigrette to moisten it generously. Taste and adjust with more salt or vinegar as needed. Put the tuna in the center of the platter(s). Separately dress the beets, potatoes, green beans, tomatoes, and cucumbers with enough of the vinaigrette to coat them; taste and adjust with more salt or vinegar as needed. (You can use the same bowl each time.) Arrange the vegetables around the tuna in separate mounds. Cut the eggs in half lengthwise. Sprinkle the eggs and radishes with a little salt and arrange them around the vegetables, tucking them where you can. Scatter the olives over all. Serve immediately, passing any extra vinaigrette.

LEMON CUCUMBERS WITH CRÈME FRAÎCHE AND CHERVIL

Serves 4

As round as a lemon and with yellow skin to boot, lemon cucumbers owe their name to their appearance, not their taste. They are crisp and mild, with no bitterness. They do have a large seed cavity, and if you scoop it out, you will not have much left to eat. Better to choose a preparation, such as this one, that incorporates the whole cucumber. If you can't find chervil, substitute dill, mint, or tarragon, adjusting the amount to taste. Serve this salad as a companion for salmon or lamb.

INGREDIENTS

1 pound lemon cucumbers

⅓ cup crème fraîche or plain whole-milk yogurt

1 clove garlic, very finely minced

2 tablespoons coarsely chopped fresh chervil

Kosher or sea salt and freshly ground black pepper

¼ cup coarsely chopped toasted walnuts (page xiv), optional

1 Trim the ends off the cucumbers and peel. Cut them in half lengthwise, then slice thinly crosswise.

2 Put the crème fraîche, garlic, and chervil in a medium bowl and whisk to blend. Whisk in salt and pepper to taste. Add the cucumbers and walnuts, then toss gently with a rubber spatula. Taste and adjust the seasoning. Serve immediately.

GRILLED EGGPLANT CANNELLONI WITH RICOTTA AND PROSCIUTTO

Serves 4 as a main course, or 6 as a first course

Lengthwise slices from a large eggplant become supple when grilled, so you can roll them around a ricotta filling as if you were making cannelloni from pasta squares. Blanketed with a homemade fresh-tomato sauce and baked until bubbly and a little crusty around the edges, the fork-tender bundles of stuffed eggplant are the ultimate Italian comfort food.

INGREDIENTS

2 large globe eggplants, 1¼ to 1½ pounds each
Kosher or sea salt
2 tablespoons extra virgin olive oil

TOMATO SAUCE
¼ cup extra virgin olive oil
½ yellow onion, minced
2 large cloves garlic, minced
1½ pounds plum (Roma type) tomatoes, chopped
   (no need to peel)
8 to 12 fresh basil leaves
1 teaspoon dried oregano
Pinch of hot red pepper flakes
Kosher or sea salt

RICOTTA FILLING
2 cups whole-milk ricotta cheese (or one 15-ounce
   container)
½ cup freshly grated pecorino or Parmigiano Reggiano
   cheese
⅓ cup minced prosciutto
2 tablespoons minced fresh Italian parsley
1 large clove garlic, minced
Freshly ground black pepper
1 large egg, lightly beaten

½ cup freshly grated pecorino or Parmigiano Reggiano
   cheese, for topping

1 Slice off the eggplants' green cap, then cut each eggplant lengthwise into slices about ⅓ inch thick. Discard the first and last slices, which are mostly skin. You should get at least 6 large slices from each eggplant. Sprinkle them generously on both sides with salt, then set the slices on a rack and let stand for 30 minutes. Moisture will bead on the surface.

continued next page

GRILLED EGGPLANT CANNELLONI WITH RICOTTA AND PROSCIUTTO continued

2 Prepare a moderate charcoal fire or preheat a gas grill to medium (375°F). Pat the eggplant slices dry with paper towels, then brush on both sides with the olive oil. Place the slices directly over the coals or gas flame and cook, turning once, until they are nicely marked by the grill and pliable, about 3 minutes per side. They do not need to be fully cooked as they will cook further in the oven. Set the slices aside on a tray to cool.

3 To make the tomato sauce, heat the olive oil in a large skillet over moderate heat. Add the onion and garlic and sauté until the onion is soft and beginning to color, 5 to 10 minutes. Add the tomatoes and cook, stirring often, until they soften and collapse into a sauce, about 10 minutes, depending on ripeness.

4 Remove from the heat, and pass the mixture through a food mill fitted with the fine disk. Return the puree to the skillet over moderate heat. Tear the basil leaves in half and add to the skillet along with the oregano (rubbing it between your fingers as you do), the hot pepper flakes, and salt to taste. Simmer gently, stirring occasionally, until the sauce is thick and tasty. Set aside.

5 To make the ricotta filling, put the ricotta, pecorino, prosciutto, parsley, and garlic in a medium bowl. Stir until blended, then season to taste with salt and pepper. Stir in the egg.

6 Preheat the oven to 350°F. Choose a shallow baking dish large enough to hold all the eggplant rolls snugly in one layer. Spread ⅓ cup of the tomato sauce on the bottom of the dish.

7 Put a generous 2 tablespoons filling on each eggplant slice and spread it evenly. Carefully roll each slice like a jelly roll, and place the rolls, seam side down, in the baking dish. Top with the remaining tomato sauce, spreading it evenly. Sprinkle the pecorino evenly over the top.

8 Bake until lightly browned and bubbling, about 45 minutes. Cool for 20 minutes before serving.

SMOKY EGGPLANT AND PEPPER SPREAD WITH PITA CRISPS

Serves 8

How fortunate that eggplants, peppers, chiles, and tomatoes all mature at the same time, since they go so well together. For this spread, the vegetables are grilled—preferably over charcoal—until their skins blacken to impart a smoky note, then peeled and chopped to a near puree. Cilantro and toasted cumin give the spread a Moroccan accent. If you don't want to make the pita crisps, serve the spread with a favorite cracker or triangles of warm pita.

INGREDIENTS

1½ pounds Italian or Japanese eggplants
1 large red sweet pepper
1 poblano chile
2 plum (Roma type) tomatoes
4 tablespoons extra virgin olive oil
2 large cloves garlic, minced
1 tablespoon finely minced fresh cilantro
¾ teaspoon cumin seed, toasted (page xiv) and crushed
   in a mortar or spice grinder
1½ to 2 teaspoons red wine vinegar
Kosher or sea salt

PITA CRISPS
4 pita breads, carefully halved horizontally
Extra virgin olive oil
Kosher or sea salt

1 Prepare a moderate charcoal fire or preheat a gas grill to medium (375°F). Place the eggplants, sweet pepper, poblano chile, and tomatoes directly over the coals or gas flame. Cover the grill and cook, turning the vegetables occasionally, until the skins are blackened and the vegetables are soft, 10 to 15 minutes. Set aside to cool.

2 Cut the eggplants in half lengthwise and scrape the flesh away from the skin with a spoon. Peel and core the sweet pepper and poblano chile and discard the seeds. Peel and core the tomatoes.

3 Chop all the grilled vegetables together to a near puree. Transfer to a bowl. Stir in 3 tablespoons of the olive oil.

4 Heat the remaining 1 tablespoon olive oil in a small skillet over moderately low heat. Add the garlic and sauté until fragrant and just beginning to color, about 1 minute.

5 Add the garlic and oil in the skillet to the vegetables. Stir in the cilantro, cumin, and vinegar and season with salt. Set the spread aside for at least 1 hour to allow the flavors to blend, or cover and refrigerate for up to 8 hours, then bring to room temperature before serving.

6 To make the pita crisps, preheat the oven to 400°F. Brush the pita halves on both sides with olive oil, then sprinkle on both sides with salt. Arrange on baking sheets and bake until crisp and golden, about 7 minutes, depending on the thickness. Watch carefully, as the pita burns easily. Cool completely on a rack.

7 Break the cooled pita into smaller pieces. Accompany the eggplant spread with the pita.

GRILLED EGGPLANT RAITA

Serves 4

Although cucumber raita is the best known of India's yogurt salads, a raita can be prepared with many different vegetables and fruits. In this recipe, you could replace the eggplant with grilled zucchini or grilled red onions, for example, or even with grilled okra (page 109). Toasting the spices in oil heightens their fragrance and is a fundamental Indian technique. Serve this raita with grilled lamb chops or kebabs, or with steamed rice and lentils for a vegetarian meal.

INGREDIENTS

1 pound Italian or Japanese eggplants, halved lengthwise
2 tablespoons peanut oil
Kosher or sea salt
1 cup plain yogurt, preferably whole milk
½ teaspoon sugar
1 serrano chile, halved lengthwise
2 cloves garlic, minced
½ teaspoon black mustard seed
¼ teaspoon cumin seed
2 tablespoons coarsely chopped fresh cilantro

1 Prepare a moderate charcoal fire or preheat a gas grill to medium (375°F).

2 Brush the eggplants all over with 1 tablespoon of the peanut oil. Season all over with salt. Place the eggplants, cut side down, directly over the coals or gas flame, cover the grill, and cook until the flesh is soft, 10 to 15 minutes.

3 Remove from the grill, cool slightly, then scrape the eggplant flesh from the skin and chop coarsely. Put it in a serving bowl. Gently stir in the yogurt, sugar, and salt to taste.

4 Heat the remaining 1 tablespoon peanut oil in a small skillet over moderate heat. Add the chile and garlic and sauté until the garlic starts to color, about 1 minute. Add the mustard seed and cumin and cook until the cumin darkens.

5 Pour the contents of the skillet over the eggplant and stir in gently along with the cilantro. Taste and adjust the seasoning. Serve warm or at room temperature.

GRILLED EGGPLANT AND MOZZARELLA PANINI

Serves 4

How many ways can you put eggplant, tomato, and mozzarella together? Dozens, certainly. Here, they meet in a panino, or Italian sandwich. The sliced eggplant is grilled first, then layered with the other ingredients between two pieces of pesto-brushed focaccia. After another brief trip to the grill to crisp the bread and melt the mozzarella, the hot panini are ready to slice and savor.

INGREDIENTS

2 small eggplants, about ½ pound each

Kosher or sea salt

2 tablespoons extra virgin olive oil

½ cup pesto (page 165)

4 pieces thick focaccia, halved horizontally, or
    8 pieces thin focaccia, each roughly 3 by
    6 inches or equivalent

8 to 12 thin tomato slices

6 ounces fresh whole-milk mozzarella cheese,
    thinly sliced

1 Slice off the eggplants' green cap, then cut each eggplant lengthwise into slices ³⁄₁₆ inch thick. Discard the first and last slices, which are mostly skin. Sprinkle the remaining slices generously on both sides with salt. Place them on a rack and let stand for 30 minutes. Moisture will bead on the surface.

2 Prepare a moderate charcoal fire or preheat a gas grill to medium (375°F). Pat the eggplant slices dry with paper towels, then brush on both sides with 1 tablespoon of the olive oil. Place the slices directly over the coals or gas flame and cook, turning once, until just tender, about 3 minutes on per side. Remove from the grill.

3 Spread 1 tablespoon pesto on one side of each focaccia piece—on the cut side if you have halved the focaccia, or on the bottom side if you have not. Layer the grilled eggplant slices, overlapping them slightly, on 4 of the pesto-topped slices. Top the eggplant with the tomato slices, then with mozzarella, dividing them both evenly. Place another piece of focaccia, pesto side down, on the sandwich.

4 Brush the sandwiches with the remaining 1 tablespoon olive oil on both sides. Place the sandwiches directly over the coals or gas flame and cook, turning once, until they are hot throughout, the focaccia is nicely toasted, and the mozzarella is molten, about 3 minutes per side, depending on the heat of the fire. Cut in half and serve immediately.

Shaved Fennel, Orange, and Arugula Salad

Serves 4 to 6

Serve this winter salad as a refreshing counterpoint to seafood, pork, or duck—after steamed mussels, a braised pork shoulder, or grilled duck breasts, perhaps. To vary it, substitute grapefruit or blood orange segments for the navel orange, add some sliced avocado, or substitute purslane or watercress for the arugula.

INGREDIENTS

DRESSING
2 tablespoons extra virgin olive oil
2 tablespoons fresh lemon juice
1 large shallot, finely minced
Kosher or sea salt and freshly ground black pepper

1 large fennel bulb, quartered lengthwise
2 navel oranges
**Large handful of arugula, stems removed, leaves torn
  smaller if large**

1 To make the dressing, in a small bowl, whisk together the olive oil, lemon juice, shallot, and salt and pepper to taste.

2 With a mandoline or other manual vegetable slicer, or with a sharp chef's knife, slice the fennel crosswise as thinly as possible. Discard the core.

3 Cut a slice off the top and bottom of each orange. Working with 1 orange at a time, set the fruit on a cutting board, one cut side down. Using a chef's knife, slice away the peel from top to bottom, following the contour of the fruit and removing all the white pith. With a small paring knife, cut the whole segments away from the membranes, allowing the segments to drop into a nonreactive bowl.

4 In a large serving bowl, combine the fennel and the orange segments, leaving any orange juice behind. Add the dress-ing and arugula and toss to coat evenly. Taste for salt. Serve immediately.

GREEN-GARLIC SOUFFLÉ

Serves 6

In its youth, well before maturity, garlic looks like a slender leek or thick green onion. The base doesn't swell into the bulb we think of as garlic until early summer. So late spring is the moment for "green" garlic, the immature stalks, which have a subtle garlicky aroma that only hints at the pungency of the mature bulb to come. The whole stalk can be thinly sliced, just as you would slice a leek. Making this soufflé in a shallow baking dish instead of in the classic deep soufflé dish produces more crust in proportion to fluffy interior.

INGREDIENTS

6 tablespoons unsalted butter, plus more for the baking dish

¼ cup plus 5 tablespoons freshly grated Parmigiano Reggiano cheese

About 2 pounds green garlic, enough to yield 4 cups sliced

Kosher or sea salt and freshly ground black pepper

3 tablespoons unbleached all-purpose flour

1 cup whole milk

4 thyme sprigs

¼ teaspoon freshly grated nutmeg

4 large egg yolks

5 large egg whites

1 Preheat the oven to 425°F. Generously butter the bottom and sides of a 13 by 9-inch oval gratin dish. Sprinkle the buttered dish evenly with 3 tablespoons of the cheese.

2 To trim the green garlic, cut off and discard the tough, dark green leafy tops, which resemble the tops of leeks. You will use only the white and pale green part of the stalks. Cut the trimmed stalk in half lengthwise, then slice thinly crosswise. Put the sliced garlic in a large pot of cold water and swish well to dislodge any dirt. Lift the garlic into a sieve or colander with your hands or with a wire-mesh skimmer. Let drain.

3 Melt 2 tablespoons of the butter in a large skillet over moderately low heat. Add the green garlic and season with salt and pepper. Stir to coat with the butter, then cover with a round of parchment paper and the lid, reduce the heat to low, and cook until the green garlic is meltingly tender, about 20 minutes, uncovering to stir occasionally.

4 While the green garlic cooks, melt the remaining 4 tablespoons butter in a small saucepan over moderately low heat. Add the flour and whisk to blend. Cook, whisking, for about 1 minute, then add the milk gradually, whisking constantly. Add the thyme sprigs. Adjust the heat to maintain a gentle bubble and cook, whisking often, for about 5 minutes to allow the béchamel to thicken and to infuse it with the herb flavor. Stir in the nutmeg. Remove from the heat and let cool for 10 minutes.

5 Whisk the egg yolks, one at a time, into the béchamel. Whisk in the ¼ cup cheese, then season with salt and pepper. Remove the thyme sprigs, and stir the cooked green garlic into the béchamel base.

6 With an electric mixer or by hand, beat the egg whites to firm but not stiff peaks. Fold the whites, one-third at a time, into the base. Transfer the soufflé mixture to the prepared baking dish, spreading it evenly. Top with the remaining 2 tablespoons cheese.

7 Bake until the soufflé is well puffed, firm to the touch, and golden brown, 17 to 18 minutes. Serve immediately.

Granby, Massachusetts

RED FIRE FARM

Ryan Voiland's entrepreneurial gene expressed itself early. Living next to a swimming hole in Amherst, Massachusetts, the youngster made serious pocket money redeeming the swimmers' discarded bottles and cans. Later, when the family moved to a rural area north of the city, Ryan began harvesting the local wild blackberries and blueberries and selling them at a roadside stand, along with his homemade jams. A family photograph shows Ryan—perhaps ten years old—and his brothers standing by the side of the road, their red wagon piled with homegrown pumpkins for sale. By the sixth or seventh grade, he was ready to expand his enterprise.

"I said, 'Dad, I'm taking over the garden. I need more stuff to sell,'" recalls Ryan.

The middle schooler mastered all the gardening skills that books at the local library offered, and by high school he had outgrown his one-acre home plot. "Before I had a driver's license, I was renting land," says Ryan, who set up a farm stand on his family's property to sell what he was harvesting two miles down the road. During summer breaks from Cornell, where he studied farm business management and horticulture, he kept the operation going.

By the age of twenty-two, when most college graduates are just starting to shape their professional lives, Ryan Voiland was a landowner. With help from the state of Massachusetts, he bought an eighty-acre former dairy farm near Granby, paying the going rate for farmland but well below the parcel's development value. The state made up the difference in return for the development rights, a creative way of ensuring that the parcel remains in agriculture. Without that assist, the land that now supplies two farmers' markets and a nine-hundred-member CSA was headed for residential development.

"Every year another farm goes out of business around here," says Ryan, who credits his thriving CSA with helping him avoid that fate. In 2009, he purchased another 120 acres along the Connecticut River to expand his production.

At a Glance

Philosophy: "I'm more interested in growing food that makes a difference in people's diets," says Ryan. "Real food, rather than specialty crops."

Biggest challenge: The 2009 tomato blight, which swiftly damaged crops throughout the eastern United States. Red Fire Farm's greenhouse tomatoes remained healthy, but the field tomatoes succumbed, a huge financial loss. "In all my years of farming, I can't remember crop losses as dramatic," says Ryan.

Farm name: A devastating fire destroyed the original farmhouse and barn in 1922. Ryan chose the farm name to commemorate the blaze.

Insight: "Farming is very time-sensitive," says Ryan. "You do things at the right time, and it works. You can't just put things off."

Favorite crops: Brocade bicolor sweet corn, Calliope and Raveena eggplants, Sarah's Choice cantaloupe, yellow-fleshed Peace watermelon, Tongues of Fire shelling beans.

Most underappreciated crops: Kale and cranberry beans. The former is "tremendously tasty," says Ryan. The latter take time to shell but reward the effort.

Each August, Red Fire Farm throws a party for the extended community—an all-day tomato festival that draws at least a thousand celebrants. Families roam the rows of zinnias, asters, and sunflowers, harvesting U-pick bouquets; line up for succulent sweet corn, charred on the grill; gather around a makeshift stage for bluegrass music; and mob the tomato-tasting tent, comparing Fabulous to Purple Russian to Chocolate Striped. Serious and not-so-serious runners compete in a 5K Tomato Trot (lots of red running shorts), while kids test their mettle in tug-of-war.

The Red Fire Farm staff makes sure the farm stand looks its best that day, its wooden shelves stocked with glistening radishes and red-tipped lettuces, flawless baby beets, frilly kales, and tomatoes in sunset colors. Most of the good-natured young people who weed, harvest, and plow the fields here—a strong, tanned, and perpetually dirty crew—envision a future in small-scale farming and have come to train with a master.

"We aim to give them learning roles on the farm," says Sarah Ingraham, Ryan's wife. A Vassar graduate, Sarah had her own one-acre CSA before she met Ryan on a Web site for vegetarian singles. "He would come over and bring his spading machine," laughs Sarah, "and tell me I had too many weeds."

In the farmhouse kitchen, Ona Lindaueur, a young Oberlin graduate, makes mid-morning muffins for the crew—raspberry-chocolate is a favorite—and prepares a vegetarian dinner for staff once a week. They sit outdoors around a plywood table, gulping water from quart canning jars, savoring gazpacho from the tomatoes they grew, and enjoying the community that forms so readily around good food. In the hands and hearts of these passionate young people, who appreciate beautiful produce and embrace hard work, the future of America's small farms lies.

Tuscan Kale with Pine Nuts and Golden Raisins

Serves 4

The crinkly-leaved greens known as Tuscan kale (or lacinato kale) get a Sicilian treatment here. The pairing of pine nuts and raisins is so commonplace in Sicily that the two are sold already mixed together. You can prepare Swiss chard, turnip greens, broccoli rabe, or spinach by the same method. If you prefer, substitute dried currants or finely diced dried apricots for the golden raisins or slivered almonds for the pine nuts. Serve with roast chicken, pork, or sausages.

Ingredients

2 tablespoons golden raisins

¼ cup hot water

1½ pounds Tuscan kale

3 tablespoons extra virgin olive oil

3 large cloves garlic, minced

2 tablespoons pine nuts, toasted (page xiv)

Kosher or sea salt

1 Put the raisins in a small bowl, add the hot water, and soften for 20 minutes. Drain.

2 Fill a sink with cold water. To remove the ribs from the kale leaves easily, hold each leaf upside down over the sink and, with a chef's knife, slice downward along each side of the rib, allowing the leafy greens to fall into the sink. Discard the tough ribs. Swish the greens in the water to dislodge any dirt, then lift them into a sieve or colander to drain.

3 Bring a large pot of well-salted water to a boil over high heat. Add the kale and cook until tender, about 5 minutes. Drain in a sieve or colander and immediately run under cold running water until cool. Drain again and squeeze to remove excess water. Chop coarsely.

4 Heat the olive oil in a large skillet over moderate heat. Add the garlic and sauté until fragrant and lightly colored, about 1 minute. Add the kale, pine nuts, and raisins and season with salt. Cook, stirring, until all the ingredients are well mixed and the kale is evenly coated with oil and hot throughout. Serve immediately.

CRISPY KALE CHIPS

Serves 4

CSA farmers who grow kale say that many of their shareholders lack recipes for this highly nutritious leafy green. Kale chips to the rescue. Roasted in the oven, the leaves crackle when you eat them and dissolve like snowflakes on the tongue. No matter how many batches you make, they will disappear in an instant. The DeLaney Community Farm blog credits Bon Appétit magazine for the idea.

INGREDIENTS

½ pound Tuscan kale or curly kale
1 tablespoon extra virgin olive oil
Kosher or sea salt

1 Preheat the oven to 250°F. With a knife, separate the kale leaves from their tough central rib and discard the ribs. Wash and thoroughly dry the kale leaves. Put them in a large bowl, drizzle with the olive oil, sprinkle with salt, and toss to coat them evenly with the oil. Arrange them on baking sheets in a single layer.

2 Bake, in batches if necessary, until the leaves become fully crisp, 25 to 30 minutes. You can serve them immediately or let them cool. They will stay crisp for at least a couple of hours.

PORTUGUESE POTATO AND KALE SOUP

Serves 8

If Portugal has a national soup, it is this one, known as caldo verde, a rustic and rib-sticking meal in a bowl. The ribbons of kale must be sliced into the finest possible shreds—as fine as a blade of grass, some say. At some markets in Portugal, shoppers can buy the kale already sliced by machine. The name caldo verde—literally, "green broth"—reflects the abundance of kale in the pot.

INGREDIENTS

¾ pound kale, preferably Tuscan kale, center rib removed

¼ cup extra virgin olive oil, plus more for drizzling

1 large yellow onion, minced

3 cloves garlic, minced

6 Yukon Gold potatoes, about 2½ pounds total, peeled and thinly sliced

1 tablespoon kosher or sea salt

2 quarts water

Freshly ground black pepper

¼ pound linguiça or Spanish-style chorizo sausage, sliced ¼ inch thick

1 Stack a few of the kale leaves at a time and slice crosswise into ribbons as fine as possible. The ribbons should be no more than 2 inches long or they will be awkward to eat.

2 Heat the olive oil in a large pot over moderate heat. Add the onion and garlic and sauté until the onion has softened, about 10 minutes. Add the potatoes, salt, and water. Bring to a simmer, cover partially, and cook until the potatoes are tender, about 30 minutes.

3 With a wooden spoon, mash the potatoes against the sides of the pot to thicken the broth. The texture does not need to be completely smooth, but most of the potatoes should be crushed.

4 Stir in the kale and several grinds of black pepper. Taste for salt. Simmer gently, uncovered, until the kale is tender, 10 to 15 minutes.

5 Fry the sausage slices in a medium, nonstick skillet over moderate heat, turning once, until crusty on both sides.

6 Ladle the soup into warmed bowls. Top each portion with 2 or 3 sausage slices. Drizzle each portion with olive oil. Offer any remaining sausage on the side. Serve immediately.

FUSILLI WITH WINTER PESTO

Serves 6

Like all good things, summer's fresh basil season comes to an end, but that doesn't mean that pesto making has to cease. Kale, especially the tender, frilly leaves of Tuscan kale, makes a delightful cold-weather pesto—as green as the one made with basil, if less aromatic. Walnuts add a toasty note, ricotta enriches it, and pecorino contributes a salty bite.

INGREDIENTS

½ pound Tuscan kale, central ribs removed

½ cup walnut pieces, toasted (page xiv)

2 cloves garlic, sliced

½ cup whole-milk ricotta cheese

½ cup extra virgin olive oil

¼ cup freshly grated pecorino cheese, plus more for the table

Kosher or sea salt and freshly ground black pepper

1½ pounds fusilli or spaghetti

1 Bring a large pot of salted water to a boil over high heat. Add the kale and boil until tender, 3 to 5 minutes. With a wire-mesh skimmer or tongs, transfer the kale to a sieve or colander and run under cold running water until cool. Drain again and squeeze to remove excess moisture. Keep the pot of water boiling.

2 Put the kale, walnuts, and garlic in a food processor and pulse until nearly smooth. Add the ricotta and pulse again until blended. With the motor running, add the olive oil through the feed tube. Transfer the pesto to a bowl and stir in the pecorino, then season with salt and pepper.

3 Add the pasta to the boiling water and cook, stirring often with tongs, until al dente. Just before the pasta is ready to drain, scoop some boiling water from the pot and use it to thin the pesto to a loose sauce consistency. Set aside an additional 1 cup boiling water to use for further thinning, if needed.

4 Drain the pasta and return it to the hot pot. Add the pesto and, using tongs, toss the pasta with the sauce, thinning with some of the reserved hot water if necessary. Divide among warmed bowls and serve immediately. Pass additional pecorino at the table.

Ham Hock Greens

A light, peppery broth made with a ham hock is ideal for cooking sturdy greens, such as mustard, turnip greens, or collards. The broth infuses the greens with meaty richness without adding much fat. You can substitute slab bacon or smoked turkey wings for the ham hock if you prefer, and you can make the broth a day or two ahead. Serve in big soup bowls with corn bread for a weekday dinner.

Ingredients

3 quarts water

1 pound ham hock, sawed into 2 or 3 pieces

½ large yellow onion

4 cloves garlic, sliced

12 black peppercorns

2 bay leaves

2 pounds mustard greens, central rib removed

Kosher or sea salt

Hot pepper vinegar, homemade (page 124) or
   store-bought

1 Put the water in a large pot, preferably one that is deeper than it is wide so that the water will cover the ham hock. Put the ham hock in the pot; the water should cover it by 1½ to 2 inches. Add the onion, garlic, peppercorns, and bay leaves. Bring to a simmer over high heat, skimming any foam, then partially cover, adjust the heat to maintain a gentle simmer, and cook until the ham hock is tender, with the meat beginning to pull away from the bone, 2½ to 3 hours.

2 Strain the broth, reserving the ham hock but discarding the onion, garlic, peppercorns, and bay leaves. You should have about 1½ quarts broth; if not, add water to make 1½ quarts. Return the broth to the pot and bring to a simmer over moderate heat.

3 Stack the mustard greens, a few at a time, and chop coarsely. Add the greens to the simmering liquid, stirring them down with a wooden spoon. Cook, uncovered, simmering steadily and stirring occasionally, until the greens are tender, 20 to 30 minutes. Season with salt. Return the ham hock to the pot and let the greens cool in their liquid. Cover and refrigerate overnight, if possible.

4 To serve, reheat the greens and ham hock over moderate heat. Divide among warmed bowls, accompanying each portion with a chunk of meat from the ham hock and some of the pot liquor (cooking liquid). Pass hot pepper vinegar separately.

BABY GREENS WITH PERSIMMONS, FENNEL, AND WALNUTS

Serves 4 to 6

Many farmers grow delicate mixed salad greens known as "cut-and-come-again" lettuces. Harvesters snip them at the base with knives or scissors rather than pull them up by the roots; if the weather cooperates, the greens will grow again. Farmers typically wash lettuces in big tubs and spin them dry—some use a washing machine on the spin cycle—but it's a good idea to repeat the washing at home. The small, squat Fuyu persimmons are firm when ripe. Their skin should be the color of pumpkin, with no sign of green.

INGREDIENTS

DRESSING

1 large shallot, minced
1 tablespoon white wine vinegar
2 tablespoons walnut oil
1 tablespoon extra virgin olive oil
Kosher or sea salt and freshly ground black pepper

½ large fennel bulb
2 ripe but firm Fuyu persimmons
¼ pound mixed baby salad greens
⅔ cup walnut halves, toasted (page xiv) and
    coarsely chopped

1 To make the dressing, put the shallot and vinegar in a small bowl. Whisk in the walnut oil and olive oil and season with salt and pepper.

2 Halve the fennel bulb again lengthwise. With a mandoline or other manual vegetable slicer, or with a sharp chef's knife, slice the fennel crosswise as thinly as possible.

3 Cut out the persimmons' cap, then peel the persimmons and cut in half through the stem end. With the mandoline or other vegetable slicer, or with the sharp chef's knife, slice each half crosswise as thinly as possible. Remove any black seeds; some persimmons have them, some don't.

4 Put the baby greens, fennel, persimmons, and walnuts in a salad bowl and toss gently to mix. Add just enough dressing to coat the salad lightly; you may not need it all. Taste for salt, pepper, and vinegar. Serve immediately.

GRILLED ROMAINE WITH A SIX-MINUTE FARM EGG

Serves 4

Why six minutes? Because that timing produces a picture-perfect boiled egg, with a firm white and a creamy, brilliant yellow yolk. If you have never grilled romaine hearts, a delightful surprise awaits. Thanks to their natural sugar, they color up beautifully on the grill. Cook them until they hover on the brink between tender and crisp. Shower with Parmigiano Reggiano and accompany with lemon wedges and your impeccable eggs. Serve as a first course or side dish for a grilled T-bone steak.

INGREDIENTS

4 large eggs, at room temperature

3 tablespoons extra virgin olive oil

4 hearts of romaine, each 5 to 6 ounces, halved
    lengthwise with the core attached

Kosher or sea salt and freshly ground black pepper

Chunk of Parmigiano Reggiano cheese, for grating

4 lemon wedges

1 Prepare a moderate charcoal fire or preheat a gas grill to medium (375°F).

2 Put the eggs in a saucepan with water to cover by 1 inch. Bring to a boil over high heat, then immediately cover and set aside for 6 minutes exactly. Drain and quickly run under cold running water until cool, then peel and set aside.

3 Put the olive oil on a tray or platter. Turn the romaine hearts in the oil to coat them all over. Season with salt.

4 Place the romaine hearts directly over the coals or gas flame. Cook, turning as needed, until they are lightly browned on both sides, crisp in spots, and tender yet still a touch crunchy, 5 to 7 minutes.

5 Transfer the romaine hearts to a serving platter or individual plates. Grind some pepper over the romaine, then grate Parmigiano Reggiano over them, using as much as you like. Cut the eggs in half and place them alongside the romaine. Sprinkle a little salt on the eggs. Accompany with the lemon wedges. Serve immediately.

Escarole Salad with Chopped Farm Eggs and Tarragon Dressing

Serves 4

The heart of a head of escarole is pale, mild, and crisp, but you must often remove a lot of sturdy, dark green leaves to get there. Don't throw them away. Save the outer leaves for cooking and the more tender inner leaves for salads such as this one. The fish sauce gives the dressing a heightened savory flavor, what taste experts call umami.

Ingredients

1 large head escarole
2 large eggs

DRESSING
1 tablespoon white wine vinegar, plus more
   if needed
1 tablespoon finely minced shallot
2 teaspoons minced fresh tarragon
1 teaspoon fish sauce (see Note, page 13), or
   2 anchovy fillets, minced to a paste
3 tablespoons extra virgin olive oil
Kosher or sea salt and freshly ground black pepper

1 Remove the tough, outer green leaves of escarole until you reach the paler, more tender leaves inside. Reserve the outer leaves for cooking. Wash and dry the inner leaves well and tear into bite-size pieces. You should have about 3 quarts loosely packed. Place the greens in a salad bowl.

2 Put the eggs in a small saucepan with water to cover by 1 inch. Bring to a boil over high heat, then immediately cover and remove from the heat. Let stand for 10 minutes. Drain and quickly run under cold running water until cool, then peel and set aside.

3 To make the dressing, in a small bowl, combine the vinegar, shallot, tarragon, and fish sauce. Whisk in the olive oil. Season with salt and pepper.

4 Add enough dressing to the escarole to coat the leaves lightly; you may not need it all. Toss well and taste. Add a splash of vinegar or more salt or pepper if needed.

5 Chop the eggs coarsely and sprinkle them over the salad. Toss gently so you don't break up the eggs too much. Serve immediately.

Farro Risotto with Jerusalem Artichokes

Serves 4 to 6

Farro is the Italian name for the ancient strain of wheat known in English as emmer. Cooked like risotto, with hot broth added a little at a time, the grains will swell and yield a creamy dish. Even when fully cooked, farro is firmer than rice; the finished risotto should be pleasantly chewy. Farro has a nutty, whole-grain flavor that complements Jerusalem artichokes; on another occasion, substitute sautéed mushrooms or leeks.

Ingredients

About 1½ quarts chicken or vegetable broth
  (if canned, use equal parts broth and water)
6 tablespoons extra virgin olive oil
1 small yellow onion, minced
1½ cups farro
1 pound Jerusalem artichokes
Kosher or sea salt and freshly ground black pepper
2 tablespoons minced fresh Italian parsley

1 Put the broth in a medium saucepan, bring to a simmer over moderate heat, then adjust the heat to keep the broth just below a simmer.

2 Heat 4 tablespoons of the olive oil in a large pot over moderate heat. Add the onion and sauté until softened and just starting to color, about 5 minutes. Add the farro and cook, stirring, until it is hot to the touch, about 1 minute.

3 Stir in 1 cup of the hot broth and adjust the heat so the liquid bubbles steadily but not vigorously. Once the farro absorbs the broth, begin adding more hot broth ½ cup at a time, stirring often and adding more liquid only when the previous addition has been absorbed.

4 While the farro simmers, peel the Jerusalem artichokes. Quarter each tuber lengthwise, then slice crosswise ¼ inch thick.

5 When the farro has cooked for 25 to 30 minutes and is beginning to soften, stir in the Jerusalem artichokes. Season with salt and pepper. Continue cooking the risotto, stirring often and adding broth gradually, until the Jerusalem artichokes just lose their crispness—don't let them get mushy—and the farro is al dente, about 10 minutes longer. You may not need all the broth; if you need more liquid, use simmering water from a tea kettle. Taste for salt and pepper. Cover and let the risotto stand for 5 minutes.

6 Stir in the remaining 2 tablespoons olive oil and the parsley. Divide the risotto among warmed bowls. Serve immediately.

ROASTED JERUSALEM ARTICHOKES WITH HERBES DE PROVENCE

Serves 6

Halved lengthwise and roasted in a hot oven, Jerusalem artichokes become crusty and browned on the cut face. Herbes de Provence, a blend that always includes dried thyme and lavender, enhances their subtle nutty taste. Serve as a side dish for roast chicken, pork chops, or leg of lamb.

INGREDIENTS

2 pounds Jerusalem artichokes, unpeeled, halved
  lengthwise
3 tablespoons extra virgin olive oil
1 tablespoon herbes de Provence
Kosher or sea salt and freshly ground black pepper

1 Preheat the oven to 425°F.

2 Put the halved artichokes in a bowl, add the olive oil and herbs, and season with salt and pepper. Toss well. Arrange, cut side down, on a large, heavy rimmed baking sheet. Bake until they are just tender when pierced and the cut side is browned, about 20 minutes. Jerusalem artichokes transition quickly from almost done to mushy, so take care not to overcook them.

3 Transfer to a serving bowl and taste for salt. Serve immediately.

SAUTÉED KOHLRABI WITH BUTTER AND DILL

Serves 4

Like turnips, which they resemble in both texture and flavor, kohlrabies make an excellent side dish for pork or duck. They must be pared thickly, down to the pale, moist flesh, but then they will cook quickly. For an even speedier version of this dish, grate the kohlrabies instead of cutting them in wedges. Vicki Westerhoff of Genesis Growers puts grated raw kohlrabi on her sandwiches for crunch. The purple- and green-skinned varieties are interchangeable in recipes.

INGREDIENTS

1½ pounds kohlrabi, thickly peeled
1½ tablespoons unsalted butter
2 cloves garlic, peeled and smashed with the side
  of a chef's knife
Kosher or sea salt and freshly ground black pepper
2 teaspoons minced fresh dill

1 Halve each kohlrabi vertically, then cut each half into thick wedges. You should get 6 to 8 wedges from a small kohlrabi, more from a larger one. The exact size of the wedges doesn't matter as long as all they are similar in size so they cook evenly.

2 Melt the butter in a large skillet over moderate heat. Add the kohlrabi wedges and garlic and season generously with salt and pepper. Toss to coat the wedges with the butter. Cover and reduce the heat to moderately low.

3 Cook until tender when pierced and golden in spots, 10 to 12 minutes; check often and adjust the heat to prevent scorching. Stir in the dill and taste for seasoning. Serve hot.

Focaccia with Leeks and Cherry Tomatoes

Makes one 12 by 17-inch focaccia

The Italian flatbread known as focaccia is a great recipe for a produce enthusiast to master because it is so adaptable. In this recipe, sautéed leeks and halved cherry tomatoes top the risen dough just before it goes into the oven. On another occasion, you could blanket the dough with thinly sliced boiled potatoes, rosemary oil, and goat cheese; or with tomato sauce and fried zucchini; or even with halved grapes and coarse sugar. Focaccia is readily portable, so it's an excellent choice for potlucks and picnics.

Ingredients

SPONGE
1 cup warm (105° to 115°F) water
1 teaspoon active dry yeast
1 cup unbleached all-purpose flour

DOUGH
½ cup lukewarm water
⅓ cup dry white wine
⅓ cup extra virgin olive oil
1 tablespoon kosher or sea salt
2 tablespoons cornmeal
2¾ cups unbleached all-purpose flour

4 tablespoons plus 2 teaspoons extra virgin olive oil

SEASONED OIL
2 tablespoons extra virgin olive oil
1 tablespoon minced fresh Italian parsley
1 small clove garlic, finely minced
Large pinch of kosher or sea salt
Large pinch of hot red pepper flakes (optional)

3 medium leeks, rinsed well and halved lengthwise, then sliced crosswise ⅓ inch thick (white and pale green parts only)
1 tablespoon minced fresh thyme
Kosher or sea salt
16 cherry tomatoes, or more if small, halved

1 To make the sponge, put the warm water in a small bowl and sprinkle the surface with the yeast. Let stand for 2 minutes to soften, then whisk with a fork to blend. Let stand until bubbly, about 10 minutes. Add the flour and stir with a wooden spoon until smooth. Cover with plastic wrap and leave at room temperature for 24 hours.

2 To make the dough, put the sponge in the bowl of a stand mixer fitted with the paddle. Add the lukewarm water, wine, olive oil, salt, and cornmeal. Mix on low speed to blend. With the mixer running, add the flour gradually. When the flour has been incorporated, raise the speed to medium and knead with the paddle for 5 minutes. The dough will be moist and a little sticky, but it will eventually clear the sides of the bowl.

3 Scrape down the sides of the bowl and the paddle. Cover the bowl with plastic wrap and let the dough rise at room temperature until doubled, about 1½ hours.

4 Using the 2 teaspoons olive oil, generously grease a 12 by 17-inch rimmed baking sheet. Punch down the dough and turn it out onto the prepared pan. With well-oiled fingers, poke and prod the dough into a rectangle that fills the pan. The dough is elastic and will want to spring back. If it resists your attempts to flatten it enough to cover the pan, let it rest for 5 minutes and try again. If it still springs back from the edges, let it rest 5 to 10 minutes longer and try once more. You should be able to flatten it sufficiently after a couple of rests. Let rise, uncovered, at room temperature until puffy, about 1½ hours.

5 About 45 minutes before you are ready to bake, position a rack in the center of the oven, then line the rack with baking tiles or a baking stone. Turn on the oven to 425°F and let it preheat for at least 45 minutes.

6 To make the seasoned oil, in a small bowl, whisk together the olive oil, parsley, and garlic. Add the salt and hot pepper flakes and set aside for at least 30 minutes to develop flavor.

7 Heat 2 tablespoons of the olive oil in a medium skillet over moderate heat. Add the leeks and thyme, season with salt, and stir well. Cover, reduce the heat to moderately low, and cook until the leeks are soft but not mushy, 12 to 15 minutes, uncovering to stir occasionally. Let cool.

8 Sprinkle the leeks evenly over the surface of the risen dough. Then nestle the cherry tomato halves, cut side up, evenly over the surface, pushing them down into the dough with your fingers. Brush the surface with the remaining 2 tablespoons olive oil and sprinkle with salt. Place the baking sheet directly on the tiles or baking stone and bake until the focaccia is golden brown, 20 to 25 minutes.

9 Loosen the focaccia with an offset spatula, then slide it out of the baking sheet and onto a rack. Brush while hot with the seasoned oil, then let cool for about 20 minutes before cutting. Serve warm.

GRILLED LEEKS WITH ROMESCO

Serves 4 to 6

In Spain's Catalonia region, people celebrate the harvest of calçots, the local sweet green onions, with an outdoor feast. The onions are blackened over a wood fire, wrapped in newspaper to steam until done, then unwrapped and served with romesco, the region's famous red pepper sauce. Leeks are not identical to calçots, but they are just as compatible with romesco, a sauce thickened with bread and almonds.

INGREDIENTS

ROMESCO

3 dried ñora chiles (see Note), or 1 large dried New
  Mexico chile

2 plum (Roma type) tomatoes, about ½ pound total,
  quartered lengthwise

2 cloves garlic, peeled

5 tablespoons extra virgin olive oil

1 slice Italian country bread, about ½ inch thick and
  4 inches long, crust removed

3 tablespoons whole natural almonds, toasted (page xiv)

2 teaspoons sherry vinegar, or more to taste

1 teaspoon pimentón de la Vera (smoked Spanish
  paprika), medium or hot

¼ teaspoon cayenne pepper

Kosher or sea salt

12 small to medium leeks, white and pale green parts

6 tablespoons extra virgin olive oil

Kosher or sea salt

1 To prepare the romesco, stem and seed the chiles. Put the chiles in a small saucepan with just enough water to cover them. Bring to a simmer over high heat, then reduce the heat and simmer gently for 5 minutes. Cover the pan, remove from the heat, and let stand until cool.

2 Preheat the oven to 400°F. Put the tomatoes and garlic in a small baking dish just large enough to hold them. Drizzle with 1 tablespoon of the olive oil and turn them in the oil to coat them evenly. Bake until the tomatoes soften and begin to caramelize, about 30 minutes. Let cool.

3 Heat 1 tablespoon of the olive oil in a small skillet over moderate heat. Add the bread and fry until golden on both sides. Cool, then break into 4 or 5 pieces.

4 Put the softened chiles (reserving the soaking liquid), roasted tomatoes and garlic, bread, almonds, vinegar, pimentón, and cayenne in a food processor or blender. Process to a paste. With the motor running, add the remaining 3 tablespoons olive oil through the feed tube (or the hole in the blender lid), processing until the mixture is nearly smooth. Transfer to a bowl and stir in salt to taste. Thin, if desired, with some of the reserved chile-soaking liquid.

5 Prepare a moderate charcoal fire for indirect grilling (page xiv) or preheat a gas grill to medium (375°F), leaving one burner unlit. Trim the root end of each leek, but keep the base intact to hold the leek together. Slice the leeks in half lengthwise and wash well between the layers. Dry thoroughly.

6 Put the 6 tablespoons olive oil on a tray or platter. Turn the leeks in the oil to coat them all over. Season with salt. Place the leeks over indirect heat, cover, and cook, turning once, until the leeks are soft and both sides are nicely colored, about 15 minutes. If necessary, put them directly over the coals or gas flame for the last couple of minutes, uncovered, to char them slightly. Serve hot or warm with a dollop of romesco, or pass the sauce separately.

NOTE: Dried ñora chiles may be ordered from www.latienda.com.

GRILLED OKRA WITH PIMENTÓN

Serves 4

What a surprise! Okra is fabulous on the grill. Barbara Frisbie, a patron of the Green Gate Farms CSA, shared this method and suggested a favorite seasoning for the charred okra: the smoky Spanish paprika (pimentón) from the region of La Vera.

INGREDIENTS

1 pound okra, preferably small
4 teaspoons extra virgin olive oil, plus more for serving
Kosher or sea salt
Pimentón de la Vera (smoked Spanish paprika), mild, medium, or hot

1 Prepare a moderate charcoal fire or preheat a gas grill to medium (375°F).

2 Trim the okra caps even with the pods. Put the olive oil on a platter. Turn the okra pods in the oil to coat them all. Season with salt.

3 Place the okra directly over the coals or gas flame, taking care to place them perpendicular to the bars of the grill rack so they do not fall through. Cover the grill and cook until the pods are tender, about 10 minutes, rolling them over halfway through cooking to brown evenly. Move them away from direct heat if they char too much before they cook through.

4 Transfer the okra to a serving platter, drizzle with a little additional oil, and sprinkle with *pimentón*. Serve immediately.

PICKLED OKRA, TEXAS STYLE

Makes 3 pints

Green Gate Farms CSA member Barbara Frisbie has adapted her grandmother's recipe for these okra pickles, using the small, firm pods she receives from this Austin farm. (She also grills okra; see page 109.) Offer these tangy, well-seasoned pickles with a hamburger, a grilled cheese sandwich, or slow-cooked pulled pork. Barbara likes them in martinis, too.

INGREDIENTS

2 teaspoons coriander seed
1 pound okra, preferably small
1 tablespoon yellow mustard seed
6 cloves garlic, peeled
6 small dried red chiles
2 cups cider vinegar
1½ tablespoons kosher or sea salt
2 cups water
1 tablespoon sugar

1 Fill a canning kettle with enough water to cover 3 wide-mouthed pint canning jars resting on the preserving rack. Bring to a boil. Wash the jars with hot, soapy water; rinse well, and keep upside down on a clean dish towel until you are ready to fill them. Put 3 new lids (never reuse lids) in a heatproof bowl and cover with boiling water.

2 Toast the coriander seed in a small, dry skillet over moderate heat until fragrant and beginning to darken. Let cool.

3 Trim the okra caps even with the pods. Divide the okra, coriander seed, mustard seed, garlic, and chiles evenly among the jars, packing the okra in tightly but neatly.

4 Put the vinegar, salt, and water in a small saucepan and bring to a boil. Add the sugar and stir until dissolved. Remove from the heat and ladle the hot liquid into the jars, leaving ½ inch of headspace. Wipe the jar rims clean with a damp paper towel. Top with the lids and then a screw band. Close tightly.

5 Place the jars on the preserving rack and lower it into the canning kettle. If the water doesn't cover the jars, add boiling water from a tea kettle. Cover the canning kettle. After the water returns to a boil, boil for 10 minutes. With a jar lifter, transfer the jars to a rack to cool completely. Do not touch the jars again until you hear the pops that indicate that the lids have sealed. You can confirm that a lid has sealed by pressing the center with your finger. If it gives, it has not sealed and the contents should be refrigerated and used within a week. Store the sealed jars in a cool, dark place for at least 1 month before using. They will keep for up to 1 year. Refrigerate after opening.

Basic Mustard-Shallot Vinaigrette

Makes a generous ¼ cup

Every cook needs to master a vinaigrette, the tangy dressing preferred in France for salad greens. To most palates, a ratio of three parts oil to one part vinegar is just about right, but feel free to adjust those proportions to suit your taste. To vary the vinaigrette, replace some of the olive oil with walnut oil or substitute sherry vinegar or lemon juice for the wine vinegar. Southeast Asian fish sauce is definitely an unconventional addition, but it adds an indescribable depth to the dressing.

This basic vinaigrette is not just for lettuces. It can dress a tomato or beet salad, grilled vegetables or fish. It will stay fresh tasting, if refrigerated, for about a day.

INGREDIENTS

1 teaspoon Dijon mustard, preferably moutarde
   de Maille
1 small shallot, finely minced
1 tablespoon red or white wine vinegar
3 tablespoons extra virgin olive oil

OPTIONAL ADDITIONS
1 teaspoon fish sauce (see Note, page 13)
1 teaspoon minced fresh tarragon or chives
1 teaspoon capers, rinsed and minced

Kosher or sea salt and freshly ground black pepper

1   In a small bowl, whisk together the mustard, shallot, and vinegar. Gradually whisk in the olive oil.

2   Whisk in any or all of the optional additions. Season to taste with salt and pepper.

CREAMY RED ONION SOUP WITH THYME   Serves 8

The slender, elongated Torpedo red onions harvested in early summer are especially mild and sweet, perfect for salads, sandwiches, and soups such as this one. Because they are high in moisture, they don't store well, so use them within a couple of weeks. Vicki Westerhoff at Genesis Growers cultivates the prized Tropea variety, a red heirloom from the southern Italian region of Calabria. Like Torpedo, Tropea is a mellow onion that would shine in this soup as well. The sharp, salty flavor of pecorino helps to balance the onions' sweetness, so it's a better choice here than Parmigiano Reggiano.

INGREDIENTS

⅓ cup extra virgin olive oil, plus more for brushing the bread

3 pounds sweet red onions, preferably Torpedo type, halved lengthwise, then thinly sliced crosswise

3 cloves garlic, sliced

Kosher or sea salt and freshly ground black pepper

1 tablespoon minced fresh thyme

1 tablespoon unbleached all-purpose flour

1½ quarts chicken broth (if canned, use equal parts broth and water), plus more if needed

8 baguette slices, about ½ inch thick, sliced at a 45-degree angle

½ cup freshly grated pecorino or Parmigiano Reggiano cheese

3 tablespoons minced fresh Italian parsley

1 Put the olive oil in a large pot over moderate heat. Add the onions and garlic and stir to coat them with the oil. Season well with salt. Cook, stirring often, until the onions become very soft and creamy, about 1 hour. They will throw some liquid at first, but after the liquid evaporates, they will begin to caramelize. Lower the heat if the onions threaten to stick to the bottom of the pan.

2 Just before the onions are ready, prepare a moderately hot charcoal fire or preheat a gas grill to medium-high (375° to 400°F).

3 When the onions are ready, add the thyme and flour and cook, stirring, for about 2 minutes. Then add the broth and bring to a simmer, stirring. Adjust the heat to maintain a gentle simmer and cook for 15 minutes to blend the flavors. Season with pepper and more salt if needed.

4 To give the soup extra body, puree about 2 cups of it (broth and onions) in a food processor or blender until smooth, then stir the puree back into the soup.

5 Brush the baguette slices on both sides with olive oil. Grill the bread on both sides directly over the coals or gas flame until golden brown.

6 Reheat the soup to serve. Divide it among warmed soup bowls. Float a grilled baguette slice on each portion, and sprinkle each slice with 1 tablespoon grated cheese. Garnish with the parsley. Serve immediately.

Glazed Cipolline Onions with Saffron and Sherry Vinegar

Serves 6

Italian cipolline (chip-oh-LEE-nay) onions are small, brown skinned, and squat, as if a weight flattened them. Peeled and braised with butter, honey, sherry, and raisins, they make an exotic sweet-tart condiment for roast pork, duck, or the Thanksgiving turkey. Saffron threads tint the onions the color of burnished gold.

Ingredients

1 pound cipolline onions

½ cup dry sherry

¼ cup golden raisins

2 tablespoons honey

1 tablespoon unsalted butter

⅛ teaspoon saffron threads

Kosher or sea salt and freshly ground black pepper

1 tablespoon pine nuts, toasted (page xiv)

2 teaspoons sherry vinegar, or more to taste

1. Bring a large pot of salted water to a boil over high heat. Prepare a large bowl of ice water. Add the onions to the boiling water and boil for 3 minutes. Drain in a sieve or colander, then transfer to the ice water to stop the cooking. When cool, drain again and peel. The skin will slip off each onion easily. Cut off the threadlike tail and trim the root end of any root hairs, but leave the root end intact to hold the onion together.

2. Combine the onions, sherry, raisins, honey, butter, saffron, and 2 tablespoons water in a 10-inch skillet. Season with salt and pepper. Bring to a simmer over moderately high heat, then cover and adjust the heat to maintain a gentle simmer. Cook for 20 minutes, then turn over the onions with tongs so they cook evenly. Re-cover and continue cooking until the onions are tender when pierced with a knife, 15 to 20 minutes longer.

3. Uncover, raise the heat to high, and cook until the juices have reduced almost to a glaze. Remove from the heat and let cool for about 15 minutes. Stir in the pine nuts and the sherry vinegar. Taste and adjust the seasoning. Serve warm.

Pickled Red Onions, Yucatán Style

Serves 6

In just one hour, these quickly made pickles develop an all-over rosy hue. They are the ever-present condiment in Yucatecan restaurants and homes, adding a tangy crunch to tacos and tostadas. Serve them with grilled skirt steak, sliced avocado, and a stack of warmed corn tortillas, or offer with sandwiches in place of a dill pickle.

Ingredients

1 large or 2 medium red onions, about 1 pound total
½ cup fresh orange juice
¼ cup fresh lime juice
1½ teaspoons kosher or sea salt
1 teaspoon dried Mexican oregano
½ teaspoon coarsely cracked black pepper

1 Trim the ends of the onion and cut in half through the stem end. Peel each half and cut away the core. Put each half, cut side down, on a cutting board and slice thinly, cutting from stem end to root end (not crosswise). Put the slices in a heatproof bowl.

2 Fill a tea kettle with water and bring to a boil. Pour the hot water over the onions and let stand for 1 minute, then drain in a sieve and immediately run under cold running water to cool. Drain well. Transfer the onions to a nonreactive bowl.

3 Add the orange juice, lime juice, salt, and oregano to the bowl, crumbling the herb between your fingers as you add it. Add the pepper and toss the onion slices to distribute the seasonings. Cover and let stand for at least 1 hour before using, stirring once or twice. For longer keeping, cover and refrigerate for up to 2 weeks.

FARMER BROWN'S PARSNIP CRISPS

Serves 6

Farmer Brown, a San Francisco soul-food restaurant, makes a delightful house salad with baby greens, shaved watermelon radishes, and these crunchy ribbons of fried parsnip. Use them to garnish your own house salad, or serve with drinks before dinner.

INGREDIENTS

2 medium parsnips
Canola oil for deep-frying
Kosher or sea salt

1 Peel the parsnips with a vegetable peeler and trim both ends. Cut away the tips if they are less than ½ inch in diameter. Cut the trimmed parsnips into roughly 3-inch lengths. Using the vegetable peeler, shave the pieces lengthwise into long, wide ribbons. Don't worry if they are not uniform.

2 Pour the canola oil in a large, heavy pot to a depth of 2 inches and heat to 360°F. Working in small batches, add the parsnip ribbons and deep-fry, agitating them constantly with a wire-mesh skimmer, until they are nut brown all over and crisp, about 1½ minutes, adjusting the heat as needed to maintain the temperature as close to 360°F as possible. (If they are not fully browned, they will not be sufficiently crisp.) With the skimmer, transfer them to a double thickness of paper towels to drain. Sprinkle with salt while hot. The crisps are best when served within a few minutes of frying, but they will stay crunchy for about an hour.

PARSNIP SOUP WITH FRIED SAGE

Serves 6

Parsnips may look like pale carrots, but their sweet, nutty flavor and slightly starchy texture are closer to chestnuts or Japanese sweet potatoes. Pureed with onions and broth, they make a velvety soup the color of ivory. Float crisp fried sage leaves on top for a dramatic garnish, or top more simply with a sliver of butter and sprinkling of chives.

INGREDIENTS

1½ pounds parsnips
2 tablespoons unsalted butter
½ large yellow onion, thinly sliced
1 large celery rib, thinly sliced
5 cups chicken or vegetable broth (if canned, use
    equal parts broth and water), plus more if needed
6 thyme sprigs
Kosher or sea salt and freshly ground black pepper

GARNISH
2 tablespoons extra virgin olive oil
12 fresh sage leaves
Kosher or sea salt

1 Peel the parsnips with a vegetable peeler and trim the thick stem end. Remove any part of the slender tip that is thinner than a pencil. Cut the trimmed parsnips into manageable lengths of about 3 inches, and then quarter lengthwise. With a paring knife, cut away and discard the hard central core. Cut the trimmed parsnips into ½-inch dice. You should have about 5 cups.

2 Melt the butter in a large, heavy pot over moderate heat. Add the onion and celery and cook, stirring often, until the onion starts to color, 7 to 8 minutes. Add the parsnips, broth, and thyme sprigs and bring to a simmer. Cover, adjust the heat to maintain a gentle simmer, and cook until the parsnips are tender, about 20 minutes.

3 Remove the thyme sprigs. Let the soup cool slightly, then puree in a blender or food processor until smooth, in batches if necessary. Return the soup to a clean pot and reheat to serve, thinning to the desired consistency with additional broth. Season with salt and pepper.

4 While the soup reheats, prepare the garnish. Heat the olive oil in a small skillet over moderately high heat. Add the sage leaves in batches and cook quickly, turning once or twice, until crisp, about 1 minute total. Transfer the leaves to paper towels to drain. Sprinkle with salt. They will crisp more as they cool.

5 Divide the soup among warmed soup bowls. Garnish each portion with 2 sage leaves. Serve immediately.

Spring Peas with Crème Fraîche and Herbs

Serves 4

It's rare to find English peas in a supermarket at that perfect stage of maturity, when they have filled out their pods and you can feel the peas distinctly but they have yet to become overlarge and starchy. Purchased from a farmers' market or through a CSA, peas are much more likely to be recently picked, moist, and sweet. They decline rapidly in storage, so freshness is paramount. In this recipe, the peas are braised with butter and spring onions and finished with thick crème fraîche to make a side dish for roast leg of lamb, lamb chops, or roast chicken. You can prepare carrots by the same method.

Ingredients

1 tablespoon unsalted butter

½ cup thinly sliced spring onions or green onions (white and pale green parts only)

2 pounds English peas, shelled (2 to 2½ cups shelled)

¼ cup water

¼ cup crème fraîche

1 tablespoon thinly sliced fresh mint, or
   2 tablespoons thinly sliced fresh chives or chopped fresh chervil

Kosher or sea salt and freshly ground black pepper

1 Melt the butter in a small, wide saucepan over moderate heat. Add the spring onions and sauté until softened, about 3 minutes. Add the peas and water and bring to a simmer. Cover and cook until tender, 8 to 10 minutes or a little longer, depending on the size and age of the peas. If the pan threatens to cook dry, add a few more tablespoons water.

2 When the peas are tender, uncover, raise the heat to high, and evaporate the excess liquid. Reduce the heat to moderate and stir in the crème fraîche and herbs. Season with salt and pepper, bring to a simmer, and serve immediately.

Peas and Pods

Serves 6

Put three different types of peas together for a side dish that's all about spring. Gloss the vegetables with butter and lavish them with the tender herbs that are just coming on strong in pea season. You can use whatever combination of herbs you like, but be a miser with tarragon. It can overtake such a delicate dish.

Ingredients

1½ pounds English peas, shelled (about 1½ cups shelled)

½ pound sugar snap peas, ends trimmed

½ pound snow peas, ends trimmed

3 tablespoons unsalted butter

2 large shallots, thinly sliced

Kosher or sea salt and freshly ground black pepper

2 tablespoons chopped fresh mixed herbs of choice (such as chervil, chives, Italian parsley, tarragon, mint, or basil, in any combination)

1 Bring a large pot of salted water to a boil over high heat. Prepare a large bowl of ice water. Add the English peas to the boiling water and boil until tender, 5 to 8 minutes, depending on their size and age. With a wire-mesh skimmer, transfer them to the ice water to stop the cooking. Add the sugar snap peas to the boiling water and cook until just tender, about 3 minutes. Transfer them to the ice water. Finally, add the snow peas to the boiling water and cook until just tender, about 2 minutes. Transfer them to the ice water with the skimmer. Set aside about 1 cup of the cooking water, then discard the rest.

2 When all the peas are cool, drain in a sieve or colander and pat dry on a kitchen towel.

3 Melt 2 tablespoons of the butter in a large skillet over moderate heat. Add the shallots and sauté until softened, about 3 minutes. Add all the peas and season highly with salt and pepper. Cook, stirring, until hot throughout, splashing them with a little of the vegetable-cooking water to moisten them. Just before serving, stir in the herbs and the remaining 1 tablespoon butter. Toss until the butter melts, then serve immediately.

Braised Peas and Fennel with Pecorino

Serves 4

Braising peas rather than boiling them produces a deeper, more savory taste. The peas don't stay brilliantly green, but they compensate with a more concentrated flavor. Fennel, braised to softness along with the peas, adds a complementary anise note, and a shower of sharp pecorino cheese relieves the sweetness. Serve as a side dish with lamb, pork, or chicken.

Ingredients

1 medium fennel bulb
2 tablespoons extra virgin olive oil
2 large shallots, thinly sliced
Kosher or sea salt and freshly ground black pepper
1 pound English peas, shelled (1 to 1¼ cups shelled)
2 tablespoons minced fresh Italian parsley
Freshly grated pecorino cheese

1 Quarter the fennel bulb lengthwise, then cut each quarter into 3 wedges, keeping the core intact to hold each wedge together.

2 Heat the olive oil in a large skillet over moderately low heat. Add the shallots and sauté until softened, 3 to 5 minutes. Add the fennel wedges, season with salt and pepper, and turn to coat with the oil. Cover and cook over low to moderately low heat for about 5 minutes. Add the peas, re-cover, and continue to cook slowly until both the peas and fennel are tender, 15 to 20 minutes longer, depending on the size and age of the peas. The vegetables should generate enough steam that you do not need to add any liquid, but if they threaten to stick, add a tablespoon or two of water.

3 Season again with salt and pepper and stir in the parsley and a generous shower of pecorino. Transfer to a serving bowl and top with a little more pecorino. Serve immediately.

GRILLED SWORDFISH WITH PEPERONATA   Serves 4

In Italy, peperonata—braised peppers with tomato and onion—is typically served as an antipasto or side dish, but it makes a superb fish topping. Substitute tuna, halibut, or cod for the swordfish, if you prefer. Swordfish should be sliced thin and cooked quickly for maximum juiciness. If your merchant has already sliced it into thick steaks, ask to have it halved horizontally, or do it at home yourself with a long, thin knife.

INGREDIENTS

PEPERONATA

3 tablespoons extra virgin olive oil

½ large red onion, thinly sliced

2 cloves garlic, minced

1 cup grated plum (Roma type) tomato (page xiv)

2 large bell peppers, 1 red and 1 gold, seeds removed
 and cut lengthwise into ¼-inch-wide strips

Kosher or sea salt

Generous pinch of hot red pepper flakes

1½ tablespoons capers, preferably salt packed,
 rinsed

Red or white wine vinegar

12 fresh basil leaves, plus more for optional garnish

4 swordfish steaks, about 6 ounces each and
 ½ inch thick

Extra virgin olive oil

Kosher or sea salt

1 teaspoon fennel seed, crushed in a mortar or
 spice grinder

1 To make the *peperonata*, heat 2 tablespoons of the olive oil in a large skillet over moderately low heat. Add the onion and garlic and sauté until the onion is soft, about 5 minutes. Add the tomato and simmer until it loses its raw taste, about 5 minutes. Add the bell peppers and season with salt and hot pepper flakes. Cover and simmer gently until the peppers are tender, about 25 minutes. Add a tablespoon or two of water if the mixture looks dry, or uncover the skillet at the end of cooking to evaporate moisture if the mixture is too juicy. The juices should be concentrated, not runny. Stir in the capers and a splash of vinegar to brighten the flavor, then taste for salt. Set aside to cool until just warm, not hot. Stir in the basil, torn into smaller pieces.

2 While the *peperonata* is cooking, prepare a moderate charcoal fire or preheat a gas grill to medium (375°F). When the *peperonata* has been set aside to cool, brush the fish generously on both sides with olive oil, then season on both sides with salt and fennel seed. Grill directly over the coals or gas flame, turning once, until the fish is white throughout but still juicy, 2 to 3 minutes per side.

3 Transfer the swordfish to a serving platter. Top each steak with some of the warm *peperonata*, mounding it attractively. Garnish with more basil, torn into smaller pieces. Serve immediately.

HOT PEPPER VINEGAR

Makes one 375-milliliter bottle

A splash of hot pepper vinegar elevates the flavor of cooked greens, green beans, cauliflower, roasted peppers, and spinach. And if you keep the bottle at the ready, you will find many other dishes that appreciate a dash. You can use any fresh chiles, or a mix of colors and types. Slitting them helps release their heat. Be careful when working with fresh chiles. Wear gloves if your skin is sensitive, avoid touching your face, and be sure to wash your hands well afterward.

INGREDIENTS

About 24 small fresh red or green chiles, or a mix
1 large clove garlic, halved
White wine vinegar

1 Leave the stems on the chiles, but cut a long slit in each chile. Pack the chiles and garlic in a clean 375-milliliter wine bottle. Use as many of the chiles as will fit comfortably.

2 Fill the bottle with the vinegar. Top with a cork-ended pour spout (available at hardware stores). Keep in a cool place. Taste occasionally to determine when the chiles have infused the vinegar sufficiently; it will probably take about 2 weeks. The vinegar will keep indefinitely.

GRILLED ROASTED PEPPER AND TELEME SANDWICH WITH ANCHOVIES AND ARUGULA   Serves 4

Who doesn't love a grilled cheese sandwich? This sophisticated one marries soft, melting Teleme cheese with sun-ripened sweet peppers, anchovies, and nutty arugula. Be careful in your choice of bread. If the texture is airy, with many openings, the cheese may drip onto the grill. Select a loaf, such as a pugliese, that is tall enough to yield slices with a lot of surface area. Depending on the bakery you patronize, ciabatta may be too flat.

INGREDIENTS

2 large sweet peppers, any color

8 slices Italian country bread (see introduction),
   about ½ inch thick

Extra virgin olive oil

½ pound Teleme or fresh whole-milk mozzarella cheese,
   cut into 4 equal pieces

Hot red pepper flakes

Dried oregano

8 anchovy fillets, torn into smaller pieces

2 ounces arugula (large handful)

1 Prepare a moderate charcoal fire or preheat a gas grill to medium (375°F). Grill the peppers directly over the coals or gas flame, turning occasionally, until blackened on all sides. When cool enough to handle, peel the peppers and remove the stem and seeds. Cut lengthwise into ½-inch-wide strips.

2 Brush the bread slices on both sides with the olive oil. Top 4 of the bread slices with the cheese, arranging each piece so that it covers the whole bread slice. Sprinkle the cheese generously with hot pepper flakes and oregano, crumbling the herb between your fingers as you add it. (Be bold with the seasonings as the cheese is bland.) Top evenly with the anchovy pieces, then with a clump of arugula and some roasted pepper strips. Top with the remaining bread slice.

3 Place the sandwiches directly over the coals or gas flame and cook, turning once, until the bread on both sides is nicely toasted and the cheese is molten, about 3 minutes per side, depending on the heat of the fire. Cut in half and serve immediately.

RED PEPPER HUMMUS

Makes about 2⅔ cups

You may find that you want to keep this hummus on hand all the time to use as a wholesome dip for crudités—try with raw kohlrabi, fennel, cucumber, or pepper strips—or as a sandwich spread. Or make a tempting meze assortment with hummus, wedges of roasted beets, Kalamata olives, and pita crisps (page 77).

INGREDIENTS

1 cup dried chickpeas

½ yellow onion

2 bay leaves

Kosher or sea salt

2 small red bell peppers

¼ cup tahini

¼ cup extra virgin olive oil

¼ cup fresh lemon juice, plus more to taste

2 cloves garlic, sliced

1 teaspoon cumin seed, toasted (page xiv) and finely ground

¼ teaspoon Spanish paprika, preferably the smoked pimentón de la Vera

1 Put the chickpeas in a medium bowl, add water to cover generously, and soak overnight. Drain and rinse, then put in a medium pot with cold water to cover by 1 inch. Bring to a simmer over moderate heat, skimming any foam. Add the onion half and bay leaves, cover, and adjust the heat to maintain a gentle simmer. Cook until the chickpeas are tender, 1 to 1½ hours. Season with salt and let cool in the liquid.

2 Prepare a moderate charcoal fire or preheat a gas grill to medium (375°F). Grill the peppers directly over the coals or gas flame, turning occasionally, until blackened on all sides. When cool enough to handle, peel the peppers and remove the stem and seeds. Cut each into quarters.

3 Drain the chickpeas and discard the onion and bay leaves. Place in a food processor along with the roasted peppers, tahini, olive oil, lemon juice, garlic, cumin, and paprika and process until smooth. Season with salt and process again. Taste and add more lemon if desired. Serve immediately or cover and refrigerate for up to 1 week, bringing to room temperature before serving.

GRILLED FINGERLING POTATOES WITH CREMA AND CHILE POWDER

Serves 4

Waxy fingerling potatoes like Russian Banana and Rose Finn Apple respond beautifully to grilling. Boil them first, then halve and sear them until they are golden brown and crusty all over. Drizzle them with crema, the thick cultured cream sold in Mexican markets, and sprinkle with chile powder to give them a Mexican accent. Serve with a grilled skirt steak, chicken, or ribs.

INGREDIENTS

1 pound fingerling potatoes, unpeeled
1 tablespoon extra virgin olive oil
Kosher or sea salt
¼ cup *crema* or sour cream
Ancho chile powder or other chile powder
1 tablespoon minced fresh cilantro

1 Prepare a moderate charcoal fire or preheat a gas grill to medium (375°F).

2 Put the potatoes in a medium pot and add water to cover by 1 inch and bring to a boil over high heat. Reduce the heat to maintain a simmer and cook just until you can pierce the potatoes easily, about 15 minutes. Drain and let cool. Cut in half lengthwise.

3 Brush the potatoes all over with the olive oil and season with salt. Place, cut side down, directly over the coals or gas flame and grill until richly browned, about 5 minutes. Turn the potatoes and grill on the skin side until nicely crisped, about 5 minutes longer.

4 Place the potatoes, cut side up, on a serving platter. In a small bowl, whisk the *crema* with just enough water to make it pourable. Drizzle the *crema* over the potatoes, then sprinkle with chile powder to taste and garnish with the cilantro. Serve immediately.

FOIL-ROASTED NEW POTATOES WITH GARLIC AND THYME

Serves 4

Choose small potatoes, about an ounce each, for roasting in foil packages directly on a bed of coals. If the potatoes are larger, they will char too much before they are done. Even small potatoes will be lightly charred, but that is part of their rustic appeal. The coals impart an irresistible smoky flavor.

INGREDIENTS

1 pound small new potatoes (12 to 16)
1 tablespoon extra virgin olive oil
Kosher or sea salt
4 generous thyme sprigs
8 large cloves garlic, unpeeled

1 Prepare a moderate charcoal fire. Toss the potatoes with the olive oil and salt. Divide them among 4 pieces of heavy-duty aluminum foil, each roughly 14 inches square. Place 1 thyme sprig and 2 garlic cloves on each packet, then fold the foil in half to enclose the potatoes. Fold the edge of the foil over all the way around to seal each packet.

2 Spread the coals into an evenly thick bed. Place the packets directly on the coals. Cover the grill and cook, vents open, for 7 to 8 minutes. Flip the packets, re-cover the grill, and continue cooking until the potatoes are tender when pierced, 8 to 10 minutes longer. The only way to know for sure that the potatoes are done is to remove a packet, carefully open it (watch for escaping steam), and pierce a potato with a skewer or paring knife. If necessary, reseal the packet and put it back on the coals.

3 At an informal outdoor meal, slit each packet to release the steam, then serve 1 packet per guest. Alternatively, slit all the packets, transfer the contents to a single bowl, and serve family style.

PURPLE POTATO CHIPS

Serves 4

If you thought you couldn't resist packaged potato chips, wait until you taste the homemade ones. They are certain to make an impression, even more so when prepared with purple-fleshed potatoes, like the Adirondack Blue variety cultivated by Vicki Westerhoff at Genesis Growers. The only difficult part is leaving some for guests.

INGREDIENTS

1 pound purple potatoes (no need to peel)
Grape seed or canola oil for deep-frying
Kosher or sea salt

1 With a mandoline or other manual vegetable slicer, or with a sharp chef's knife, slice the potatoes 1/16 inch thick. Put the potatoes in a large bowl of ice water to remove the surface starch and let soak for 30 minutes. Drain and pat thoroughly dry on kitchen towels. (If the potatoes are not dry, they will spatter in the hot oil.)

2 Pour the oil into a large, deep pot to a depth of 2 to 3 inches and heat to 360ºF. Working in small batches, add the potato slices and deep-fry, agitating them constantly with a wire skimmer, until they are lightly browned, 2 to 3 minutes, adjusting the heat as needed to maintain the oil temperature as close to 360ºF as possible. With the skimmer, transfer them to a double thickness of paper towels to drain. Sprinkle with salt while hot. Serve as soon as possible. They will remain crisp for about an hour.

SKILLET-COOKED CREAMER POTATOES WITH ROSEMARY

Serves 4

In the world of the potato farmer, creamers are the smallest new potatoes, ranging in size from a marble to a Ping-Pong ball. In less cholesterol-conscious times, cooks probably simmered them in cream—hence the name—but olive oil makes a more heart-healthy choice today. Cooked in a covered skillet with a sprig of rosemary and whole cloves of garlic, they brown beautifully and absorb the aromas of the seasonings. Potato enthusiasts can make a whole meal of them with a salad and a piece of cheese but, of course, they can be a side dish, too.

INGREDIENTS

1½ pounds creamer potatoes

2 tablespoons extra virgin olive oil

1 rosemary sprig, 6 inches long

6 cloves garlic, peeled

Kosher or sea salt

1 Put the potatoes, olive oil, rosemary, and garlic in a heavy skillet just large enough to hold the potatoes in a single layer. Season with salt. Cover and cook over moderately low heat, shaking the skillet occasionally to rotate the potatoes, until the potatoes are tender when pierced, about 30 minutes, depending on their size.

2 Remove the rosemary sprig and sprinkle with more salt. Serve immediately.

GOLDEN EARTHWORM ORGANIC FARM

Home sites on the desirable North Fork of Long Island can sell for a million dollars, making it hard to justify growing potatoes there. Most farmers have cashed in, selling family land that had been in agriculture for generations. But a handful of holdouts remain, which is why Matthew Kurek, Maggie Wood, and James Russo could piece together eighty acres of leased land for Golden Earthworm, their organic farm on Peconic Bay in Jamesport.

Among the partners, only James felt called to farming at an early age and took a direct path there—a college degree in plant and soil science, followed by a viticulture job on a Long Island vineyard. Matthew and Maggie, now married, traveled less obvious routes. Maggie, the daughter of music professionals, played classical flute seriously; Matthew studied oboe with an eye on a music career. Both eventually put aside their instruments for other pursuits: architecture for Maggie (she still has a part-time design practice), cooking for Matthew.

After a few years working in Manhattan restaurants and hanging out at the Union Square Greenmarket, Matthew moved back to his childhood home on the North Fork with the vague notion of growing produce for restaurants. "It was a complete experiment," admits Matthew, who had no farming background. Eliot Coleman's books on organic farming provided inspiration, and New Age notions of human potential—if you can imagine it, you can do it—gave him confidence.

By 1999 he had a small CSA—perhaps twenty-five members—and was selling some of his organic produce at the farmers' market in Port Washington, on the west end of Long Island. Maggie's mother, who founded the market, told her daughter about the handsome young vendor.

In 2005, the year the couple married, James joined the farming partnership, disheartened by the chemical spraying that most Long Island wine grapes require. With Maggie handling marketing and communications, the Golden Earthworm CSA has mushroomed to sixteen hundred shares, plus a waiting list. The United Way in Queens accounts for a few hundred of those shares, distributing the just-picked produce to soup kitchens.

Matthew and James no longer try to grow the fashionable produce that leading chefs want—"fluffy stuff" Matthew calls it. Harvesting edible flowers for elite diners isn't nearly as satisfying, in their view, as growing kale, broccoli, beets, and tomatoes for regular folks. "You can spend your time on the 'wow' factor, or you can give people a lot of good food," says Matthew.

The farm delivers CSA boxes to numerous sites on Long Island and in Queens, and still participates in farmers' markets. A thrice-weekly farm stand on the Jamesport property draws neighbors and a few shareholders who pick up their boxes on the farm. Hoping to encourage families to visit, the farmers keep a few rare-breed animals as pets: Gloucestershire Old Spots pigs, Navajo-Churro sheep, and Angora goats. Some CSA members turn the wool into sweaters, and local teachers use it in the classroom to demonstrate the technique of carding, or preparing wool for spinning.

At a Glance

Farm name: Earthworms are treasured laborers on an organic farm. They aerate the soil, and their castings (droppings) are high in plant nutrients. To farmers trying to operate without chemical fertilizers, earthworms are as good as gold.

Insight: Not everyone is a good CSA member, says Maggie. If you're not willing to be flexible in the kitchen, shop at a farmers' market.

Favorite crops: Hakurei turnip, Primetime tomato, Purple Majesty potato, wild purslane— a weed to some, but to others, "the most coveted crop of the season," says Maggie. "People have complained about getting tomatoes instead of purslane."

Kitchen motto: When in doubt, mash it.

Teachable moment: "CSA sounds great. But will I need to cook the vegetables?"

Because they don't own the land they farm, the partners hesitate to invest in infrastructure, the permanent fences, structures, and outbuildings that would make their work easier. Purchasing acreage in the area is nothing short of a fantasy, but farming on leased land can keep a grower awake at night.

In the meantime, the partners take pride in running a sustainable organic farm without trust funds, grants, or bank loans. They pay employees decently, they say, and still turn a profit. They maintain organic certification only because they would farm organically anyway, says Maggie, and because it's easier to be certified than to explain to customers why you're not.

But the work is relentless. Beginning in May, Matthew and James can work seven days a week. "I don't see my husband again until the end of October," jokes Maggie. Although the farm operates through the winter—supplying a few hundred customers with produce shares—the pace slows. Maggie and Matthew, who live across the street from the farm, in a home on the beach, spend more time together then. "We do the things other people do during the summer," says Maggie. "We have lunch together every day; we make fires and read." And these two music lovers go to the opera in New York City, a world away from digging potatoes on the North Fork.

GRILLED RADICCHIO WITH BAGNA CAUDA

Serves 4

What Italians know as bagna cauda—literally, "hot bath"—is the world's most aromatic dip: hot olive oil with anchovies and garlic melted in it. Although Italians typically dunk raw vegetables, such as fennel or celery, into bagna cauda, in this recipe it is used as a sauce. Because you need a generous portion of oil to cover the garlic in the pan, it is easier to make a large quantity of bagna cauda than it is to make a small amount. Reserve the remainder for tossing with pasta or spooning over boiled broccoli rabe, cauliflower, or spinach or a grilled steak. It will keep refrigerated for 1 week.

INGREDIENTS

BAGNA CAUDA
½ cup extra virgin olive oil
8 large cloves garlic, minced
8 anchovy fillets, finely minced

3 tablespoons extra virgin olive oil
2 heads radicchio, about ½ pound each, quartered through the core and leaving the core attached
Kosher or sea salt
Minced fresh Italian parsley, for garnish
4 lemon wedges

1 Prepare a moderate charcoal fire for indirect grilling (page xiv) or preheat a gas grill to medium (375°F), leaving one burner unlit.

2 To make the *bagna cauda*, put the ½ cup olive oil and garlic in a small saucepan and place over low heat. Cook until the garlic is very soft and fragrant, about 30 minutes. Remove from the heat, add the anchovies, and stir until the anchovies dissolve. Return the saucepan to low heat and keep warm.

3 Put the 3 tablespoons olive oil on a tray or platter. Turn the radicchio wedges in the oil to coat them all over. Season with salt.

4 Place the radicchio over indirect heat, cover the grill, and cook, turning occasionally, until softened and crisp in parts, about 10 minutes.

5 Transfer the radicchio to a platter and drizzle with the warm *bagna cauda*, using about half of it and reserving the remainder for another use. Garnish with the parsley and accompany with the lemon wedges. Serve immediately.

VIETNAMESE-STYLE CARROT AND DAIKON PICKLE

Serves 8

Crunchy and sweet-tart, these refreshing pickles are a staple in Vietnamese restaurants, where they often accompany grilled meats and are always layered with cold sliced meats in bánh mì, the Vietnamese baguette sandwich. Serve in place of a cucumber pickle with a sandwich or in place of relish with a hot dog. The julienned pickles will keep for about 1 week in the refrigerator before the flavor deteriorates.

INGREDIENTS

½ pound daikon, peeled
½ pound large carrots, peeled
1 teaspoon kosher or sea salt
1 cup unseasoned rice vinegar
2 tablespoons plus 2 teaspoons sugar
1 cup water

1 Cut the daikon and carrots into roughly 2½-inch lengths. With a mandoline or V-slicer fitted with the julienne attachment, or by hand with a chef's knife, cut the daikon and carrots into matchsticks. Put them in a sieve, sprinkle with the salt, and toss to coat evenly with the salt. Set the sieve over a bowl or over the sink and let the vegetables drain for 1 to 2 hours. They should be soft enough to bend without breaking but still retain some crunch. Rinse well, then pat dry.

2 In a bowl, stir together the vinegar, sugar, and water until the sugar dissolves. Add the vegetables and stir to coat evenly. Let marinate for 1 hour before serving.

SHAVED WATERMELON RADISHES, WATERCRESS, AND FENNEL

Serves 6

With their pale green skin, watermelon radishes give no hint of the peppermint pink flesh inside. Although the interior is rarely as deeply colored as watermelon, it is eye-catching when contrasted with white fennel and deeply hued greens. A mandoline, V-slicer, or other manual vegetable slicer makes it easy to shave the vegetables. Well-grown watermelon radishes are crunchy and mild, never spongy or hot.

INGREDIENTS

2 large bunches watercress or arugula, tough stems removed (about 3 lightly packed quarts after trimming)

1 small fennel bulb, halved lengthwise

1 large watermelon radish, about the size of a baseball, thickly peeled and halved

DRESSING

3 tablespoons extra virgin olive oil

1 tablespoon fresh lemon juice, or more to taste

1 teaspoon fish sauce (see Note, page 13)

1 clove garlic, finely minced

Kosher or sea salt and freshly ground black pepper

3 ounces ricotta salata cheese

1 Put the watercress or arugula in a large salad bowl. With a mandoline or other manual vegetable slicer, or by hand with a chef's knife, shave the fennel thinly crosswise. Do the same with the radish halves. Put the shaved fennel and radish in the salad bowl and toss with your hands to mix.

2 To make the dressing, in a small bowl, whisk together the olive oil, lemon juice, fish sauce, garlic, and salt and pepper to taste.

3 Toss the salad with just enough of dressing to coat the vegetables lightly; you may not need it all. Taste and add more lemon juice if desired. With a cheese plane or vegetable peeler, shave the ricotta salata thinly into the salad. Toss gently so as not to break up the cheese too much. Serve immediately.

FLATBREAD WITH RADISHES, FETA, AND SPRING HERBS

Serves 6

When late spring brings the first flush of tender herbs, edible flowers, and mild radishes, this Persian hors d'oeuvre should be in your repertoire. The concept is simple: you spread a little creamy feta on warm flatbread, then wrap it around green onions, radishes, herbs, edible flowers, toasted nuts, or any combination of these crisp and fragrant foods. The recipe is intentionally vague because the precise amount of each ingredient is unimportant. Focus instead on composing a beautiful painting of the fresh spring produce available to you.

INGREDIENTS

Lavash (Middle Eastern flatbread) or pita bread

Whipped feta (page 31, pepper flakes and mint optional)

Toasted walnut halves (page xiv)

Radishes, trimmed

Green onions, trimmed, halved lengthwise if large, and cut into 3-inch lengths (white and pale green parts only)

Herb sprigs (such as basil, dill, mint, tarragon, Italian parsley, and cilantro), thick stems removed but leaves left whole

Edible flowers such as nasturtiums or borage

1 If using *lavash*, warm according to package directions until soft and pliable. If using pita bread, preheat the oven to 350°F. Wrap the pita bread in aluminum foil and bake until hot throughout, about 10 minutes.

2 Put the feta in a serving bowl. On a large platter, arrange the walnut halves, radishes, green onions, herbs, and flowers attractively, either in individual mounds or mixed.

3 Serve the warm bread with the platter of cheese and herbs. Invite diners to spread a small piece of bread with the feta, then wrap the bread, taco style, around any of the other ingredients, preferably in combination.

GLAZED RUTABAGA WEDGES

Serves 4

These well-browned rutabagas make an ideal companion for a holiday rib roast or a weeknight roast chicken. Their natural sugar will caramelize on the surface as they cook, then melt into a glaze when you add a touch of broth at the end. Rutabagas appreciate a generous hand with the black pepper.

INGREDIENTS

2 large rutabagas, about 1½ pounds total
1½ tablespoons unsalted butter
Kosher or sea salt and freshly ground black pepper
⅓ cup chicken broth, or more if needed
1 tablespoon minced fresh Italian parsley (optional)

1 Peel the rutabagas thickly with a paring knife. Quarter the rutabagas—cut lengthwise and then crosswise—and then cut each quarter into 4 thick wedges.

2 In a skillet that will hold all the rutabaga wedges in a single layer, melt the butter over moderately low heat. Add the wedges, season generously with salt and pepper, and toss to coat with the butter. Place the wedges with one cut side down, cover, and cook until richly colored on that side, about 10 minutes, adjusting the heat to prevent scorching. Turn the wedges so that another cut side is down. Re-cover and cook until almost tender when pierced, about 5 minutes.

3 Add the broth and stir with a wooden spoon to release any caramelized bits stuck to the skillet. Cover and simmer until the broth has evaporated and the wedges are nut brown, lightly glazed, and tender, about 3 minutes longer. If the broth evaporates before the wedges are tender, add a little more. Taste and adjust the seasoning. Add the parsley, toss gently, and serve immediately.

Spinach Salad with Queso Fresco, Sesame Seeds, and Tortilla Crisps

Serves 4

Toasted sesame seeds and moist queso fresco produce a fresh take on spinach salad. The combination is a favorite at Fonda, an Albany, California, restaurant that specializes in Latin American–inspired small plates. Fried tortilla ribbons add a pleasing crunch.

INGREDIENTS

DRESSING

3 tablespoons extra virgin olive oil

1 tablespoon fresh lemon juice

1 teaspoon fish sauce (see Note, page 13)

1 small clove garlic, minced to a paste

Kosher or sea salt

Canola oil, for deep-frying

2 corn tortillas, about 6 inches in diameter

Kosher or sea salt

2 tablespoons sesame seeds

½ pound baby spinach

¼ pound queso fresco, crumbled (about ¾ cup)

1 lime, halved

1 To make the dressing, in a small bowl, whisk together the olive oil, lemon juice, fish sauce, garlic, and salt to taste.

2 Pour the canola oil into a small, heavy saucepan to a depth of 2 inches and heat to 375°F. While the oil heats, cut the tortillas in half, then stack the 4 halves. With the straight side facing you, cut them vertically into ½-inch-wide strips. Discard the end pieces, which will be too short.

3 Working in small batches, add the tortilla strips to the hot oil and deep-fry until they darken in color, about 1 minute, adjusting the heat as needed to maintain the temperature as close to 375°F as possible. Lift them out with a wire-mesh skimmer onto a double thickness of paper towels to drain. Sprinkle with salt while still hot.

4 Put the sesame seeds in a small, dry skillet and toast over moderate heat, shaking the skillet frequently, until the seeds are golden brown, about 4 minutes. Let cool.

5 Put the spinach in a large salad bowl. Add the toasted sesame seeds and queso fresco and toss to mix. Add just enough dressing to coat the spinach lightly; you may not need it all. Toss well and taste. The salad will probably need a squeeze of lime juice. Add the fried tortilla strips, toss gently, and serve immediately.

GRILLED SCALLOPS WITH WILTED SPINACH AND LEMON-CAPER BUTTER

Serves 4

In just a few moments on the stove, a potful of rough fresh spinach leaves wilts down into a silky bed for grilled scallops. A composed butter enlivened with capers and lemon zest creates a simple sauce as it melts on the hot greens and shellfish. Be sure to warm the dinner plates for a few minutes in a low oven to keep the food hot. Both the spinach and the scallops cool off quickly otherwise.

INGREDIENTS

LEMON-CAPER BUTTER

½ cup unsalted butter (1 stick), softened
2 tablespoons capers, preferably salt packed, rinsed
  and finely minced
2 teaspoons grated lemon zest
2 tablespoons minced fresh Italian parsley
Kosher or sea salt

1 pound sea scallops
Kosher or sea salt and freshly ground black pepper
1 tablespoon unsalted butter, melted
3 bunches (12 to 14 ounces each) spinach, thick
  stems removed
4 lemon wedges

1 Prepare a moderate charcoal fire or preheat a gas grill to medium (375°F). To make the lemon-caper butter, put the butter, capers, lemon zest, and parsley in a bowl and stir with a wooden spoon until smooth. Season to taste with salt.

2 Remove the "foot" or small muscle on the side of each scallop. Halve the scallops horizontally, or slice them in thirds if they are jumbo scallops, so the slices are no more than ½ inch thick. Season all over with salt and pepper and brush with the melted butter.

3 Put the spinach in a large pot with just the washing water clinging to the leaves. Cover and cook over moderate heat, stirring with tongs once or twice, until the spinach is barely wilted, about 3 minutes. Drain in a sieve or colander. Do not press on the leaves or squeeze them to extract more liquid; you want to leave them fairly moist. Return them to the same pot and add half of the lemon-caper butter. Toss with tongs over low heat so that the butter melts and coats the spinach. Taste for salt. Keep the spinach warm while you grill the scallops.

4 Grill the scallops directly over the coals or gas flame, turning once, until they are nicely marked by the grill and no longer translucent, about 5 minutes total.

5 Divide the spinach among warmed dinner plates. Arrange the scallops on top, and immediately slather the scallops with the remaining butter. The butter will melt from the heat of the shellfish. Garnish each serving with a lemon wedge and serve immediately.

GRILLED QUESADILLAS WITH MOZZARELLA AND SQUASH BLOSSOMS

Serves 4

Squash blossoms vary greatly in size depending on whether they come from zucchini or from winter squash. You can use small or large ones here. Some farmers sell baby zucchini with blossoms still attached. For this recipe, twist off the blossoms and reserve the zucchini for another dish.

INGREDIENTS

16 large or 24 small squash blossoms
2 tablespoons canola oil, plus more for brushing
1 small white onion, minced
2 cloves garlic, minced
1 teaspoon dried Mexican oregano
Kosher or sea salt
1 small avocado, ripe but firm
4 flour tortillas, 9 inches in diameter
½ pound low-moisture whole-milk mozzarella
   cheese, grated on the large holes of a box grater
Grilled Tomatillo Salsa (page 160)
Fresh cilantro leaves, for garnish

1 Prepare a moderate charcoal fire or preheat a gas grill to medium (375°F). Tear the squash blossoms in half lengthwise and inspect for ants. Dunk the blossoms in a large bowl of cold water, swish well, then lift them out into a sieve or colander to drain. Pat dry. If the blossom halves are large, tear each one lengthwise into 2 or 3 pieces.

2 Heat the canola oil in a large skillet over moderately low heat. Add the onion, garlic, and oregano, crumbling the herb between your fingers as you add it. Sauté until the onion is soft, about 10 minutes. Add the squash blossoms, season with salt, and cook, stirring to coat them with the seasonings, just until the blossoms begin to soften, about 1 minute. Do not let them wilt.

3 Halve and pit the avocado. With a large spoon, scoop both halves out of the peel in 1 piece and put, cut side down, on a cutting board. Slice thinly lengthwise.

4 Brush one side of a flour tortilla with canola oil, then place it, oiled side down, on a rimless baking sheet. Top one-half of the tortilla with one-quarter of the cheese, then with one-quarter of the squash blossom mixture. Fold like a turnover. Repeat with the remaining tortillas. Slide the folded tortillas onto the grill directly over the coals or gas flame. Cook until browned on the bottom, about 1 minute, then turn and grill until the quesadilla browns on the second side and the cheese melts, about 1 minute longer.

5 Top each quesadilla with a drizzle of salsa, a few slices of avocado, and a sprinkling of cilantro leaves. Serve immediately.

SUMMER SQUASH CARPACCIO WITH ARUGULA, PECORINO, AND ALMONDS

Serves 4

When shaved thinly, vegetables that you might not normally eat raw present new possibilities. Long, straight-sided summer squashes like green and yellow zucchini look like wide ribbons when shaved for this salad. A brief rest in a garlicky vinaigrette renders them supple, so they can be tossed with arugula and shavings of salty cheese. Zephyr squash, a straightneck variety popular at Austin's Green Gate Farms, would be ideal for this recipe because each squash has both yellow and green markings.

INGREDIENTS

¼ cup sliced almonds, toasted (page xiv)

1 pound small zucchini, preferably a mix of green
    and yellow varieties, no more than 5 inches long

2½ tablespoons extra virgin olive oil

1½ tablespoons fresh lemon juice

1 small clove garlic, minced to a paste

Kosher or sea salt and freshly ground black pepper

2 handfuls of arugula (about 3 ounces)

Chunk of pecorino toscano, ricotta salata, or other
    medium-aged pecorino cheese, for shaving

1 Preheat the oven to 350°F. Toast the almonds on a baking sheet until golden brown and fragrant, 10 to 15 minutes. Let cool.

2 Trim the ends of the zucchini. With a mandoline or other manual vegetable slicer, or a vegetable peeler, shave the zucchini thinly lengthwise. Discard the first and last slices of each squash, which are mostly skin. Put the zucchini ribbons in a large bowl.

3 In a small bowl, whisk together the olive oil, lemon juice, garlic, and salt to taste. Add the dressing to the shaved zucchini and toss with your hands to coat it evenly. Taste and add more salt if necessary. Let stand for 5 minutes to allow the zucchini to soften.

4 Add the arugula to the zucchini. With a cheese plane or vegetable peeler, shave about 3 ounces of cheese, or as much as you like, into the bowl. Add several grinds of black pepper, then toss gently with your hands. Transfer the salad to a serving platter, leaving any watery juices behind. Top with the toasted almonds. Serve immediately.

Pita Sandwich with Grilled Zucchini and Red Pepper Hummus

Serves 4

A pita pocket makes a handy holder for grilled vegetables of many types. Instead of the grilled zucchini suggested here, try grilled peppers, leeks, radicchio, or eggplant. You can also replace the hummus with guacamole, if you like.

Ingredients

2 medium green zucchini, as straight as possible
2 medium yellow zucchini, as straight as possible
2 tablespoons extra virgin olive oil, or more
   if needed
Kosher or sea salt
4 red onion slices, about ½ inch thick
4 pita breads, halved
1 cup Red Pepper Hummus (page 126)
8 to 12 thin tomato slices
½ cup fresh cilantro leaves

1 Prepare a moderate charcoal fire or preheat a gas grill to medium (375°F).

2 Trim the ends of the zucchini. Slice each one lengthwise about 3/16 inch thick. Brush the slices with olive oil on both sides, then season with salt. From opposing directions, insert 2 toothpicks horizontally into each red onion slice; the toothpicks will hold the onion layers together on the grill. Brush the onion slices with olive oil on both sides, then season with salt.

3 Grill the zucchini and onion slices directly over the coals or gas flame, turning once, until they are nicely marked by the grill and just tender, about 3 minutes per side for the zucchini, a little longer for the onions. Remove the toothpicks from the onions. Cut the zucchini slices in half crosswise.

4 Wrap the pita in aluminum foil and warm the package on the grill or in a moderate oven until the bread is hot.

5 To assemble the sandwiches, spread the interior of each pita half with the hummus, using about 2 tablespoons per half. Tuck some zucchini, red onion, tomato, and cilantro leaves into each pita half, dividing them evenly. Serve immediately.

GRILLED PATTYPAN SQUASH WITH CHORIZO AND COTIJA CHEESE

Serves 4

The scallop-edged summer squashes known as pattypan or scallopini are ideal for this preparation because, halved horizontally, their broad surface begs for a topping. Grill the squashes, then garnish with crema (Mexican-style cultured cream), warm crumbled chorizo, and grated Cotija cheese to make a summer side dish for grilled chicken or a main dish accompanied by rice and beans.

INGREDIENTS

1 pound pattypan squashes
1 tablespoon olive oil
2 teaspoons dried Mexican oregano
Kosher or sea salt
¼ pound Mexican-style chorizo
2 tablespoons *crema*, crème fraîche, or sour cream
2 tablespoons coarsely chopped fresh cilantro
⅓ cup freshly grated Cotija or pecorino romano cheese

1 Prepare a moderate charcoal fire for indirect grilling (page xiv) or preheat a gas grill to medium-high (375° to 400°F), leaving one burner unlit.

2 Trim the ends from the squashes so they will sit upright, then cut in half horizontally. Brush on both sides with the olive oil. Season both sides with the oregano, crumbling it between your fingers as you add it, and with salt.

3 Remove the chorizo from its casing and crumble into a small, nonstick skillet on the stove. Cook over moderately low heat, stirring, until the chorizo is fully cooked, 5 to 7 minutes. Keep warm.

4 Place the squash halves on the grill over indirect heat, cover, and cook, turning to brown both sides, until tender, about 20 minutes. Uncover the grill and move the squashes directly over the coals or gas flame for the final few minutes to color them nicely, if necessary.

5 Transfer to a serving platter. Whisk the *crema* until it is pourable, adding a little water if necessary. Drizzle over the squash halves. Top with the hot chorizo, then with the cilantro and cheese. Serve immediately.

ROASTED BUTTERNUT SQUASH SOUP WITH TOASTED PUMPKIN SEEDS

Serves 6 to 8

Butternut squash has dense, creamy, sweet flesh that you can easily scrape from the skin after baking. Puree it with sautéed onions and broth to make a silky, pumpkin-colored soup, then stir in some minced chipotle chiles to warm it up. Garnish with a flurry of grated Cotija cheese—a hard, well-aged cow's milk cheese sold in Mexican markets—and a sprinkle of toasted pumpkin seeds.

INGREDIENTS

1 butternut squash, 2½ to 3 pounds
3 tablespoons extra virgin olive oil
1 large yellow onion, minced
2 large cloves garlic, minced
1 teaspoon ancho chile powder or other chile powder
5 cups chicken broth (if canned, use equal parts broth and water), plus more if needed
Kosher or sea salt
2 teaspoons finely minced canned chipotle chile in adobo sauce, or more to taste
Freshly grated Cotija cheese, for garnish
Hulled, roasted, and salted pumpkin seeds, for garnish
Coarsely chopped fresh cilantro, for garnish

1 Preheat the oven to 375°F. With a cleaver or heavy chef's knife, cut off the stem end of the squash, then cut the squash into 8 roughly equal pieces. Discard the stringy matter and seeds in the seed cavity. Using 1 tablespoon of the oil, grease a baking dish just large enough to hold the squash in a single layer. Put the squash in the baking dish, cut side down. Cover with aluminum foil and bake until tender when pierced, 45 to 50 minutes. Cool completely, then scrape the flesh away from the skin with a spoon.

2 Heat the remaining 2 tablespoons olive oil in a large pot over moderately low heat. Add the onion and sauté until softened, about 10 minutes. Add the garlic and chile powder and sauté for 1 minute to release the garlic fragrance.

3 Add the squash flesh and the broth to the pot. Bring to a simmer, stirring. Adjust the heat to maintain a gentle simmer and cook for 5 minutes to blend the flavors.

4 Let the soup cool slightly, then puree in a blender or food processor, in batches if necessary. Return to a clean pot. If the soup is too thick for your taste, thin with additional broth. Season with the salt and chile.

5 Reheat the soup to serve. Divide among warmed soup bowls, and garnish each portion with the cheese, pumpkin seeds, and cilantro. Serve immediately.

Roast Acorn Squash with Maple Glaze

Serves 4

Any hard-shelled winter squash can be prepared this way, as long as the squash wedges have a cavity to hold the butter and maple syrup. Serve with pork chops, roast chicken, or roast duck.

Ingredients

1 acorn squash, about 2½ pounds
Kosher or sea salt
4 teaspoons unsalted butter
4 teaspoons maple syrup
¼ cup water

1 Preheat the oven to 375°F. With a cleaver or heavy chef's knife, cut across the top of the squash to remove the stem, then quarter the squash lengthwise and remove the seeds and stringy fibers in the seed cavity.

2 Put the squash quarters, cavity side up, in a baking dish just large enough to hold them comfortably. Season the squash with salt, then put 1 teaspoon butter and 1 teaspoon maple syrup in each cavity. Pour the water into the baking dish, then cover the dish and bake until the squash is tender when pierced, about 45 minutes.

3 Pour any juices from the squash cavities into the baking dish, then transfer the squash quarters to a serving platter. Transfer all the juices from the baking dish into a small pan and place over high heat. Cook until reduced to a syrup, then spoon the syrup over the squash. Let rest for 10 to 15 minutes before serving. The squash is best when it is not piping hot.

SPICY RED LENTIL SOUP WITH MUSTARD GREENS AND BUTTERNUT SQUASH

Serves 8

Despite their name, red lentils are coral, and they turn yellow when cooked. Here, they are simmered with fragrant Indian spices until they collapse into puree. Nuggets of pumpkin-colored squash and forest green ribbons of mustard greens are stirred in to complete the soup. Look for the lentils in Indian markets. Brown lentils are not a good substitute, as they don't break down as readily as the red lentils do.

INGREDIENTS

2 tablespoons canola oil

1 medium yellow onion, minced

4 cloves garlic, minced

1-inch piece fresh ginger, peeled and minced

1 teaspoon ground turmeric

1 teaspoon cumin seed, toasted (page xiv) and finely ground

1 dried red chile, broken in half

2 cups Indian red lentils, rinsed

1 bay leaf

1 quart chicken or vegetable broth (if canned, use equal parts broth and water)

1 quart water

Kosher or sea salt and freshly ground black pepper

2 cups peeled butternut or kabocha squash, in ½-inch dice

⅓ pound mustard greens, ribs removed and cut crosswise into ½-inch-wide ribbons

1 Heat the canola oil in a large pot over moderate heat. Add the onion, garlic, ginger, turmeric, cumin, and chile and sauté until the onion is soft, about 10 minutes. Add the lentils, bay leaf, broth, and water and bring to a simmer, skimming any surface foam. Cover and adjust the heat to maintain a gentle simmer. Cook until the lentils are soft, about 30 minutes.

2 Season the lentils with salt and pepper. Stir in the squash. Cover and simmer until the squash is almost tender but still slightly firm, about 8 minutes. Stir in the mustard greens, re-cover, and remove the soup from the heat. Let stand until the mustard greens soften and the squash is fully cooked, 5 to 10 minutes.

3 Remove the bay leaf and chile. Taste and adjust the seasoning. Divide the soup among warmed bowls. Serve immediately.

SWEET POTATOES ON THE GRILL

Serves 4

Add these sweet potatoes to the menu when you're grilling pork chops or a pork tenderloin. They can cook alongside the meat and need no attention, other than an occasional turn to prevent the skin from blackening. They need to cook with the grill lid on so that the grill emulates an oven. You can use moist, orange-fleshed sweet potatoes (sometimes called yams), but the Japanese varieties with pale, dry flesh are even tastier because they are not candy-sweet. Cooked this way, the drier varieties taste almost like roasted chestnuts.

INGREDIENTS

4 sweet potatoes, each about 10 ounces
Unsalted butter
Kosher or sea salt and freshly ground black pepper
Whole nutmeg, for grating

1 Prepare a moderate charcoal fire for indirect grilling (page xiv) or preheat a gas grill to medium-high (375° to 400°F), leaving one burner unlit.

2 Prick each sweet potato in several places with a fork. Place them on the grill over indirect heat. Cover the grill (leaving the vents open on a charcoal grill) and cook, turning occasionally, until the sweet potatoes are tender when pierced, 40 to 45 minutes.

3 Slit each sweet potato and tuck a large nugget of butter inside. Season with salt, a couple of grinds of black pepper, and a scraping of nutmeg. Serve immediately.

SWEET POTATO AND KABOCHA SQUASH PUREE

Serves 4 to 6

Harvested in fall at about the same time, dry-fleshed sweet potatoes and dense-meated winter squashes like kabocha make a heavenly puree. The potatoes, more nutty than sweet, help to cut the sweetness of the squash, and they give the puree more body. Serve with pork chops, ham, roast duck, or the Thanksgiving turkey. The puree can be made a few hours ahead and reheated.

INGREDIENTS

1 large Japanese sweet potato (satsumaimo) or other
  dry-fleshed sweet potato, about 1 pound
1- to 1¼-pound piece kabocha or butternut squash,
  seeds removed
2 tablespoons unsalted butter
Kosher or sea salt

1 Preheat the oven to 375°F. Pierce the sweet potato in several places with a fork, then put on a tray or in a baking dish to catch any drips. Bake until tender when pierced, about 1 hour.

2 Cut the squash into 2 equal pieces to speed the cooking. Place in a lightly oiled baking dish, flesh side up. Cover tightly with aluminum foil and bake alongside the sweet potato until the squash is tender when pierced, 45 minutes to 1 hour.

3 When the sweet potato is cool enough to handle, halve lengthwise and scoop the flesh into a food processor, leaving the skin behind. Scoop the squash flesh into the processor as well, leaving the skin behind. Add the butter and puree until smooth.

4 Transfer the puree to a saucepan and reheat over moderately low heat, stirring often, until hot. Season with salt and serve immediately.

GRILLED TOMATILLO SALSA

Makes about 1⅓ cups

Grilling all the vegetables for this salsa verde—"green salsa"—adds an alluring smoky note. Once you have grilled the components, you can make the salsa in a couple of minutes. Serve with quesadillas (page 149), tacos, or chips, or as a garnish for corn soup. At the market, choose tomatillos that feel firm and have an intact husk.

INGREDIENTS

½ pound tomatillos (about 5 medium)
½ small white onion, peeled
1 or 2 cloves garlic, unpeeled
1 jalapeño chile
6 cilantro sprigs
Kosher or sea salt

1 Prepare a moderate charcoal fire or preheat a gas grill to medium (375°F). Remove the husks from the tomatillos and wash them to remove any stickiness. Dry well.

2 Grill the tomatillos, onion half, garlic, and chile directly over the coals or gas flame, turning as needed, until charred on all sides. They don't need to be thoroughly blackened, but they should have plenty of toasty char.

3 Put the tomatillos and onion in a blender. Peel the garlic and add to the blender along with the chile and cilantro. Blend until smooth. Transfer to a small bowl and stir in salt to taste. Thin to a pleasing consistency with a few tablespoons of water.

MEXICAN PORK STEW WITH TOMATILLOS   Serves 4

You could add hominy, chickpeas, or potatoes to this succulent pork stew, but it's substantial without them. The pork is fork-tender, bathed in a highly seasoned tomatillo sauce that is even better the second day. Serve with hot corn tortillas and a bowlful of radishes.

INGREDIENTS

2 pounds boneless pork shoulder, cut into 1-inch cubes

2 quarts water

24 black peppercorns

1 large white onion, halved through the stem end

2 teaspoons kosher or sea salt, plus more as needed

1 pound tomatillos, husked and rinsed

4 large cloves garlic, unpeeled

1 serrano chile

3 tablespoons canola oil

⅓ cup chopped fresh cilantro, plus more for garnish

1 teaspoon cumin seed, toasted (page xiv) and finely ground

1½ teaspoons dried Mexican oregano

1 Put the pork and water in a large pot over moderate heat. Bring to a simmer, skimming any foam. Add the peppercorns, an onion half, and the salt and simmer gently for 45 minutes, skimming as needed. Strain, reserving the meat and broth separately. Discard the onion half and peppercorns.

2 Prepare a moderate charcoal fire or preheat a gas grill to medium (375°F). Cut the remaining half onion in half again through the stem end. Put the 2 onion wedges, the tomatillos, the garlic cloves, and the chile on the grill directly over the coals or gas flame. Grill, turning as needed, until softened and charred all over. Watch carefully and remove the tomatillos before they split and lose their juices.

3 Peel the garlic cloves. Put the garlic, onion, tomatillos, and chile in a blender and blend until smooth.

4 Heat the canola oil in a large, deep skillet or Dutch oven over moderate heat. Add the tomatillo puree, cilantro, cumin, and oregano, crumbling the herb between your fingers as you add it. Simmer, stirring often, for 15 minutes to develop the flavor, adjusting the heat as needed to prevent scorching. If necessary, add a little pork broth to keep the sauce from sticking.

5 Add the pork and enough of the pork broth to achieve a saucelike consistency, 2 to 2½ cups. Cover and adjust the heat to maintain a gentle simmer. Cook until the pork is tender, about 45 minutes.

6 Taste and adjust the seasoning. If the sauce is too thick, thin with pork broth. If it is too thin, simmer, uncovered, for a few minutes. Transfer to a serving dish and garnish with cilantro. Serve immediately.

Yellow Tomato Gazpacho

Serves 6

With ripe tomatoes harvested in so many riveting hues these days, gazpacho no longer has to be red. Surprise guests with this golden version, a puree of all the classic gazpacho vegetables—tomatoes, cucumbers, onions, sweet peppers (yellow, of course)—thickened with bread, heightened with vinegar, and scented with cumin. Float a slice of hard-cooked egg and a drizzle of green olive oil on each serving to make a chilled soup with eye appeal. For the tomatoes, look for super-tasty slicing varieties like Lemon Boy, Taxi, Pineapple, Persimmon, or Gold Medal.

Ingredients

½ pound dense, day-old French or Italian country bread, crust removed, cut into 1-inch cubes

¼ cup Champagne vinegar or white wine vinegar

2½ pounds yellow or gold tomatoes, peeled, cored, and diced, with juices

1 small cucumber, about ½ pound, peeled and cut into 1-inch cubes

½ large yellow or gold bell pepper, seeded and cut into 1-inch cubes

½ small red onion, sliced

1 large clove garlic, minced

½ teaspoon cumin seed, toasted (page xiv)

2 teaspoons kosher or sea salt

¼ cup extra virgin olive oil, plus more for garnish

1 tablespoon sherry vinegar (optional)

2 hard-cooked eggs

1 small red tomato, sliced into ½-inch wedges

Pimentón de la Vera (smoked Spanish paprika), mild, medium, or hot, or other paprika

1 Put the bread in a large bowl and sprinkle with the Champagne vinegar. Toss to coat the bread with the vinegar. Add the tomatoes, cucumber, bell pepper, onion, garlic, cumin, salt, and olive oil. Toss well. Let stand at room temperature for 1 hour to draw the juices out of the tomatoes.

2 Puree the mixture thoroughly in a blender, in batches. Strain through a medium-mesh sieve to remove the tomato seeds and pepper skins, pressing on the solids. Taste for salt and stir in the sherry vinegar. If the soup seems too thick, thin with cold water. Cover and chill thoroughly.

3 Slice the eggs and set aside 6 pretty slices that include both white and yolk.

4 Divide the soup evenly among bowls. Top each portion with an egg slice, tomato wedge, drizzle with olive oil, and sprinkle with *pimentón*. Serve immediately.

ROASTED TOMATO SAUCE

Makes about 3½ cups

The meaty San Marzano tomatoes that Shari Sirkin grows at Dancing Roots Farm would be ideal for this recipe. Slow baking in a low oven drives off their moisture and deepens their flavor, just as it does in Slow-Roasted Tomatoes with Oregano and Feta (page 172). Pureed, they yield a thick sauce with heightened sweetness and a rich, mellow taste. Note that you need a food mill to separate the tomato pulp from the skins and seeds. You can use the sauce on pasta or as a braising medium for chicken, baby back ribs, or beans.

INGREDIENTS

5 pounds plum (Roma type) tomatoes, cored and
   halved lengthwise
⅓ cup extra virgin olive oil
10 cloves garlic, finely minced
1 tablespoon kosher or sea salt

1 Preheat the oven to 300°F. In a large bowl, toss the tomato halves with the olive oil, garlic, and salt. Arrange the tomato halves, cut side up, in a single layer, in large baking dishes. (You will probably need two.) Transfer to the oven and bake, brushing once or twice with the juices that collect in the baking dish, until the tomatoes are very soft and beginning to caramelize, about 3 hours. Do not let the juices blacken.

2 Puree the tomatoes in a food mill fitted with the fine disk to eliminate the skins and seeds. Taste for salt. Use immediately, or cover and refrigerate for up to 3 days or freeze for up to 6 months.

GRILLED TOMATOES WITH PESTO

Serves 4

This recipe yields more pesto than you need for the tomatoes, but why make just a little? You will have enough pesto left over to sauce 3/4 pound of pasta the next day, a head start on dinner for four. Serve the tomatoes with grilled fish or steak.

INGREDIENTS

PESTO

1½ cups firmly packed fresh basil leaves

2 cloves garlic, sliced

¼ cup pine nuts, toasted (page xiv)

½ cup extra virgin olive oil

6 tablespoons freshly grated Parmigiano Reggiano
  or pecorino cheese, or a mix

Kosher or sea salt

3 large, firm tomatoes, 10 to 12 ounces each

1 tablespoon extra virgin olive oil

Kosher or sea salt

1 Prepare a moderate charcoal fire or preheat a gas grill to medium (375°F).

2 To make the pesto, put the basil, garlic, and pine nuts in a food processor and pulse until well chopped. With the motor running, add the olive oil gradually through the feed tube, stopping once or twice to scrape down the sides of the work bowl. Puree until the pesto is almost but not completely smooth. Transfer to a bowl and stir in the cheese. Season to taste with salt.

3 Core the tomatoes. Slice off the rounded top and bottom of each tomato, then cut the remainder into ¾-inch-thick slices. Brush with olive oil on both sides and sprinkle on both sides with salt.

4 Grill the tomatoes directly over the coals or gas flame, turning once, just until hot throughout, 2 to 3 minutes per side. Do not overcook or they will become mushy. Transfer the tomato slices to a serving platter and slather them with the pesto, using 1 heaping teaspoon per slice (reserve the remaining pesto for another use), and serve immediately.

Greek Salad with Heirloom Tomatoes and Grilled Pita Crisps

Serves 4

Made with the splashy, brilliantly colored tomatoes grown by small farms such as Full Belly in Guinda, California, a Greek salad becomes a visual feast. Mix orange varieties like Golden Jubilee with purplish Black Krim, striped Green Zebra, and the incomparable Sun Gold, a hybrid cherry tomato the color of a sunset. Pita crisps, made on the grill, add crunch to this summer salad, a merging of Greek horiatiki with Lebanese fattoush.

INGREDIENTS

DRESSING

4 tablespoons extra virgin olive oil

2 tablespoons red wine vinegar

1 large clove garlic, minced

1 teaspoon fish sauce (see Note, page 13), optional

Kosher or sea salt

2 pita breads

Extra virgin olive oil

Kosher or sea salt

1½ pounds heirloom tomatoes in mixed colors and sizes

½ pound cucumbers, peeled (unless skin is thin and tender), halved or quartered lengthwise, and cut into ½-inch chunks

½ cup thinly sliced red onion

Freshly ground black pepper

¼ pound Greek, French, Bulgarian, or Israeli feta cheese

16 Kalamata olives, preferably unpitted

12 fresh basil leaves

1 Prepare a moderate charcoal fire or preheat a gas grill to medium (375°F).

2 To make the dressing, in a small bowl, whisk together the olive oil, vinegar, garlic, and fish sauce. Season with salt.

3 By hand, tear each pita bread in half to make 2 half-moons. Use your fingers to separate the two layers of each half-moon, giving you a total of 8 half-moons. Brush both sides of each half-moon with olive oil and sprinkle both sides with salt. Grill directly over the coals or gas flame, turning once, until the pita is lightly charred and crisp. Cool, then break into smaller pieces.

4 Cut large tomatoes into wedges. Cut cherry tomatoes in half. In a large bowl, combine the tomatoes, cucumbers, and red onion. Add the dressing and several grinds of black pepper and toss to mix. Taste and adjust the seasoning. Add the feta in chunks and the pita crisps and toss again gently. Transfer the salad to a shallow bowl or rimmed platter. Garnish the salad with the olives and the basil, torn into smaller pieces. Serve immediately so the pita remains crisp.

BUTTERMILK SALAD DRESSING WITH DRIED TOMATOES

Makes about 1⅓ cups

Dried tomatoes, so intense on their own, can play a background role in a salad dressing. In this creamy ranch-style blend, they contribute sweetness, body, and an appetizing blush. They are hardly discernible, but the dressing would be less compelling without them. Spoon it over hearts of romaine, heirloom tomatoes, beets, or an old-fashioned iceberg wedge. It also makes a tasty dip for crudités.

INGREDIENTS

½ ounce dried tomatoes (about 6 tomato halves), homemade (page 174) or store-bought, preferably without sulfur

½ cup boiling water

½ cup mayonnaise

½ cup buttermilk

2 green onions, white and pale green parts only, minced

2 teaspoons minced fresh dill

1 small clove garlic, minced to a paste

½ to 1 teaspoon white wine vinegar

Kosher or sea salt and freshly ground black pepper

1 Put the tomatoes in a small heatproof bowl, add the boiling water, and let stand until softened, 10 minutes or more. Drain in a sieve and squeeze to remove excess moisture. Chop finely.

2 In a bowl, whisk together the mayonnaise and buttermilk, then whisk in the green onions, dill, garlic, and 2 tablespoons chopped tomato. (If you have a little extra tomato, mix with some extra virgin olive oil and spread on a baguette slice.) Add the vinegar to taste, then season with salt and pepper. If you used store-bought mayonnaise, you may not need additional salt. Use the dressing immediately, or cover and refrigerate for up to 3 days.

BLT: The Salad

Serves 4

When heirloom tomatoes start to flood the market in their vivid Technicolor hues, it's time to deconstruct the bacon, lettuce, and tomato sandwich. Such tomatoes are too eye appealing to hide between slices of bread. Make them the stars of the BLT, drizzling them with a creamy dressing, then topping them with some wispy greens and crisp-fried bacon. Use the tastiest tomatoes you can find, preferably in a variety of colors, sizes, and shapes. Offer bread on the side for mopping up the flavorful juices.

Ingredients

Tomatoes in a variety of colors and sizes, including
  cherry, grape, or pear tomatoes, to serve 4
Kosher or sea salt and freshly ground black pepper
Red or white wine vinegar
4 thick slices apple wood–smoked bacon, cut into
  1-inch pieces
½ cup Buttermilk Salad Dressing with Dried Tomatoes
  (page 168), made without the dried tomatoes
4 small handfuls of arugula, mizuna, or other soft
  baby greens

1 Slice the large tomatoes and arrange them on a serving platter. Season with salt and pepper and sprinkle with vinegar. Cut small tomatoes in half and set aside.

2 Put the bacon in a large cold skillet and set over moderately low heat. Cook, turning the bacon often with tongs, until the pieces are crisp, about 8 minutes. Using a slotted spoon, transfer to paper towels to drain.

3 Spoon the dressing over the tomatoes. Top with the arugula, and scatter the halved small tomatoes and the crisp bacon on top. Serve immediately.

NITTY GRITTY DIRT FARM KETCHUP   Makes 1½ pints

When Robin Raudabaugh makes this richly spiced tomato ketchup, only the seasonings and the vinegar are store-bought. All the vegetables and herbs come from her Nitty Gritty Dirt Farm; even the honey is harvested from farm hives.

INGREDIENTS

5 pounds ripe red tomatoes, coarsely chopped (no need to peel)

2 cups finely chopped yellow onion

2 cups finely chopped red bell pepper

¼ cup minced fresh Italian parsley

4 cloves garlic, finely chopped

2 tablespoons kosher or sea salt

2 bay leaves

1 whole clove

1 teaspoon yellow mustard seed

1 teaspoon whole allspice

1 teaspoon coriander seed

1 teaspoon black peppercorns

1 cinnamon stick

¼ cup honey

2 tablespoons cider vinegar

1 Put the vegetables, parsley, garlic, and salt in a large pot. Bring to a simmer over moderate heat, stirring occasionally. Adjust the heat to maintain a brisk simmer and cook until the tomatoes are soft, about 30 minutes. Pass the mixture through a food mill fitted with the fine disk and return the puree to the pot.

2 Put the bay leaves, clove, mustard seed, allspice, coriander seed, peppercorns, and cinnamon stick on a square of cheesecloth, then tie with kitchen twine to make a spice bag. Add to the pot with the honey. Simmer over moderate heat, stirring occasionally, until the mixture has reduced by half, about 1 hour. Remove the spice bag and add the vinegar. Continue to simmer, stirring as needed to prevent sticking, until the mixture reaches the desired thickness, or about 3 cups.

3 Fill a canning kettle with enough water to cover 3 half-pint canning jars (or 1 pint jar and 1 half-pint jar) resting on the preserving rack. Bring to a boil. Wash the jars with hot, soapy water; rinse well, and keep upside down on a clean dish towel until you are ready to fill them. Put 3 new lids (never reuse lids) in a heatproof bowl and cover with boiling water.

4 Using a ladle and a funnel, transfer the ketchup to the jars, leaving ½ inch headspace. Wipe the rims clean with a damp paper towel. Top with lids and then a screw band. Close tightly.

5 Place the jars on the preserving rack and lower it into the canning kettle. If the water doesn't cover the jars, add boiling water from a tea kettle. Cover the canning kettle. After the water returns to a boil, boil for 15 minutes. With a jar lifter, transfer the jars to a rack to cool completely. Do not touch the jars again until you hear the pops that indicate that the lids have sealed. You can confirm that a lid has sealed by pressing the center with your finger. If it gives, it has not sealed and the contents should be refrigerated and used within a week. Store the sealed jars in a cool, dark place for at least 2 weeks before using. They will keep for up to 1 year before opening. Refrigerate after opening.

Slow-Roasted Tomatoes with Oregano and Feta

Serves 8

Baking tomatoes slowly in a low oven caramelizes their sugars and concentrates their sweetness. They remain moist—not chewy, like sun-dried tomatoes—but with their flavor intensified. Strew them with grated feta while they are warm and serve them with lamb chops, roast chicken, or a bulgur pilaf. Andrew Brait, who oversees tomato production at California's Full Belly Farm, loves Brandywine and Cherokee Purple heirloom varieties and the hybrid Early Girl. You can also use Roma-type tomatoes, such as San Marzano. Leftover roasted tomatoes are sublime on a sandwich. The warm, feta-topped roasted tomatoes are good chopped and tossed with pasta, too.

INGREDIENTS

4 large slicing tomatoes, about ½ pound each

Kosher or sea salt

¼ cup extra virgin olive oil

1 tablespoon minced fresh oregano

2 cloves garlic, finely minced

2 to 3 ounces Greek, French, Bulgarian, or Israeli feta cheese

1 Preheat the oven to 300°F. Core the tomatoes, then cut them in half horizontally. Put the 8 halves, cut side up, in a baking dish just large enough to hold them. Sprinkle generously with salt. Combine the olive oil, oregano (crumbling the herb between your fingers as you add it), and garlic, then spoon the mixture over the tomatoes, dividing it evenly.

2 Bake the tomatoes, basting every half hour or so, until they are very soft and just beginning to caramelize, about 3 hours.

3 Using an offset spatula, transfer the tomatoes to a serving platter, spooning any pan juices over them. Grate the feta over them. Serve warm, not hot.

HOME-DRIED TOMATOES IN HERBED OLIVE OIL

Makes ½ pint

Serve these plump, moist tomatoes on a sliced baguette or bruschetta, add them to sandwiches, or enjoy as a topping for pizza bianca (a pizza without tomato sauce). It is not safe to keep garlic and fresh herbs under olive oil for a long time, even under refrigeration, so make a batch of these marinated tomatoes as you need them and use within a week.

INGREDIENTS

¼ cup white wine vinegar

1 teaspoon kosher or sea salt

½ cup water

14 to 16 dried tomato halves (following)

¼ cup extra virgin olive oil, plus more as needed

1 large clove garlic, thinly sliced

1 teaspoon fennel seed, crushed in a mortar or spice grinder

2 rosemary sprigs, 2 inches long

1. In a small bowl, combine the vinegar, salt, and water. Stir until the liquid is clear again, indicating that the salt has dissolved. Put the tomato halves in another small bowl and pour the vinegar mixture over them. Weight the tomatoes with an overturned saucer or jar lid so they remain submerged. Let stand until they soften and are pliable but not so long that they become mushy; begin checking them after 1 hour, though some may need up to 2 hours to soften, depending on dryness. Remove them to paper towels to drain as they are done. Let them dry for 1 hour.

2. Put the olive oil, garlic, fennel seed, and 1 of the rosemary sprigs in a small skillet and set over moderate heat until the garlic begins to color, 1 to 2 minutes. Set aside to cool. Strain the oil through a fine-mesh sieve.

3. Pack the tomatoes in a clean half-pint jar. Top with the remaining rosemary sprig and the strained oil. Fill the jar with enough additional olive oil to cover the tomatoes completely. Cover with a lid. Let stand at room temperature for 1 day before using. For longer keeping, refrigerate but bring to room temperature before using. They will last in the refrigerator for up to 1 week.

DRIED TOMATOES: Choose meaty, elongated plum tomato varieties, such as Roma or San Marzano. Cut in half lengthwise. Place, cut side up, in a dehydrator with the temperature set at 135°F. Leave in the dehydrator until the tomatoes are dry and stiff, with no moist or soft spots, 12 to 24 hours. Check often. Cool, then refrigerate in heavy-duty storage bags or plastic containers. They will keep indefinitely.

LEBANESE PICKLED TURNIPS

Makes 1 quart

Every Middle Eastern market sells jars of crunchy pickled turnips tinted the rosy color of beets. The pickles are easy to duplicate, their garnet hue achieved by adding a slice or two of raw beet to each jar. Serve with sandwiches or hamburgers in place of a store-bought dill pickle, or with sliced salumi (Italian-style cured meats) or pâté. Or offer them with olives and toasted nuts as an accompaniment to drinks. The small, thin-skinned Tokyo turnips work well here.

INGREDIENTS

PICKLING MIXTURE

1¾ cups water

1 tablespoon plus 1 teaspoon kosher or sea salt

1 clove garlic, halved

1 small dried red chile (optional)

½ cup white wine vinegar

¾ to 1 pound turnips, preferably no larger than
  a golf ball, greens removed

1 small red beet, peeled

1 To make the pickling mixture, in a small saucepan, combine the water, salt, garlic, and chile. Set over moderate heat and stir until the salt dissolves. Set aside to cool. When cool, stir in the vinegar.

2 If the turnips are small and thin skinned, you do not need to peel them. Simply scrub them well and quarter them through the stem end. If they are larger and thick skinned, peel them thickly and cut each one into 6 wedges. Cut the beet into pieces of approximately the same size as the turnips.

3 Pack the vegetables into a clean 1-quart jar. Pour the pickling mixture over them, tucking the garlic halves and chile down into the jar. You should have just enough pickling mixture to cover the vegetables and fill the jar. Cover and refrigerate for 1 week before tasting. The pickled turnips will keep in the refrigerator for at least 2 weeks longer.

DeLaney Community Farm

The rain began gently, a cold drizzle on a gray morning, but soon the crew at DeLaney Community Farm was harvesting in a downpour. Worse, the mid-September day seemed to be getting chillier by the minute. As they dug beets, cut chard, and pulled muddy carrots with icy hands, the drenched young interns began to laugh at their plight. Improbably, the driving rain had turned to snow, the first of the season, and they still had eggplants and tomatoes to pick.

Hours later, when this Denver-area farm's CSA shareholders arrived to load their canvas bags with the weekly share, they saw no evidence of that morning's misery. They found only big galvanized tubs full of flawless chard, bins of glossy green peppers, and scrubbed carrots with perky greens. The interns who huddled in a circle in the greenhouse after the harvest, their lips trembling and their hands piled on top of each others' to thaw, knew the effort that went into getting that pristine produce from field to barn, but consumers witnessed only the outcome.

The mission of DeLaney, an unusual nonprofit CSA, is to bridge that gap, to reconnect city people with the land that nourishes them. "That's why

ANNOUNCEMENTS

FRUIT SHARE:
1 JAR APPLESAUCE
1 BAG APPLES *(only for those who purchased a fruit share!! Thank you)*

EXTRAS: Kale, Radishes, Broccoli, Broccoli Bouquets, Eggplant, Soybeans (Edamame)

WORK NEEDS DOING:

VEGGIES	half share	full share
onions	2	4
red onions	4	8
garlic	1	2
beets	1 bunch	2 bunch
carrots	1 bunch	2 bunch
turnips	1	2
parsnips	1 bunch	2 bunch
daikon radish		2
bell peppers	LG-2 SM-1	LG-4 SM-2
hot peppers	2 hot, 1 paprika	4 hot, 2 paprika
tomatoes	green 2, red 5	green 4, red 10
collards	1	2

we're here," says Heather DeLong, program coordinator for the farm. "We're trying to get kids to understand that lettuce doesn't grow in the back of the supermarket."

To that end, DeLaney's shareholders are expected to volunteer on the farm—planting, harvesting, weeding, or helping out on pickup day. One shareholder, an herbalist, has created a hand salve and herb teas for the farm to sell. Another, an avid home canner, teaches a preserving workshop for CSA members.

Sessions on beekeeping and honey harvesting, composting, and organic gardening also lure the public to this three-acre parcel. Schoolkids regularly tour the farm, learning how to dig potatoes or mobbing the glass-fronted demonstration beehive. Plants might get trampled by these novice helpers, the herbs might not get clipped in the right spot, but that's okay, staffers say. Only by engaging shareholders and their children in the chores of the farm will they understand the challenges farmers face.

Food Donations for Pantries & Meal Sites

☆ the aspen place
☆ colorado AIDS project
☆ operation frontline
☆ project angel heart

For many members of CSA farms, the experience is simply a financial transaction—money now for produce later. "DeLaney is everything but that," says Michael Buchenau, the executive director of Denver Urban Gardens (DUG), whose staff manages the farm. A Harvard-educated landscape architect, Michael has helped DUG establish more than ninety community gardens in the city. When the City of Aurora approached DUG about establishing a small farm on the DeLaney site—a historic, 160-acre farmstead bequeathed to Aurora—Michael recognized its potential as an educational community center.

The farm has a three-year waiting list for the roughly sixty spots in its CSA. Even so, shareholder revenue does not cover operating costs, in large part because of the farm's philanthropy. Staffers deliver shares every week to a nearby residence for low-income seniors, to a commercial kitchen that provides meals for people with life-threatening illness, and to a food pantry for people living with AIDS. Participants in WIC—a federal nutrition program for low-income women with young children—are encouraged to volunteer on the farm in return for just-picked produce.

For many of these WIC mothers, DeLaney provides rare access to really fresh vegetables. And to get even more produce into needy communities, DUG operates a Mobile Market. Traveling by bicycle, an employee transports DeLaney crops to two sites frequented by low-income residents and sets up a mini-farm stand.

Local farms partner with DeLaney to provide egg, meat, goat's milk, honey, and fruit shares; in late summer, DeLaney's own beehive yields enough to provide every member with a small ration. In October, the city turns off the farm's water, the CSA season ends, and shareholders are invited to come glean what remains.

At a Glance

Favorite crops: Royal Burgundy bush bean, Masai haricot vert; Eight Ball zucchini (for stuffing), Red Long of Tropea onion, Rhubarb Swiss chard, French Fingerling potato, Fish pepper.

Shareholder insight: "We're eating better, and we're saving money, and we're getting an edible education," says Sasha Addams, a DeLaney shareholder and mother who was on the waiting list for three years.

Drying herbs: In warm shade, place fresh herbs on window screens, stacking the screens on bricks. Herbs will dry in two to five days.

Kitchen tip: Take pesto beyond basil. Substitute spinach, kale, or garlic scapes for some or all of the basil.

Wish list: Changes to city zoning laws to permit more community gardens and greenhouse cultivation, and to allow for keeping bees and chickens in urban areas. "For a quarter-century, we've separated city and countryside," says Michael. Maybe, he argues, it's time to rethink that.

Mobile Market

Buy fresh fruits & veggies from
DeLaney Community Farm
& other local farmers.

Now Accepting
Food Stamps
& Debit Cards!

brought to you

Without the profit demands of private CSA farms, DeLaney can pour resources into building community, and the results are obvious. During the September snowfall that took the harvest crew by surprise, Heather got a call from a concerned shareholder. "I just wanted to make sure you all were warm," said the caller.

Like other farmers grappling with a short growing season and weather extremes, DeLaney's young staff has learned to rebound from setbacks. One year, a sudden August hailstorm shredded the kale and pummeled the winter squash as the interns watched in shock. "It was so violent," recalls intern Abbie Harris. "It was warm and raining, then cold and raining, then the barrage. And I thought, ohmigod, the chard."

Shareholders immediately stepped in to help replant and grasped that the harvest would come up short for a while. "That's what CSA means," says Abbie. "In sickness and in health."

FRUITS

Eating locally engages home cooks in the cycle of the growing season. Unlike supermarket shoppers, who expect strawberries to be available year-round, people who patronize farmers' markets or belong to a CSA know that many fruits are fleeting. When creamy Comice pears appear in the market, it's time to snap them up for a pear sorbet (page 230). When the local peaches and blueberries ripen, it's the moment for cobbler (page 223), crisp (page 224), or clafouti (page 193). These precious and perishable fruits beg to be "put up" for the future—perhaps as fig and lemon preserves (page 211) or a brandy-spiked cherry sauce (page 197) for ice cream. Some of them shine on the grill, too. Try grilling nectarines (page 225) to partner with mascarpone ice cream or tucking slices of Asian pear into a grilled prosciutto and goat cheese sandwich (page 232). In the following pages, you'll find recipes that celebrate the fruits of every season.

Hot Spiced Apple Cider

Serves 8

An old-fashioned winter beverage that never loses its appeal, spiced cider on the kitchen stove will perfume the whole house. To maintain the disappearing autumn ritual of cider production, Red Fire Farm in Granby, Massachusetts, holds a cider pressing day in October. Locals are encouraged to bring their own homegrown apples, or to purchase cider apples from the farm. A scarecrow contest and a potluck conclude the festivities.

Ingredients

2 quarts apple cider (unfiltered apple juice)

¼ cup honey

1 navel orange, quartered

2 cinnamon sticks

8 whole allspice

6 quarter-sized coins peeled fresh ginger

4 ounces (½ cup) dark rum or Calvados (optional)

1 Put the cider, honey, and orange quarters in a large saucepan. Put the cinnamon sticks and allspice on a square of cheesecloth. Smack the ginger coins with the side of a chef's knife to release their juice, then put the coins on the cheesecloth square, too. Tie the cheesecloth with kitchen twine to make a spice bag and add it to the saucepan.

2 Bring the mixture to a simmer over moderately low heat, stirring to dissolve the honey. Cover partially and simmer gently for 30 minutes to marry the flavors.

3 Put ½ ounce (1 tablespoon) rum in each of 8 mugs. Divide the hot cider among the mugs and serve immediately.

Heirloom Apple Tart with Almond Filling and Calvados Cream

Makes one 9-inch tart, to serve 8

Unlike the apple varieties sold in most supermarkets, selected for their ability to store for months, heirloom apples may not be good keepers. But when fresh off the tree, as you will find them at farmers' markets and in CSA shares, they have a perfume and juicy sweetness that few storage apples can match. If you have a choice, taste first to find a variety whose flavor you like; with tart varieties, you may want to sweeten with a little more sugar.

Ingredients

TART DOUGH

1 cup unbleached all-purpose flour

1 tablespoon sugar

½ teaspoon kosher or sea salt

6 tablespoons unsalted butter, chilled, in small pieces

3 tablespoons ice water

ALMOND FILLING

4 tablespoons unsalted butter, at room temperature

4 ounces almond paste, at room temperature, crumbled

1 large egg, at room temperature

¼ cup unbleached all-purpose flour

1 pound apples, peeled, quartered, cored, and thinly sliced lengthwise

1 tablespoon fresh lemon juice

1 tablespoon sugar

1 tablespoon unsalted butter, melted

2 tablespoons apple jelly or honey

CALVADOS CREAM

1 cup heavy cream

1 tablespoon plus 1 teaspoon sugar

¼ teaspoon vanilla extract

2 teaspoons Calvados or brandy, or to taste

1 To make the tart dough, put the flour, sugar, and salt in a food processor and pulse several times to blend. Add the butter and pulse until the bits of butter are no larger than a pea. Drizzle the ice water over the mixture and pulse until the dough begins to come together; it will be crumbly. Transfer the dough to a sheet of plastic wrap and use the wrap, rather than your hands, to help you gather and shape the dough into a ¾-inch-thick disk. Enclose with the plastic wrap and refrigerate for at least 1 hour or up to 1 day.

2 Remove the dough from the refrigerator and place it between 2 sheets of parchment paper at least 12 inches square. With a rolling pin, flatten the dough into an 11-inch circle. To prevent sticking, occasionally lift the top sheet of parchment and lightly flour the dough, then replace the parchment and invert the dough so the bottom sheet is on top. Peel back that sheet of parchment and lightly flour the dough, then replace the parchment and continue rolling.

3 When the circle is large enough, fold it gently in quarters to make it easy to lift. Transfer it to a 9-inch tart tin with a removable bottom, unfold it, and gently press it into place. Roll the rolling pin across the top of the tin to remove any excess dough. Prick the dough in several places with a fork, then place in the freezer for 30 minutes.

continued next page

Heirloom Apple Tart with Almond Filling and Calvados Cream **continued**

4 Preheat the oven to 400°F. To keep the tart dough in place as it bakes, put a sheet of parchment paper in the tart shell and add enough pie weights or dried beans to cover the bottom of the shell and press up against the sides. Bake until the sides are golden brown, about 25 minutes. Lift the parchment paper to remove the weights; the shell will still be pale on the bottom. Cool on a rack. Leave the oven on.

5 To make the almond filling, put the butter and almond paste in a bowl and beat with an electric mixer on medium speed until well blended. Add the egg and beat until creamy. Add the flour and beat just until well mixed. Spread the filling evenly in the cooled tart shell.

6 In a large bowl, toss the apples with the lemon juice to prevent browning. Sprinkle with the sugar and toss again. Arrange the apples over the filling in concentric circles, working from the outside in and overlapping the slices slightly. Brush the apples with the melted butter.

7 Bake until the filling is puffed and firm to the touch and the apples are browned on the edges, about 40 minutes. Transfer to a rack.

8 While the tart is still hot, warm the jelly in a small saucepan until it liquefies. Brush this warm glaze over the apples.

9 Serve the tart warm, not hot. Just before serving, make the Calvados cream: In a bowl, with a whisk or a handheld mixer, beat together the cream, sugar, and vanilla until the mixture visibly thickens and begins to hold a shape. Whisk in the Calvados. Cut the tart into wedges, and serve a dollop of the cream alongside each serving.

Summer Fruit Macedonia with Anisette

Serves 8

Fruit salad is too often a pedestrian dessert made with overripe, flavorless, or out-of-season fruits, carelessly cut up and presented. Who would want that? But prepared in the Italian fashion, using a well-chosen mix of the best summer fruits and a hint of anise or maraschino liqueur, fruit salad—macedonia in Italian—becomes a truly grand finale. Use any fruit but strawberries, which quickly turn mushy. Serve the chilled macedonia in your most beautiful stemware or crystal to show off the gemlike colors of the fruit.

Ingredients

1½ cups dry white wine

½ cup sugar

1½ cups water

6 cups mixed summer fruits, pitted and cut into
   bite-size pieces as needed, such as 4 apricots,
   3 nectarines, 2 plums, ¾ cup each blueberries
   and blackberries, and 24 cherries

About 2 teaspoons anise liqueur such as anisette or
   Sambuca, kirsch, maraschino, or other liqueur
   of choice

1 Put the wine, sugar, and water in a small saucepan and bring to a simmer over moderate heat, stirring to dissolve the sugar. Simmer until reduced to 2 cups. Cool the syrup, then cover and refrigerate until cold.

2 Combine the syrup and the fruits in a large bowl, stirring gently. Add the liqueur and again stir gently. Cover and refrigerate for at least 2 hours or up to 8 hours. Serve in martini glasses, balloon wineglasses, or footed compotes.

Mixed Summer Berries with Honey Sabayon

Serves 8

Like the Italian zabaglione, a French sabayon calls for whisking eggs, a sweetener (in this case, honey), and wine over simmering water until the mixture becomes pale and frothy and grows dramatically in volume. Sabayon is typically served warm, but if you chill the mixture and fold in whipped cream, you have a luscious, fluffy sauce for summer fruit. Use any combination of berries, or add in other warm-weather fruits, such as apricots, peaches, nectarines, or figs.

Ingredients

SABAYON
¾ cup heavy cream
6 large egg yolks
¼ cup honey
¾ cup muscat wine

2 pints mixed berries (such as blueberries, raspberries, blackberries, and strawberries)
Superfine sugar
Brandy

1 To make the sabayon, in a bowl, whisk the cream until soft peaks form. Cover and refrigerate.

2 Have ready a large bowl of ice water. In the top pan of a double boiler, using a whisk or a handheld mixer fitted with beaters, whip together the egg yolks and honey until pale. Set over the lower pan of simmering water, making sure the top pan remains above, not touching, the water. (Or use a heatproof bowl that fits snugly in the top of a saucepan of simmering water, again with the bottom of the bowl not touching the water.) Whip until the mixture is light and thick, about 3 minutes. Add the wine gradually, whisking constantly, then continue to whisk until the mixture is pale, thick, fluffy, and about doubled in volume, about 10 minutes. Do not let the mixture get too hot or the eggs can scramble.

3 Place the top pan of the double boiler in the bowl of ice water to chill the mixture quickly. Whisk the mixture occasionally to cool it faster. When cool, fold in the whipped cream. Cover and refrigerate until needed; you can make the sabayon up to 6 hours ahead.

4 Put the berries in a large bowl, slicing the strawberries first, if using. Add superfine sugar to taste and a splash of brandy to heighten the flavor. Toss and let stand for about 15 minutes to draw out some juices.

5 To serve, divide the berries evenly among footed compote dishes or balloon wineglasses. Top each portion with a generous dollop of the sabayon. Serve immediately.

BLUEBERRY CLAFOUTI

Serves 6

A classic from rural French kitchens, clafouti is traditionally made with fresh cherries. But when the blueberry season gets under way, this homespun dessert should be top of mind again. Resembling a cross between a custard and a puffy pancake, clafouti comes together quickly and is best when still warm. Try one for a weekend breakfast or brunch in place of waffles or pancakes. Pronounce it clah-foo-tee, with every syllable accented evenly.

INGREDIENTS

1 teaspoon unsalted butter, softened

⅓ cup plus 1 tablespoon granulated sugar

¾ pound blueberries (about 2½ cups)

3 large eggs

1 cup whole milk

½ cup unbleached all-purpose flour

½ teaspoon vanilla extract

¼ teaspoon almond extract

Pinch of kosher or sea salt

¼ cup sliced almonds, toasted (page xiv)

Confectioners' sugar, for dusting

1 Preheat the oven to 325°F. Using the butter, grease the bottom and sides of a 9 by 2-inch round baking dish, or another low-sided baking dish with a 1½-quart capacity. Sprinkle the bottom and sides with the 1 tablespoon granulated sugar. Put the blueberries in the prepared dish in an even layer.

2 Put the eggs, milk, flour, vanilla and almond extracts, salt, and the remaining ⅓ cup granulated sugar in a blender. Blend until smooth. Pour carefully over the berries so as not to dislodge them. Scatter the almonds over the surface.

3 Bake until the *clafouti* is puffed and firm to the touch, about 35 minutes. Cool on a rack for about 20 minutes, then dust thickly with confectioners' sugar. The *clafouti* is best when served warm.

GRILLED POUND CAKE WITH
STRAWBERRY-RHUBARB SAUCE

Serves 8

Many fans of pound cake know that toasting it heightens the cake's buttery flavor. Grilling works the same magic, so when you have the grill going for a summer dinner, why not grill dessert, too? Be sure to brush the grill rack clean first.

INGREDIENTS

POUND CAKE

1 cup (2 sticks) unsalted butter, softened, plus more for preparing the pan

2 cups sifted unbleached all-purpose flour, plus more for preparing the pan

½ teaspoon kosher or sea salt

¼ teaspoon baking powder

1½ cups sugar

5 large eggs, at room temperature

1 tablespoon freshly grated lemon zest

1 tablespoon poppy seeds

STRAWBERRY-RHUBARB SAUCE

1 pint strawberries, cored and quartered lengthwise

½ pound rhubarb, trimmed and cut crosswise into ½-inch pieces

2 tablespoons fresh orange juice

6 to 8 tablespoons sugar

Mascarpone Ice Cream (page 197) or store-bought vanilla ice cream

1 To make the cake, preheat the oven to 325°F. Lightly grease a 9 by 5 by 3-inch loaf pan with butter. Coat the bottom and sides with flour and shake out the excess.

2 Sift together the flour, salt, and baking powder into a medium bowl.

3 In the bowl of a stand mixer fitted with the paddle, or in a large bowl with a handheld mixer, cream the butter on medium speed until smooth. Add the sugar gradually, beating constantly until the mixture is light and fluffy. Beat in the eggs, one at a time, beating well after each addition and scraping down the sides of the bowl once or twice, then beat in the lemon zest and poppy seeds. On low speed, add the dry ingredients gradually, beating just until blended. Transfer the batter to the prepared pan, spreading it evenly.

4 Bake until the cake is firm to the touch and beginning to pull away from the sides of the pan, about 1¼ hours. A cake tester inserted in the middle should come out clean. Cool the cake in the pan on a rack for 15 minutes, then invert onto a rack. Invert again so the top is up and finish cooling on the rack.

5 To make the strawberry-rhubarb sauce, put the berries, rhubarb, orange juice, and 6 tablespoons sugar in a medium saucepan. Set over moderate heat and heat, stirring until the sugar dissolves. Cover, adjust the heat to maintain a gentle simmer, and cook, stirring occasionally, until the fruit softens and forms a sauce, about 10 minutes. Keep a close eye on the saucepan, reducing the heat if the mixture threatens to bubble over. Cool slightly, then taste and add more sugar if desired. Transfer to a bowl, cover, and chill thoroughly.

6 Prepare a moderately hot charcoal fire or preheat a gas grill to medium-high (375° to 400°F). Cut the ends off the cake, then cut the cake into 8 equal slices. Grill directly over the coals or gas flame, turning once, until lightly toasted on both sides, about 2 minutes per side.

7 Put about ⅓ cup of the sauce on each dessert plate. Top with a slice of toasted cake and a scoop of ice cream. Serve immediately.

Warm Cornmeal Shortcake with Farm Stand Berries

Serves 8

Traditional biscuit-based shortcake tastes best when the biscuits are hot from the oven, making it a last-minute dessert. With this golden cornmeal loaf, you can bake the cake hours ahead, then slice and toast it just before serving. With cool, juicy berries spooned over it and a dollop of soft-whipped cream, the cake may well become your go-to summer dessert.

Ingredients

CORNMEAL CAKE

¾ cup (1½ sticks) unsalted butter, softened,
   plus more for preparing the pan

1½ cups sifted unbleached all-purpose flour,
   plus more for preparing the pan

2 teaspoons baking powder

1 teaspoon baking soda

⅔ cup yellow cornmeal

½ cup fine semolina

½ teaspoon kosher or sea salt

⅔ cup sugar

2 large eggs, at room temperature

½ teaspoon almond extract

1 cup buttermilk

3 pints mixed juicy berries (such as boysenberries,
   strawberries, and raspberries)

¼ cup plus 1 tablespoon sugar

1 tablespoon plus 1 teaspoon brandy, or to taste

1 cup heavy cream

¼ teaspoon vanilla extract

1 To make the cake, preheat the oven to 375°F. Lightly grease a 9 by 5 by 3-inch loaf pan with butter. Coat the bottom and sides with flour and shake out the excess.

2 Sift together the flour, baking powder, and baking soda into a medium bowl. Whisk in the cornmeal, semolina, and salt until well blended.

continued next page

WARM CORNMEAL SHORTCAKE WITH FARM STAND BERRIES continued

3 In the bowl of a stand mixer fitted with the paddle, or in a large bowl with a handheld mixer, beat the butter on medium speed until smooth. Add the sugar gradually, beating constantly until the mixture is pale and light and scraping down the sides of the bowl once or twice. Beat in the eggs, one at a time, beating well after each addition, then beat in the almond extract.

4 On low speed, add half of the dry ingredients and beat just until blended. Add the buttermilk and beat just until blended, then add the remaining dry ingredients and beat just until blended. Transfer the batter to the prepared pan.

5 Bake until the cake is firm to the touch and beginning to pull away from the sides of the pan, 45 to 50 minutes. A cake tester inserted in the middle should come out clean. Cool the cake in the pan on a rack for 15 minutes, then invert onto a rack. Invert again so the top is up and finish cooling on the rack.

6 In a bowl, combine the berries, ¼ cup of the sugar, and the brandy. Stir gently with a rubber spatula. Let macerate at room temperature for 1 hour to dissolve the sugar and draw out the fruit juices, stirring occasionally.

7 In a bowl, whisk together the cream, the remaining 1 tablespoon sugar, and the vanilla until soft peaks form. Cover and refrigerate until serving.

8 Preheat the oven to 375°F. Cut the ends off the cake, then cut the cake into 8 equal slices. Arrange the slices in a single layer on a baking sheet and toast in the oven until hot throughout and slightly crusty, about 5 minutes. Transfer the slices to individual dessert plates. Spoon some of the macerated berries and their juices over the cake. Top each serving with a dollop of the cream. Serve immediately.

Mascarpone Ice Cream Sundae with Brandied Cherry Sauce

Serves 8

When sweet cherries are in season, make this sauce in quantity. You can freeze it, or you can preserve it using the standard water-bath processing procedure. It's divine over ice cream and can be used to dress up an angel food cake or pound cake.

Ingredients

BRANDIED CHERRY SAUCE

1/3 cup sugar
1 1/2 teaspoons cornstarch
2/3 cup water
1 pound sweet cherries, pitted and halved
   (about 3 cups)
1 tablespoon brandy
Fresh lemon juice, if needed

MASCARPONE ICE CREAM

1 cup half-and-half
1 cup heavy cream
1/2 vanilla bean (halved crosswise)
6 large egg yolks
2/3 cup sugar
Pinch of kosher or sea salt
1 cup mascarpone cheese

3/4 cup heavy cream
2 tablespoons sugar
Brandy
3/4 cup sliced almonds, toasted (page xiv)

1 To make the cherry sauce, combine the sugar, cornstarch, and water in a saucepan. Simmer over moderate heat, whisking constantly until the mixture thickens. Add the cherries. Simmer, stirring often, until the cherries soften and the sauce develops a deep burgundy color and rich cherry flavor, about 10 minutes. Set aside to cool.

2 Stir in the brandy and lemon juice. Set aside until ready to serve, or cover and refrigerate for up to 1 week.

3 To make the ice cream, put the half-and-half and cream in a medium saucepan. Cut the halved vanilla bean in half lengthwise and scrape the seeds into the saucepan, then add the bean pod as well. Bring to a simmer over moderate heat, remove from the heat, cover, and let steep for 15 minutes.

4 In a bowl, whisk the egg yolks, sugar, and salt until pale and thick. Add the contents of the saucepan gradually, whisking constantly, then return the mixture to the saucepan and set over moderate heat.

5 Cook, stirring constantly with a wooden spoon, until the custard reaches 178°F on an instant-read thermometer. It will visibly thicken and coat the spoon. Do not let it boil or it will curdle. Immediately remove from the heat, stirring for a minute or two to cool the custard rapidly. Cool for 15 minutes, then remove the vanilla bean pod and whisk in the mascarpone. Cover the custard and refrigerate until well chilled, then freeze the custard in an ice-cream maker according to the manufacturer's directions. Transfer the ice cream to a freezer container and freeze for at least 30 minutes to allow it to firm up before serving.

6 In a bowl, whisk the cream until soft peaks forms. Whisk in the sugar and brandy to taste.

7 To serve, warm the cherry sauce gently in a small saucepan over low heat. Put about 2 tablespoons warm sauce in the bottom of each of parfait glass or footed compote. Top each pool of sauce with 1/2 cup ice cream. Spoon the remaining sauce over the ice cream, dividing it evenly. Top each portion with a dollop of the whipped cream, then scatter on the almonds. Serve immediately.

WARM CHERRY UPSIDE-DOWN CAKE

Makes one 9-inch cake, to serve 8

Canned pineapple and bottled cherries were the garnish for upside-down cake in times past. Thank goodness that era is over. Fresh cherries, pitted and halved, make a more contemporary topping for a delicate butter cake with a particularly tender crumb. Apricots, figs, or blackberries could stand in for the cherries.

INGREDIENTS

¾ cup (1½ sticks) unsalted butter, softened
1½ cups sugar
1 tablespoon fresh lemon juice
¼ cup sliced almonds, toasted (page xiv)
½ pound cherries, pitted and halved
1½ cups sifted all-purpose flour
1½ teaspoons baking powder
½ teaspoon kosher salt
2 large eggs, at room temperature
1 teaspoon vanilla extract
½ teaspoon almond extract
⅔ cup whole milk

1 Preheat the oven to 350°F. Grease the sides (not the bottom) of a 9-inch round cake pan.

2 Melt 4 tablespoons of the butter in a small saucepan over moderately low heat. Add ½ cup of the sugar and the lemon juice and cook, stirring, just until the sugar dissolves and the mixture bubbles. Pour into the prepared pan and swirl the pan to coat the bottom evenly with the mixture.

3 Scatter the toasted almonds evenly over the bottom of the pan. Put the cherries, cut side up, in the pan in concentric rings.

4 Sift together the flour, baking powder, and salt into a bowl.

5 In a stand mixer fitted with the paddle, or in a large bowl with a handheld mixer, beat the remaining ½ cup butter on medium speed until smooth. Add the remaining 1 cup sugar gradually, beating constantly until pale and light and scraping down the sides of the bowl once or twice. When the mixture is no longer grainy, add the eggs, one at a time, beating well after each addition, then beat in the vanilla and almond extracts.

6 On low speed, add half of the dry ingredients and beat just until blended. Add the milk and beat just until blended, then add the remaining dry ingredients and beat just until blended. Transfer the batter to the prepared pan, spreading it evenly.

7 Bake until the cake is well risen, golden brown, firm to the touch, and beginning to pull away from the sides of the pan, 45 to 50 minutes. A toothpick inserted in the middle should come out clean.

8 Remove from the oven and immediately invert the cake onto a serving platter. Leave the cake pan upside down over the cake for about 2 minutes, then lift it off. If a few almonds or cherries have stuck to the bottom of the pan, set them in place on top of the cake. Serve warm.

Rainbow, California

MORNING SONG FARM

For the one hundred households in Southern California that subscribe to the Morning Song Farm CSA, fresh macadamia nuts, crisp and buttery, are among the more recognizable items in the weekly delivery.

Donna Buono, who owns Morning Song Farm, claims to have the only rare-fruit CSA in the nation, harvesting yuzu and Oro Blanco citrus, Pakistani mulberries, kumquats, feijoas, passion fruit, and pomegranates on her twenty acres in northern San Diego County. Little wonder that her customers' most frequent question is, "Donna, what is this?"

A self-described "carpool mom in cowboy boots," Donna straddles two worlds: the prosperous suburban community of San Clemente, where she lives; and the more arduous realm of the small farmer, struggling with challenges that can sometimes seem insurmountable.

But the woman whom customers call Farmer Donna is nothing if not feisty. The farm may have started as a husband-subsidized project, but it is now, following divorce, a serious business that must support her and two children.

The money-losing macadamia farm that she purchased in 2000 is a more diverse operation now, with 200 lime trees, 160 avocado trees, and 50 kumquat trees. Trial plantings of more obscure items like Buddha's hand citron, loquats, dragon fruit, and Lavender Gem (a citrus cross, also called wekiwa) provide novelties for her CSA customers.

"I want to try everything," admits Donna. "There probably isn't any weird fruit I'm not aware of."

On the farm's few flat parcels, she plants tomatoes, chard, carrots, beans, green onions, arugula, and other row crops to make her CSA box more varied and useful. But what excites her is growing the offbeat, like yard-long beans and fiery Kung Pao chiles. When she and her former husband bought the acreage so she could turn her rare fruit-growing hobby into a small business, she named it Morning Song Farm because "it felt so joyous," says Donna. "I was so excited."

Initially, she focused her sales effort on farmers' markets, but profits eluded her. It took years of losses for Donna to realize that she was effectively paying customers to take her produce. "Passion fruit for everybody!" jokes Donna now.

Forsaking farmers' markets for CSA has put Donna on more stable financial footing. She still sells a lot of her harvest wholesale, but despite her farm's location in the town of Rainbow, there is no pot of gold here. "It will never provide an affluent lifestyle," says Donna. "The only future for little farms like mine is having a relationship directly with the consumer."

Imports from Mexico have cut into sales of her organic avocados and limes. She can't compete, she says, with growers just across the border who operate with many fewer regulations. But probably the biggest threat to her farm's survival is lack of water. The more residential development in her rapidly urbanizing county, the less water for her. "A farm is worthless without water rights," says Donna.

Crops are harvested year-round at Morning Song Farm, although the pace slows in August. The thermometer can hit 120°F then, hot enough to melt the asphalt. When that happens, the farms' four llamas take refuge in their shady corral. Purchased as weed eaters and manure producers, they are valued members of the crew. And Donna adores them. When one was bitten in the face by a snake and the veterinarian determined that nothing could be done, Donna pulled a mattress into the barn and slept with the injured llama for two nights, until the animal died. "I'm kind of a tough cookie," says Donna, "but that was hard."

From the highway, the winding road up to Morning Song Farm leads past palm-tree nurseries and modest ranch homes landscaped with agave and bougainvillea. At one point, the steep road crests and a driver can no longer see the end, a fitting metaphor for the route Donna has chosen.

CSA Pick-up: Straight Ahead

At a Glance

Favorite crops: "Customers don't like kumquats, and they're one of my favorite things in the world," says Donna. "If you don't cook them, you don't understand them." Her tangy kumquat sauce (page 208) elevates pancakes, waffles, and crepes.

Produce tip: When fully ripe, limes develop a yellow cast. "They're still tart, but they have a more complex flavor then," says Donna. A wholesale customer once returned thousands of ripe limes to her because "they weren't green enough."

Farm wisdom: "Uniformity has essentially no value," says Donna. "In my boxes, the avocados are all different. The price of uniformity is that either you have to pay more or I have to make less."

In Donna's freezer: Peeled and diced melon for use in smoothies and sorbets. Frozen fruit makes especially flavorful smoothies because you don't have to add ice.

In Donna's pantry: Lemon verbena sugar. In a food processor, puree a dozen lemon verbena leaves with a cup of sugar. Let stand 24 hours, then strain. Use the fragrant sugar on fruit or in iced tea.

Mixed Citrus Compote with Pomegranate Seeds

Serves 6

You can use any combination of citrus you like in this compote, but for maximum appeal, aim for a mix of colors. It's the ideal dessert after a robust winter stew or braise—light, refreshing, and compellingly scented with cardamom and cinnamon.

Ingredients

1 cup dry white wine

½ cup plus 1 tablespoon sugar

1 cinnamon stick

1 cup water

10 cardamom pods

2 large navel oranges

2 large blood oranges

1 ruby grapefruit

1 Cara Cara orange or 1 additional navel orange

¾ cup fresh pomegranate seeds

½ teaspoon rose water (optional)

1 In a small saucepan, combine the wine, sugar, cinnamon stick, and water. In a mortar or with a rolling pin, lightly pound the cardamom pods to crack the hulls and crush the seeds lightly. Add them to the saucepan. Bring to a simmer over moderate heat, stirring to dissolve the sugar. Continue simmering until reduced to 1½ cups, 10 to 15 minutes. Strain through a fine-mesh sieve to remove the spices and set aside to cool.

2 Cut a slice off the top and bottom of each citrus fruit. Working with 1 fruit at a time, set it on a cutting board, one cut side down. Using a chef's knife, slice away the peel from top to bottom, following the contour of the fruit and removing all the white pith. With a small paring knife, cut the whole segments away from the membranes, allowing the segments to drop into a nonreactive bowl. Remove any visible citrus seeds. Gently stir in the pomegranate seeds.

3 When the syrup is cool, pour off any citrus juices that have accumulated in the bowl and reserve for a beverage. Pour the syrup over the fruit. Stir in the rose water. Cover and chill thoroughly.

4 At serving time, spoon the compote and syrup into individual serving bowls or balloon wineglasses. Serve immediately.

CREPES WITH A WARM KUMQUAT SAUCE

Makes 16 crepes, to serve 8

Donna Buono, proprietor of Morning Song Farm, makes these crepes for breakfast, topping them with a syruplike reduction of pureed kumquats and sugar. For an appealing dessert, fold the warm, unfilled crepes in quarters, drizzle with the warm kumquat reduction, and top with a scoop of vanilla ice cream. Kumquats have a pleasantly bitter edge because you eat both the pulp and the peel.

INGREDIENTS

CREPE BATTER
1 cup unbleached all-purpose flour
½ cup whole milk
½ cup water
2 large eggs
2 tablespoons unsalted butter, melted
½ teaspoon kosher or sea salt
½ teaspoon vanilla extract

KUMQUAT SAUCE
½ pound kumquats, halved
½ cup sugar

2 cups whole-milk ricotta cheese (one 15-ounce container), sweetened to taste with sugar
1 tablespoon unsalted butter, melted

1 To make the crepe batter, put all the ingredients in a blender and blend until smooth. You should have about 2 cups batter. You can make the batter several hours ahead and refrigerate, but bring to room temperature before using.

2 To make the kumquat sauce, put the kumquats in the blender and add water to come just to the level of the fruit. Puree, then strain through a fine-mesh sieve. Put the strained puree in a small saucepan with the sugar, stirring to blend. Set over moderate heat and simmer until reduced to about 1 cup; the reduction should have a pourable consistency similar to maple syrup. Set aside to cool slightly.

3 Put the ricotta in a bowl and beat with a wooden spoon until smooth.

4 To cook the crepes, put the batter in a liquid measuring cup with a spout, or other container with a pour spout. Set an 8-inch nonstick skillet or crepe pan over moderate heat. Brush lightly with some of the melted butter. When the skillet is hot, add about 2 tablespoons batter, swirling the pan at the same time so the batter covers the skillet in a thin, even layer. Cook until the crepe colors lightly on the bottom and begins to separate from the skillet, 15 to 20 seconds; the surface will no longer look moist. Loosen the edges of the crepe with a heatproof rubber spatula, then flip the crepe with your fingers and cook on the second side until it is mostly dry and lightly colored, about 15 seconds. Transfer to a plate.

5 Continue cooking the crepes, stacking them as you go with a piece of waxed paper separating each, until you have used all the batter. You should have 16 crepes in all. Brush the skillet lightly with butter between crepes only if they are threatening to stick. Adjust the heat as needed to produce crepes that are lightly colored but still pliable, not crisp.

6 To serve, reheat the kumquat sauce if necessary until it is warm but not piping hot. Spread one side of each crepe with 2 tablespoons of the sweetened ricotta, then fold the crepe in half. Place 2 crepes on each serving plate, and drizzle each crepe with about 1 tablespoon of the kumquat sauce. Serve immediately.

BABY GREENS WITH GRILLED FIGS, BLUE CHEESE, AND WALNUTS

Serves 6

Warming figs on the grill seems to heighten their sweetness, slightly caramelizing their natural sugar. Serve them as a companion to blue cheese at the end of a meal or, as here, in a salad with crumbled blue cheese and toasted walnuts.

INGREDIENTS

DRESSING

3 tablespoons extra virgin olive oil

1 tablespoon fresh lemon juice, or more if needed

1 large shallot, minced

Kosher or sea salt and freshly ground black pepper

9 figs, halved lengthwise

1 tablespoon unsalted butter, melted

½ pound mixed baby salad greens

¾ cup walnut halves, toasted (page xvi) and coarsely chopped

3 to 4 ounces blue cheese, firm enough to crumble

1 Prepare a moderate charcoal fire or preheat a gas grill to medium (375°F).

2 To make the dressing, in a small bowl, whisk together the olive oil, lemon juice, and shallot. Season to taste with salt and pepper.

3 Using wooden skewers, skewer the fig halves lengthwise, putting as many on a skewer as will fit. Brush lightly with the melted butter. Grill directly over the coals or gas flame, turning once, just until hot throughout.

4 Put the baby greens and walnuts in a large bowl. Add the blue cheese, crumbling it as you add it. Add just enough dressing to coat the greens lightly; you may not need it all. Toss to coat the greens evenly. Taste and adjust the seasoning. Add another squeeze of lemon, if needed.

5 Divide the salad among individual salad plates or arrange on a platter. Nestle the warm figs among the greens. Serve immediately.

FRESH FIG AND LEMON PRESERVES

Makes 2 to 2½ pints

The plump Brown Turkey figs that Amy Hicks brings to farmers' markets for customers of Amy's Garden would be luscious in this easy jam, but any fresh figs will work. A finely chopped lemon, minus the seeds, helps balance the figs' honeyed sweetness. Serve on English muffins, toast, or biscuits, or as an accompaniment to blue cheese.

INGREDIENTS

1 medium lemon
2 cups sugar
2 pounds black or green figs, stem ends removed

1 Fill a canning kettle with enough water to cover the top of widemouthed canning jars (half-pints or mix of pints and half-pints) resting on the preserving rack. Bring to a boil. Wash the jars with hot, soapy water; rinse well, and keep upside down on a clean dish towel until you are ready to fill them. Put new lids (never reuse lids) in a heatproof bowl and cover with boiling water.

2 Remove the tips of the lemon and quarter it lengthwise. Cut away the white core. Pick out and discard any seeds. Cut the quarters in half and put them in a food processor with 1 cup of the sugar. Process as fine as possible. Add the figs and process until they are well chopped but not fully pureed. It is nice to leave the preserve a little coarse.

3 Transfer the contents of the processor bowl to a large nonreactive pot and stir in the remaining 1 cup sugar. Bring to a simmer over moderate heat, stirring, then simmer gently until the temperature reaches 200°F on an instant-read thermometer, about 15 minutes. You can also test for doneness by spooning a small amount of jam onto a chilled saucer. Return the saucer to the freezer until the jam is cold, then test to see if it has the consistency you like. It should be neither soupy nor stiff.

4 Ladle the hot jam into the jars, leaving ½ inch headspace. Wipe the jar rims clean with a damp paper towel. Top with the lids and then a screw band. Close tightly.

5 Place the jars on the preserving rack and lower it into the canning kettle. If the water doesn't cover the jars, add boiling water from a tea kettle. Cover the canning kettle. After the water returns to a boil, boil for 10 minutes. With a jar lifter, transfer the jars to a rack to cool completely. Do not touch the jars again until you hear the pops that indicate that the lids have sealed. You can confirm that a lid has sealed by pressing the center with your finger. If it gives, it has not sealed and the contents should be refrigerated and used within a month. Store the sealed jars in a cool, dark place for up to 1 year. Refrigerate after opening.

Mexican Cantaloupe Cooler

Makes about 1½ quarts, to serve 6

You can use any sweet melon for this summer thirst quencher, but cantaloupes and watermelons produce particularly appetizing hues. In taquerias, these refreshing coolers, known as aguas frescas, are often displayed in big glass jars to show off their gemlike colors. Put your cooler in your prettiest clear pitcher and serve it with lamb burgers (page 266), pork tacos (page 278), or any warm-weather meal. It's a wholesome alternative to soda. To make a more adult beverage, add a splash of tequila or rum to your glass.

Ingredients

2 quarts seeded cantaloupe chunks (from
    about 4 pounds unpeeled)
¼ cup fresh lime juice, or more to taste
2 tablespoons superfine sugar, or more to taste
Pinch of salt
1 cup water
6 lime slices

1 Put the melon, lime juice, sugar, salt, and water in a blender, in two batches if necessary, and puree until smooth. Taste and adjust with more sugar or lime if needed, and adjust the thickness with water.

2 Cover and chill thoroughly. Serve in tall glasses over ice and garnish with a lime slice.

WATERMELON, WATERCRESS, AND FETA

Serves 6

Sweet melon and salty feta are a popular meze in Turkey and Greece, which should surprise no one who enjoys the pairing of prosciutto and melon, or melon with salt. Adding watercress and a lemony dressing transforms the combination into a summer salad, an unexpected accompaniment for lamb chops or hamburgers on the grill.

INGREDIENTS

DRESSING

¼ cup extra virgin olive oil

2 tablespoons fresh lemon juice

Kosher or sea salt and freshly ground black pepper

⅓ pound watercress (about 6 small handfuls),
thick or long stems removed

About 2½ cups peeled watermelon in
¾-inch cubes

¼ small red onion, thinly sliced

12 large mint leaves, torn into smaller pieces

⅓ pound Greek, French, Bulgarian, or Israeli
feta cheese

1 To make the dressing, in a small bowl, whisk together the olive oil, lemon juice, and salt and pepper to taste.

2 Put the watercress, watermelon, onion, and mint in a salad bowl. Add enough of the dressing to coat the ingredients lightly; you may not need it all. Toss well, then crumble the feta into the bowl and toss again gently. Taste and adjust the seasoning. Serve immediately.

Guinda, California

FULL BELLY FARM

It's a searing summer day at Full Belly Farm, but the dragonflies have found their Eden: the long, lush rows of zinnias, cosmos, and sunflowers that are among this diversified farm's sought-after crops. The graceful creatures float over the floral carpet, then dive into the lipstick-pink and blood-red blossoms, in search of an insect lunch.

"We probably have fifteen different species of dragonflies," says Dru Rivers, one of four partners who have nurtured the biodiversity on this 200-acre Northern California farm. Predators like dragonflies are among the complex layers of life on the farm—from the microorganisms that inhabit its soil to the employees who till it, an integrated but fragile ecosystem.

"It takes twenty years to bring a farm to this stage," says Judith Redmond, another partner, "and it could fall apart in two."

Of all the achievements that Full Belly can claim—among them, a 1,500-member CSA and a roster of customers that includes some of the San Francisco Bay Area's best restaurants—the partners seem most proud of providing jobs for fifty people year-round. "Many agriculture workers in

California are unemployed in the off-season and impoverished," says Judith. "That's very unhealthy for rural communities."

But at Full Belly, harvest happens 360 days a year, with a brief break around Christmas. Nature has no off-season in the Capay Valley, a fertile twenty-five-mile-long sliver two hours northeast of San Francisco. Winter CSA boxes hold cauliflower, leeks, broccoli, walnuts, and cabbage. Spring means carrots, asparagus, lettuces, and herbs, followed by the heirloom tomatoes, beans, melons, and corn that signify full-blown summer. Peppers, pumpkins, and other winter squashes bring up the rear, along with the farm's locally famous almond butter. Excess peaches, tomatoes, and onions are arrayed on old wooden commercial prune-drying racks and dehydrated in the valley's fierce summer heat. Cut flowers are bundled and hung upside down to dry, in preparation for Dru's fall wreath-making classes.

Dru and her husband, Paul Muller, began farming the property in 1984, refugees from California's Central Valley. In that vast agricultural plain, they were surrounded by farm neighbors who sprayed chemical pesticides, making it difficult to claim that their own farm was truly organic. In the remote Capay Valley, they could be more certain of their harvest's purity, a critical issue to a couple who first met at an ecological farming conference. ("We square-danced, and that was the end of that," recalls Dru.)

Today, the partners harvest more than eighty crops a year, which they sell to demanding restaurants like Chez Panisse, to their CSA shareholders, and to the discriminating shoppers at three Bay Area farmers' markets. Sheep cycle through the farm pastures, controlling weeds, enhancing soil fertility, and eventually providing meat for subscribers.

At a Glance

Favorite crops: Royal Blenheim apricot, Delicata and Red Kuri winter squashes, Sungold and Sweet 100 cherry tomatoes. "There's not a better cherry tomato than those two," claims Andrew.

Inputs: Two million pounds of compost a year, roughly ten thousand pounds per acre

Lunch on the farm: Always communal; the crew takes turns cooking. One summer day's menu featured homemade hummus, boiled sweet corn, lentils with roasted cipolline onions, green beans with sesame seeds, fresh melon, and corn tortillas.

Insight: "The beautiful thing about CSA is that it's a community of people saying, 'We'll share the risk with the farmer,'" says Paul. "That's something agriculture has never had before."

On recycling: "We take tons and tons from this farm," says Judith. "How can we replace all that fertility and nutrition? Industrial agriculture doesn't ask that question. If a farm doesn't use compost, it's not trying to close that circle."

Hard-earned wisdom: "When my friends scoff at the prices at the farmers' market, I say, 'You come pick with me in 100-degree heat,'" says Rachel Dixon, a Full Belly intern.

The farm animals also enhance the experience for the city kids who participate in Full Belly's week-long summer camp sessions. Overseen by Dru and Paul's daughter Hallie, the youngsters collect eggs, milk the cows, make butter, plant seeds, pack CSA boxes, swim in the creek, and work in teams to make lunch. On the last day of each session, they hold a farmers' market for their parents.

In October, more than five thousand people descend on the farm for the annual Hoes Down festival, a day-long celebration of rural life, with hayrides, workshops, a farmers' market, and music. "It's an exhausting thing to do at the end of the summer, but it's the teachable moment," says Andrew Brait, the fourth partner.

People come to the CSA for wholesome food, says Judith, but they remain for the sense of community. "Some of our charter members are still members," says Judith of the CSA the farm started in 1994. "Just like they need a family doctor,

they need a family farmer." Full Belly is "their" farm, and they help fight its political battles and rally support in times of need.

The round-bellied Buddha on the farm's logo reflects the partners' concern with Right Livelihood, the idea that one's work should never compromise one's ideals. The business of farming, as Full Belly does it, provides many moments of satisfaction, like watching a farmers' market customer select the perfect bouquet. Or touring the peach orchard in July and snitching a ripe White Lady peach, the kind so drippy that you need to eat it over the sink.

"My mom calls them bend-over peaches," says Dru as she patrols the orchard on a summer morning, half-eaten peach in hand. "I could stay here all day and eat fruit."

PEACH AND BOYSENBERRY COBBLER

Serves 6

Consider this recipe a template for any summer cobbler made with stone fruit and berries. Use nectarines, plums, or Pluots instead of (or in addition to) peaches. Replace boysenberries with blackberries or blueberries. The flaky biscuit topping will welcome any warm, juicy fruit underneath. Serve with ice cream, frozen yogurt, or lightly sweetened whipped cream.

INGREDIENTS

2 pounds peaches, peeled, halved, pitted, and
   sliced lengthwise ½ inch thick
½ cup granulated sugar
1½ tablespoons cornstarch
½ pound boysenberries (about 1½ cups)

BISCUIT TOPPING
1½ cups unbleached all-purpose flour
2 tablespoons granulated sugar
2½ teaspoons baking powder
½ teaspoon kosher or sea salt
6 tablespoons unsalted butter, chilled,
   in 12 pieces
½ cup whole milk, plus more for brushing
About 2 teaspoons sparkling sugar (coarse
   decorating sugar)

1 Preheat the oven to 425°F. Put the peaches in a large bowl. In a small bowl, whisk together the sugar and cornstarch until well blended. Add to the peaches and toss to coat evenly. Add the boysenberries and toss gently. Put the fruit in a 9 by 2-inch round baking dish or other baking dish with a 1½-quart capacity.

2 To make the biscuit topping, put the flour, granulated sugar, baking powder, and salt in a food processor and pulse several times to blend. Add the butter and pulse until the bits of butter are no larger than a pea. Transfer the mixture to a bowl and stir in the milk with a fork, tossing gently just until the dry ingredients are moistened. Knead gently with your hand, just until the mixture forms a cohesive dough. Turn it out onto a work surface and pat it into a ½-inch-thick round.

3 Using a 2½-inch round biscuit or cookie cutter, cut out 6 biscuits and place them on top of the fruit, spacing them evenly. Brush the top of the biscuits lightly with milk and sprinkle with the sparkling sugar.

4 Bake until the biscuits are nicely browned and the fruit is bubbling, 30 to 35 minutes. Transfer to a rack to cool slightly. Serve warm.

PEACH AND RHUBARB CRISP

Serves 8

Rhubarb's frank tartness can be overwhelming to some, even when it is tamed with sugar. Pairing it with sweet fruit, such as peaches, puts that acidity to good use. In this crisp, the tangy rhubarb balances an old-fashioned dessert that might otherwise seem cloying. If your peaches are very sweet, you can reduce the sugar in the filling by 1 to 2 tablespoons. Serve the crisp warm with whipped cream, ice cream, or frozen yogurt.

INGREDIENTS

TOPPING

¾ cup unbleached all-purpose flour

3 tablespoons brown sugar

2 tablespoons granulated sugar

¼ teaspoon ground cinnamon

Pinch of kosher or sea salt

6 tablespoons unsalted butter, cool but not chilled, cut into 12 pieces

½ cup coarsely chopped toasted walnuts (page xiv)

⅓ cup old-fashioned rolled oats

1½ to 1¾ pounds peaches, peeled, halved, pitted, and cut into ½-inch chunks

½ pound rhubarb, trimmed and cut crosswise into ½-inch pieces

½ cup plus 2 tablespoons granulated sugar

2 tablespoons quick-cooking tapioca

1 To make the topping, put the flour, brown sugar, granulated sugar, cinnamon, and salt in a stand mixer fitted with the paddle. Mix on low speed until well blended. Add the butter and mix until the mixture resembles coarse crumbs. On medium-low speed, add the walnuts and oats and mix until the mixture begins to clump, 2 to 3 minutes. You can also prepare the topping in a food processor, but the mixer is preferable. Set aside.

2 Preheat the oven to 375°F. Put the peaches, rhubarb, granulated sugar, and tapioca in a large bowl and stir to blend. Let stand for 10 minutes to draw some juices from the fruit.

3 Transfer the fruit to a 10-inch pie pan or other baking dish of similar capacity and spread it evenly. Sprinkle the topping evenly over the surface. Put the pie pan on a baking sheet to catch any drips.

4 Bake until the topping is nicely browned and the filling is bubbling, about 50 minutes. Cool on a rack. Serve warm, not hot.

GRILLED NECTARINES WITH MASCARPONE ICE CREAM AND CRUSHED AMARETTI

Serves 6

If you've never grilled nectarines or other stone fruits (such as peaches, apricots, and plums), you are in for a treat. The direct heat caramelizes the surface, softens the flesh, and releases the sweet juices; with a scoop of ice cream snuggled up against the warm fruit, you have a luscious dessert. Crushed amaretti, the almond-flavored Italian cookies, add a crunchy contrast. To crush them easily, put them in a heavy plastic bag and smash with a rolling pin.

INGREDIENTS

3 nectarines, halved and pitted

1 tablespoon unsalted butter, melted

Mascarpone Ice Cream (page 197) or store-bought
vanilla ice cream

6 heaping tablespoons coarsely crushed amaretti

1 Prepare a moderate charcoal fire or preheat a gas grill to medium (375°F).

2 Brush the nectarine halves on both sides with the melted butter. Place the nectarines, cut side down, on the grill directly over the coals or gas flame. Cover the grill and cook until the nectarines are hot throughout, lightly caramelized on the surface, and slightly softened, 5 to 10 minutes. If they char too much before they soften, move them away from the coals or flame to finish cooking.

3 Put a nectarine half in each compote dish or stemmed glass. Top each nectarine half with a scoop of ice cream and a heaping tablespoon of crushed amaretti. Serve immediately.

Nectarine and Raspberry Galette

Serves 8

You can adapt this galette to other summer fruits, such as apricots or plums. In the fall, fill it with apples or pears. The beauty of a galette—a tart with a wide rim of dough folded over the fruit—is its rusticity. It should look like a grandmother, not a pastry chef, made it.

Ingredients

GALETTE DOUGH

2 cups unbleached all-purpose flour

¾ teaspoon kosher or sea salt

½ cup plus 7 tablespoons unsalted butter, chilled,
    cut into small pieces

About ¼ cup ice water

1½ pounds nectarines, halved, pitted, and sliced
    lengthwise

½ pint raspberries

3 tablespoons granulated sugar

1 large egg yolk whisked with 1 teaspoon water,
    for egg wash

About 1 tablespoon sparkling sugar (coarse
    decorating sugar)

1 To make the galette dough, put the flour and salt in a food processor and pulse a few times to blend. Add half the butter and pulse just until the fat is evenly distributed and coated with flour. Add the remaining butter and pulse a few times, just until it is coated with flour. There should still be pieces of flour-coated butter about the size of large peas. Transfer the mixture to a bowl. Drizzle in the ice water while tossing with a fork, adding water just until the mixture begins to come together. Gather the dough with your hands and knead gently if necessary to get it to hold together. Resist the temptation to add more water. Handling the dough as little as possible, shape it into a thick disk like a hamburger patty, then wrap it in plastic wrap and refrigerate until chilled, at least 2 hours or up to 1 day.

2 Preheat the oven to 425°F. If you have a baking stone, put it in the oven on the middle rack to preheat for at least 45 minutes.

3 Remove the dough from the refrigerator about 10 minutes before you are ready to roll it to allow it to soften slightly. If it is too cold, it will be brittle and difficult to roll. Unwrap the dough and place it between 2 sheets of parchment paper at least 16 inches square. With a rolling pin, flatten the dough into a 15-inch circle. To prevent sticking, occasionally lift the top sheet of parchment and lightly flour the dough, then replace the parchment and invert the dough so the bottom sheet is on top. Peel back that sheet of parchment and lightly flour the dough, then replace the parchment and continue rolling.

continued next page

Nectarine and Raspberry Galette   continued

4 When the circle is large enough, remove the top sheet of parchment and transfer the dough, still on the bottom sheet of parchment, to a rimless baking sheet. Working 2 inches from the edge of the dough, place the nectarine slices in concentric rings. Scatter the raspberries evenly over the nectarines. Sprinkle the fruit with the granulated sugar.

5 Using a palette knife or other broad knife to help you lift the dough off the parchment, gently fold the uncovered edge of the dough over the fruit to make a wide, rough-edged rim. Make sure there are no cracks in the dough for juices to seep through. Brush the rim with the egg wash, then sprinkle the rim with the sparkling sugar. With scissors, cut off the exposed parchment paper. (It's okay if a little paper is exposed.)

6 If you have a baking stone in the oven, slide the galette, still on the bottom sheet of parchment, directly onto the stone. If you do not have a baking stone, bake the galette on the rimless baking sheet. Bake until the crust is golden and the nectarines are juicy, about 50 minutes. Slide the galette onto a rack to cool slightly. To serve, slide it from the rack onto a cutting board and cut into wedges. Serve warm.

Wine-Poached Pears with Ricotta Cream

Serves 4

Poached in a light red-wine syrup, pears don't immediately take up the color. But over several hours of steeping, they develop a deep burgundy hue. That color is just surface deep, however. When you slice and fan the pears, their creamy interior looks lovely against the ruby red syrup. Serve with a dollop of whipped and sweetened ricotta or with whipped cream.

Ingredients

1 cup dry red wine with rich color such as Zinfandel
1 cup water
⅓ cup sugar
1 orange zest strip
2 ripe but firm pears

RICOTTA CREAM
1 cup whole-milk ricotta cheese
1 tablespoon sugar
¼ teaspoon vanilla extract

1 tablespoon very finely minced pistachios

1. Put the wine, water, sugar, and orange zest in a small saucepan. Bring to a simmer over moderate heat, stirring until the sugar dissolves. Peel the pears with a vegetable peeler. Add them to the simmering liquid, setting them on one side. Cover with a round of parchment paper and tuck the edges of the parchment under the liquid to keep the paper in place. Adjust the heat to maintain a gentle simmer and cook for 15 minutes.

2. Lift the parchment and turn the pears to the other side, then replace the parchment cover. Simmer until the pears are just tender when pierced, 10 to 12 minutes longer. They will continue to cook as they cool so don't overcook.

3. With a slotted spoon, transfer the pears to a refrigerator container. Simmer the poaching liquid until reduced to ¾ cup. Cool the syrup completely, then pour it over the pears. Cover and refrigerate for at least 8 hours or up to 1 day, turning the pears in the syrup every couple of hours so they color evenly.

4. To make the ricotta cream, put the ricotta, sugar, and vanilla in a food processor and process until smooth.

5. . At serving time, cut each pear in half lengthwise and core with a melon baller. Put each pear half on a cutting board, cut side down. Thinly slice lengthwise, leaving the slices attached at the stem end.

6. Put a pear half on each dessert plate. Gently press on each pear half with your hand to fan the slices. Put a dollop of ricotta cream alongside and sprinkle the ricotta cream with the pistachios. Spoon a little of the poaching syrup over the pears.

Pear Sorbet with Champagne

Makes about 1½ quarts

Thanks to their creamy texture, ripe pears make a particularly plush sorbet. Adding a little brandy to the pear puree keeps the sorbet from freezing hard. For maximum effect, top each serving with a splash of Champagne at the dinner table.

Ingredients

3 pounds ripe pears, preferably Comice

¼ cup water

About 1½ cups sugar

¼ cup fresh lemon juice

2 tablespoons brandy

Champagne or other sparkling wine, well chilled

1 Peel the pears with a vegetable peeler. Quarter the pears lengthwise, core, and cut into large chunks. Put the chunks in a large saucepan with the water. Bring to a simmer over moderate heat, then cover, adjust the heat to maintain a gentle simmer, and cook until the pears are tender, about 10 minutes.

2 Transfer the pears to a food processor and puree until completely smooth. Measure the volume, then return the puree to the food processor. Add sugar in the ratio of 1½ cups sugar to 4 cups puree. Add the lemon juice and brandy and puree until the mixture is completely smooth and the sugar has dissolved. Transfer to a bowl, cover, and refrigerate until thoroughly chilled.

3 Freeze the chilled puree in an ice-cream maker according to the manufacturer's directions. Because of the alcohol, the sorbet will not freeze hard. Transfer the sorbet to a freezer container and freeze for at least 30 minutes to allow it to firm up before serving.

4 Scoop the sorbet into martini glasses or parfait glasses. Top each portion with 1 ounce (2 tablespoons) of Champagne. Serve immediately.

GRILLED GOAT CHEESE SANDWICH WITH ASIAN PEARS AND PROSCIUTTO

Makes 4 sandwiches

Asian pears vary greatly in color, size, and shape, with skins ranging from pale yellow to caramel. Even when ripe, they don't become soft and creamy like regular pears. Instead, they are as crunchy as an apple, but juicier. Slice them into salads or tuck a few thin wedges into a grilled cheese sandwich. Here, they are paired in a toasted sandwich with prosciutto and fresh goat cheese.

INGREDIENTS

- 4 teaspoons unsalted butter, softened, plus 2 tablespoons, melted
- 8 slices dense country bread such as pugliese, about ¼ inch thick
- ¼ pound fresh goat cheese, cream cheese, or mild blue cheese, at room temperature
- 1 Asian pear, peeled, quartered, cored, and thinly sliced
- Freshly ground black pepper
- 4 thin slices prosciutto

1 Prepare a moderate charcoal grill or preheat a gas grill to medium (375°F).

2 Using the softened butter, butter 4 slices of bread on one side only. Top the remaining 4 bread slices with the cheese, spreading it evenly. Top the cheese on each slice with 3 or 4 pear slices. Add a few grinds of black pepper, then top with the prosciutto. Put the buttered bread, buttered side down, over the prosciutto. Brush the sandwiches with melted butter on both sides.

3 Place the sandwiches directly over the coals or gas flame and cook, turning once, until the bread turns golden brown and the cheese softens, about 1 minute per side. Cut in half and serve immediately.

PERSIMMON-GINGER SMOOTHIE

Makes 3 cups, to serve 2

The heart-shaped Hachiya persimmon is ripe when it is jelly soft. Keep firm ones at room temperature until they reach that squishy stage, which may take a week or more. Then halve them and enjoy them for breakfast with a squeeze of lemon or lime, or put them, whole, in the freezer for future smoothies. Persimmons give luscious body to a smoothie; you won't need a banana to achieve a thick and creamy texture. Prepared with buttermilk, which is low in fat, this smoothie makes a wholesome breakfast for people on the go.

INGREDIENTS

1 fully ripe, soft Hachiya persimmon (about
   6 ounces), chilled (partially thawed if frozen)
2 cups buttermilk
2 tablespoons honey
½ teaspoon ground ginger
⅛ teaspoon vanilla extract
About 4 ice cubes

1 Remove the persimmon's cap, then quarter the fruit and remove any visible black seeds. (Some Hachiyas have none.)

2 Put the persimmon quarters, buttermilk, honey, ginger, vanilla, and ice cubes in a blender. Puree until smooth and creamy. Pour into 2 tall glasses and serve immediately.

Persimmon-Nut Muffins

Makes 12 muffins

These tender muffins perfume the kitchen with the scent of cinnamon as they bake. Prepare them for a weekend breakfast (you can mix the dry ingredients the night before), or put them in the freezer and reheat one a day at a midmorning coffee break.

Ingredients

Nonstick cooking spray, for preparing the muffin tin

1 fully ripe, soft Hachiya persimmon

1 cup sifted unbleached all-purpose flour

1 cup sifted cake flour

2 teaspoons baking powder

1 teaspoon ground cinnamon

½ teaspoon baking soda

¼ teaspoon kosher or sea salt

1 large egg

½ cup buttermilk

1 cup plus 2 tablespoons granulated sugar

⅓ cup canola oil

1⅓ cups coarsely chopped toasted walnuts or pecans (page xiv)

About 1 tablespoon sparkling sugar (coarse decorating sugar)

1. Preheat the oven to 400°F. Coat a 12-cup standard muffin tin with nonstick cooking spray.

2. Remove the persimmon's cap, then halve the fruit and remove any visible black seeds. (Some Hachiyas have none.) Put the persimmon halves in a food processor, skin and all, and puree until smooth. Measure out ½ cup puree and set aside.

3. Sift together the all-purpose flour and cake flour into a bowl, then resift with the baking powder, cinnamon, and baking soda. Stir in the salt.

4. In a large bowl, whisk together the egg, buttermilk, granulated sugar, oil, and ½ cup persimmon puree. Stir in 1 cup of the walnuts.

5. Add the dry ingredients to the persimmon mixture and stir with a rubber spatula just until blended; do not overmix. Divide the batter evenly among the prepared muffin cups; it will almost fill the cups. Top each muffin with about ¼ teaspoon sparkling sugar and with the remaining ⅓ cup walnuts, divided evenly.

6. Bake until the muffins are golden brown and firm to the touch, 18 to 20 minutes. Cool in the tin on a rack for 5 minutes, then gently loosen the muffins with a knife and transfer them to a rack to cool.

GRILLED PRUNE PLUMS WITH ANISE ICE CREAM

Serves 6

Prune plums are the small, intensely sweet varieties preferred by commercial dryers for making prunes. Sometimes known as French prunes or Italian prunes (depending on the variety), they are a late-summer treat that. Other plums tend to be too tart and watery to grill well, but you can pair this luscious ice cream with another grilled stone fruit, such as apricots, peaches, or nectarines.

INGREDIENTS

ANISE ICE CREAM

2 cups half-and-half

1 teaspoon aniseed, lightly crushed in a mortar

6 large egg yolks

⅔ cup sugar

Pinch of kosher or sea salt

1 cup heavy cream

18 prune plums, halved and pitted

1½ to 2 tablespoons unsalted butter, melted

1 To make the ice cream, combine the half-and-half and aniseed in a medium saucepan. Bring to a simmer over moderate heat. In a bowl, whisk the egg yolks, sugar, and salt until pale and thick. Add the contents of the saucepan gradually, whisking constantly, then return the mixture to the saucepan and set over moderate heat. Cook, stirring constantly with a wooden spoon, until the custard reaches 178°F on an instant-read thermometer. It will visibly thicken and coat the spoon. Do not let it boil or it will curdle.

2 Immediately transfer the custard to a bowl and cool for 15 minutes, then stir in the heavy cream. Cover the custard and refrigerate until well chilled.

3 Whisk the custard to distribute the aniseed evenly, then freeze in an ice-cream maker according to the manufacturer's directions. Transfer to a freezer container and freeze for at least 30 minutes to allow it to firm up before serving. You will have about 1 quart of ice cream, which is more than you need for this recipe. The remainder will keep for up to 1 week.

4 Prepare a moderately hot charcoal fire or preheat a gas grill to medium-high (425°F). Thread the plums on wooden skewers. Brush with the melted butter. Grill, cut side down, directly over the coals or gas flame until the flesh begins to caramelize, 3 to 4 minutes, then turn and grill on the skin side until hot, 1 to 2 minutes.

5 Put a scoop of ice cream in each compote dish. Remove the hot plums from the skewers and divide them evenly among the dishes. Serve immediately.

RUBY YACHT

Pomegranate juice makes an elegant Champagne cocktail the color of a costly sparkling rosé. One sip and you may want to make this festive beverage your house specialty. It is lovely to look at and entirely too easy to drink.

INGREDIENTS

½ ounce (1 tablespoon) Fresh Pomegranate Juice (following)

½ ounce (1 tablespoon) Simple Syrup (following)

4 ounces (½ cup) dry Champagne or other sparkling wine, well chilled

1 orange twist

1 Chill a Champagne flute by filling it with ice water. Let stand for one minute, then drain.

2 Put the pomegranate juice and the syrup in the flute, then top with Champagne. Add the orange twist and serve at once.

FRESH POMEGRANATE JUICE: Choose an unblemished pomegranate with no cracks. With the heel of your hand, roll the pomegranate around on a cutting board, pressing firmly to crush the internal cells. You will hear the crackle of popping membranes. Keep rolling and pressing until the pomegranate feels slightly flaccid, taking care not to breach the skin, or the juice—which stains fiercely—will squirt out. Hold the softened pomegranate over a bowl and, with a wooden or metal skewer, pierce it gingerly in one spot, releasing the juice into the bowl. Squeeze the pomegranate to release more juice. You should have about ⅓ cup.

SIMPLE SYRUP: In a small bowl, pour ½ cup boiling water over ½ cup superfine sugar. Stir until the sugar dissolves and the syrup becomes clear. Chill thoroughly. Keep leftover syrup in a tightly covered container in the refrigerator for up to 2 weeks. Makes about ¾ cup.

Charles City, Virginia

AMY'S GARDEN

In the beginning, Amy's Garden *was* a garden: a few heirloom tomatoes and some culinary herbs nurtured by newly married city dwellers.

But in an extreme case of mission creep, the tomato plants soon numbered one hundred. Armed with business cards, Amy Hicks began peddling her excess to natural-food stores near her Richmond, Virginia, home. Predictably, the budding enterprise quickly outgrew the backyard.

So Amy and her husband, George Ferguson, a contractor, purchased a larger parcel in Quinton, between Richmond and Williamsburg. George had grown up on a Virginia farm and understood soil, tillers, and tractors. Amy, an art-history graduate and daughter of a floral designer, had the eye for display that lures customers at farmers' markets.

The organic specialty produce the couple took to market was a novelty for Richmond in the late 1990s. One mother told her inquisitive youngster that Amy's striped heirloom tomatoes were odd looking "because they're organic."

A decade later, Amy's fruits, vegetables, and cut flowers are still often the only certified organic crops at the market, but patrons no longer think of her farm

as a hippie endeavor. At the farmers' market in Colonial Williamsburg, where Amy's five-year-old towheaded niece Bella helps pack pints of Sungold tomatoes, the booth for Amy's Garden has the longest line of all.

"We don't think of organic as fringe anymore," a state agricultural advisor finally told her. Imagine that.

In 2002, George persuaded Amy to try selling CSA shares. To her astonishment, forty families sent checks, the seed money that CSA farms rely on to finance operations. Amy, fearing failure, put all their money aside in case she had to give it back.

On the contrary, operations have expanded to a sunny seventy-acre parcel in Charles City, near the James River and the storied Civil War–era plantations. Here she and George produce most of the crops for their sixty-member CSA and farmers' markets customers.

In just a few years, with the help of soil-enhancing cover crops and massive additions of compost, Amy and George have transformed a conventionally farmed soybean field into a healthy and diverse organic farm. After the morning mist lifts, the sun illuminates a landscape planted with sixty-five hundred tomato vines;

At a Glance

Motto: "We grow for flavor," says George. "If it doesn't taste good, I don't care how much it produces."

Favorite crops: Juliet tomato, Sun Jewel and Ha-Ogen melons, Caroline raspberry, Yummy orange sweet pepper, Sugar Pearl corn, Kiowa blackberry

Underappreciated crops: Radishes, napa cabbage, escarole, radicchio. "People here are not in touch with the bitter side of their palates," says Amy.

Clueless customers: "A lot of people think green beans should be ninety-nine cents a pound," says Amy. "They don't understand the bent-over, backbreaking picking."

Kitchen tip: Cut unpeeled sweet potatoes into thick fingers, like thick-cut fries. Toss with olive oil in a cast-iron pan. Cook in a hot oven until crusty and tender.

Crafters' tip: The extra-long pods of Star of David okra make a stunning ornament for wreaths and centerpieces. Dry the pods on the plant, then cut and hang until completely dry. Spray gold or silver for holiday decor.

southern specialties like okra, butter beans, and crowder peas; exotic melons; old-fashioned pole beans; edamame; slender Jimmy Nardello frying peppers; fragrant raspberries, enormous blackberries, and juicy Chandler strawberries.

"'You can't grow strawberries organically,'" says George, mimicking the local farm advisors. "That's straight from the university."

Having rejected the "spray and pray" philosophy of most of their Virginia farming neighbors, Amy and George have restored layers of life to the farm. Soil that they couldn't penetrate with a walk-behind tiller is now friable. Beneficial wasps circle the bean blossoms, looking for aphids, while bees swarm the buckwheat. Butterflies head for the cutting flowers, a vast playground of sunflowers, lisianthuses, zinnias, celosias, and tuberoses. Birds supply the farm soundtrack, with overdubbing from George, who whistles mightily whenever he's on the tractor. He is happiest behind the scenes, while Amy is the public face of the farm, whose superb produce makes the case weekly for organic practices.

Poultry, Meat, and Eggs

For many CSA members and farmers' market shoppers, eating locally extends beyond produce. When their regional landscape allows it, they prefer to buy poultry, meat, and eggs from local producers, too. And in many communities, this option exists. Farms that produce only vegetables are partnering with neighboring chicken or hog farmers or cattle ranchers to offer CSA customers fresh eggs and meat from conscientious suppliers. For consumers, that translates to eggs with yolks the color of persimmons, grass-fed beef, and full-flavored pork and chicken from pasture-raised animals. Such fine raw materials deserve respectful treatment in the kitchen. Show off their quality in dishes like Braised Chicken with Apple Cider, Tarragon, and Cream (page 262); Grilled Country Pork Chops with Bourbon-Basted Grilled Peaches (page 276); or Frittata with Zucchini, Cherry Tomatoes, and Goat Cheese (page 264). With the recipes in this chapter, you can showcase the humanely raised meat and farm-fresh eggs available to you.

Bollito Misto with Salsa Verde

Serves 8

The Italian bollito misto, or "mixed boil," usually includes a variety of meats. In this version, the variety comes from the vegetables. A slow-cooked brisket is sliced and served with a colorful garland of winter root vegetables and cabbage, all cooked in the meaty broth derived from the brisket. A salsa verde, or green sauce, thick with parsley, anchovies, capers, and bread crumbs, provides a zesty complement. Many cultures prepare similar nutritious meals in winter, flooding the kitchen with warmth and beefy aromas on a chilly day. Serve the flavorful broth as a first course with a few noodles or chickpeas in it, or reserve it for another day. You can replace the brisket with beef tongue or shanks or even a whole chicken, if you prefer, although the chicken will cook much more quickly.

Ingredients

BRISKET

1 (4-pound) well-trimmed beef brisket

5 quarts water, or more if needed

2 yellow onions, halved

2 carrots, peeled and cut into large chunks

2 celery ribs, cut into large chunks

12 Italian parsley sprigs

2 bay leaves

2 tablespoons kosher or sea salt

SALSA VERDE

1½ cups finely minced fresh Italian parsley

2 teaspoons minced fresh tarragon

1½ cups extra virgin olive oil

12 anchovy fillets, finely minced

¼ cup capers, preferably salt packed, rinsed and finely chopped

2 large cloves garlic, minced

2 teaspoons freshly grated lemon zest

2 tablespoons fresh lemon juice

1 cup fresh bread crumbs

Kosher or sea salt and freshly ground black pepper

8 small waxy potatoes, peeled if desired

2 small rutabagas, peeled and quartered

4 small turnips, peeled and halved

8 small whole carrots, peeled

1 small head Savoy cabbage

1 To cook the brisket, put it and the water in a large stock-pot. If the meat is not covered with water, add more as needed. Bring to a simmer over moderate heat, carefully skimming any foam. Add the onions, carrots, celery, parsley, bay leaves, and salt. Cover partially and adjust the heat to maintain a bare simmer. Cook for 3 hours, then test for doneness by probing the meat with a fork. If it does not seem tender, cook for 1 hour longer.

2 To make the *salsa verde*, in a bowl, combine the parsley, tarragon, olive oil, anchovies, capers, garlic, and lemon zest and juice. Stir in the bread crumbs, and season with salt and pepper. Set aside until serving.

3 With tongs, carefully remove the brisket to a tray. Strain the broth through a fine-mesh sieve and return it to the pot. Discard the contents of the sieve. Taste the broth and adjust with salt. Return the brisket to the broth and keep warm over low heat.

4 Put the potatoes, rutabagas, turnips, and carrots in a large pot and add enough of the broth to cover them. Bring to a simmer over high heat, then cover partially and adjust the heat to maintain a gentle simmer. Cook until tender when pierced, about 10 minutes, removing them as they are done to a platter. Meanwhile, cut the cabbage into 8 wedges, keeping the core intact to hold each wedge together. Put the cabbage wedges in a large skillet and add broth to a depth of ¼ inch. Bring to a simmer over moderate heat, cover, and adjust the heat to maintain a gentle simmer. Cook until the cabbage is tender, about 5 minutes.

5 To serve, remove the meat from the broth to a cutting board. Slice the meat and arrange on a platter. Arrange the vegetables on a separate platter. Moisten the meat and the vegetables with a little hot broth, then serve immediately. Pass the *salsa verde* separately.

Grilled Flank Steak with Old-Fashioned Creamed Spinach

Serves 4

A classic steak-house favorite, creamed spinach blossoms with a dash of an anise-scented spirit, such as Pernod or pastis. Simmered in cream-enriched béchamel, it is rich and indulgent but worth every calorie.

Ingredients

1 flank steak, about 1½ pounds
¼ cup extra virgin olive oil
¼ cup dry red wine
4 cloves garlic, thinly sliced
1 tablespoon Dijon mustard
1 tablespoon minced fresh rosemary

CREAMED SPINACH

2 pounds spinach, thick stems removed
1½ tablespoons unsalted butter
1½ tablespoons unbleached all-purpose flour
¾ cup whole milk
¼ cup heavy cream
Whole nutmeg, for grating
Kosher or sea salt and freshly ground black pepper
2 teaspoons Pernod or pastis

1 Place the flank steak flat in a nonreactive container. In a small bowl, whisk together the olive oil, wine, garlic, mustard, and rosemary. Pour this marinade over the meat and turn the meat to distribute the seasonings evenly. Cover with plastic wrap and refrigerate for 8 hours, turning the meat once halfway through.

2 Remove the meat from the refrigerator about 1 hour before you plan to grill it. Prepare a moderate charcoal fire or preheat a gas grill to medium (375°F).

3 To make the creamed spinach, bring a large pot of salted water to a boil over high heat. Add the spinach, pushing it down into the water with tongs. As soon as it wilts—less than 30 seconds—drain in a sieve or colander and immediately run under cold running water until cool. Drain again and squeeze to remove excess moisture. Chop finely.

4 Melt the butter in a medium saucepan over moderately low heat. Add the flour and whisk until well blended and bubbling, about 1 minute. Whisk in the milk and cream and bring to a simmer. Adjust the heat to maintain a gentle simmer and cook, whisking often, for about 5 minutes to eliminate the raw flour taste.

5 Add the spinach and season with several scrapings of nutmeg and salt and pepper. Gently simmer the spinach for about 10 minutes to blend the flavors, stirring often with a wooden spoon. Stir in the Pernod and reduce the heat to low. Keep warm while you grill the steak.

6 Remove the steak from the marinade and season it on both sides with salt and pepper. Grill directly over the coals or gas flame, turning once, for about 5 minutes per side for rare to medium-rare. Because it is so lean, flank steak is best if not cooked beyond medium-rare. Let the meat rest for 10 minutes before slicing.

7 To slice the steak, hold a chef's knife at an angle of about 30 degrees to the cutting board to make broad, wide slices. Serve with the creamed spinach on the side.

Austin, Texas

GREEN GATE FARMS

The big green gate is open at Skip Connett and Erin Flynn's Austin farm, although perhaps you can't see it. Until Erin finds time to build it, welding the scrap metal she has been amassing, the gate remains just a vision, like so many of the ambitious plans the couple has for Green Gate Farm. "Skip and I talk about our dreams for the farm so often that sometimes we see things that aren't there yet," Erin admits.

In the meantime, the farm's name helps convey their intentions: to operate a sustainable, open-door venture that embraces the community, involving anyone who cares to participate in farm life. Local artists will come here to sketch, Erin imagines. Children will come to feed the piglets or learn about seed saving. Austin's high-tech engineers, who spend their workdays in a cubicle, will come to decompress in a rural setting only eight miles east of downtown.

"If you can farm in Texas, you can farm anywhere," says Skip, who grew up on an immaculate farm in Pennsylvania Dutch country. "Hail is inevitable. You might have a heat wave in April and you won't set a single bean. All farmers ever talk about is the weather, and I understand that now."

Why a young couple with established careers in Atlanta would choose to replant themselves in such challenging circumstances is a question their own parents posed. But Skip had wanted to farm since childhood and had grown weary of hearing colleagues at the Centers for Disease Control, where he worked as a speechwriter, talk about combating obesity with more research. He wanted to *do* something. Erin, who worked for the American Cancer Society, had her own daily encounters with the data linking diet and disease. Growing organic vegetables, they figured, would put them on "the happy side of public health."

Today, their five-acre farm nourishes about seventy-five local families who participate in its CSA, and many more people who shop at its weekend farm stand. On a morning in early June, sunflowers frame the edge of a field of Hungarian Hot Wax peppers and Honey Bear acorn squash. Plumes of amaranth, like burgundy feather dusters, dance in the breeze. On bushy okra plants, mature pods stand stiffly upright, looking like rockets ready to launch.

At a Glance

Favorite crops: Cherokee Purple tomato, Suyo Long cucumber, Zephyr zucchini

Chief worry: Water. Getting enough and paying for it. Because of the farm's location, the couple pays city rates for agricultural water.

Peak moments: "When the fields are weeded and the windmill is turning and we can stop and enjoy a fiery sunset," says Erin.

Handiest farm skill: Repurposing stuff . . . from Goodwill, customers, and friends. "Once you get into that mind-set, it becomes a game," says Erin. "Skip can make a penny scream."

Inspirations: Author/poet/farmer Wendell Berry; Virginia farmer Joel Salatin, advocate for pasture-raised meat; organic farmer, author, and CSA pioneer Elizabeth Henderson

Insight: "People have to take their enthusiasm for local food to the next step," says Erin. "They have to do more than just buy it; they have to become activists."

Summer lunch on the farm: Just-picked tomatoes, cucumbers, hot peppers, and basil, local goat feta, and a fresh baguette.

On this steamy June day, garlic dominates the farm stage. Every gentle wind carries its scent, and the weathered red barn is literally filled to the rafters with dangling clusters of drying elephant garlic. In the cool of the barn, Rosie, a tubby Hampshire sow, sprawls on matted leaves, breathing rapidly. Eight-year-old Avery kneels down beside her and strokes her as tenderly as a city youngster would pet a cat.

"Their entertainment is nature," says Erin of her two children, whose playmates include pigs, rare-breed chickens, and goats. The chickens fertilize the fields; the pigs grow to market weight on produce unsuitable for sale. And the animals visibly enthrall visiting youngsters.

"A four-year-old will pick up a chicken egg and shriek, 'It's warm!' because they're used to eggs coming from the fridge," says Erin.

Once a week, the farm hosts a "5-H" program for local kids who have no ties to farming. The youngsters "adopt" a piglet, naming it, caring for it, and bringing it scraps from home. In 4-H, kids learn conventional practices such as cutting pigs' tails and clipping their teeth. "We didn't want to do any of that," says Erin. "So I added 'humane' and we made it 5-H."

Skip and Erin don't deliver their produce. Instead, CSA members come to the farm to fetch their share, part of the couple's strategy to enlist people in the Green

Gate community. By midafternoon on pickup day, farm employees have stocked the makeshift farm stand with baskets and galvanized buckets of lemon basil, cucumbers, zucchini, shallots, red onions, fennel, potatoes, and hot peppers. Customers gather their share of the day's harvest, putting any vegetables they dislike in the swap box and trading recipe ideas. Who knew you could make sorbet with lemon basil or ice cream scented with fennel fronds?

In what must seem like a prior life, Erin worked in Manhattan for a global public-relations firm. Now she spends her workday in overalls, her long hair pinned on top of her head, her face possibly spattered with mud from showering a nine-hundred-pound hog with a hose.

"When we wrote our marriage vows, we said we would honor each other's dreams," says Erin, who came to farming reluctantly. Fortunately for Austin residents, the couple's dreams for Green Gate nurture the entire community.

GRILLED FIVE-SPICE CHICKEN

Serves 4

Popular at Vietnamese restaurants, this dish is easy to replicate at home. You can use the same marinade on chicken parts, but a whole butterflied chicken is dramatic and less trouble to maneuver on a grill. Because the marinade contains sugar, the chicken skin will char easily if placed directly over the coals or gas flame, so cook the bird over indirect heat the entire time. The exterior will still develop a honey brown gloss thanks to the soy sauce and five-spice powder.

INGREDIENTS

1 whole chicken, 3½ to 4 pounds

MARINADE

6 cloves garlic, thinly sliced

1 large shallot, coarsely chopped

2 tablespoons minced lemongrass

1 tablespoon peeled and minced fresh ginger

1 tablespoon plus 1 teaspoon light brown sugar

¼ cup soy sauce

¼ cup fish sauce (see Note, page 13)

1 teaspoon five-spice powder

½ teaspoon freshly ground black pepper

1 To butterfly the chicken, you need to remove the back-bone. You can do this with poultry shears or a chef's knife. If using poultry shears, turn the chicken, breast side down, on a cutting board and cut from the neck to the tail along both sides of the backbone to release it. If using a chef's knife, turn the chicken, breast side up, on a cutting board. Insert the chef's knife into the body cavity and cut along both sides of the backbone to release it. With the breast side up, press on the breastbone with the heel of your hand to flatten the bird. Cut off the wing tips and discard.

2 To make the marinade, put the garlic, shallot, lemon-grass, ginger, and sugar in a food processor and pulse until very finely chopped. With the motor running, add the soy sauce through the feed tube and puree until the paste is as fine as possible. Transfer to a bowl and whisk in the fish sauce, five-spice powder, and pepper.

3 Place the flattened chicken in a large baking dish, pour the marinade over it, and turn the bird to coat on both sides. Cover with plastic wrap and refrigerate. Alternatively, you can put the chicken and its marinade in a 1-gallon heavy-duty resealable food storage bag and refrigerate. Marinate for 6 to 8 hours.

4 Remove the chicken from the refrigerator about 1 hour before you plan to grill. Prepare a moderate charcoal fire for indirect grilling (page xiv) or preheat a gas grill to medium (375°F), leaving one burner unlit for indirect grilling.

5 Remove the chicken from the marinade, reserving the marinade. Brush the skin side of the chicken with some of the marinade. Place the chicken, skin side down, over indirect heat. Cover the grill and cook until the skin is richly browned and crisp, 15 to 20 minutes. Brush the flesh side of the chicken with the remaining marinade, then turn the chicken, skin side up, cover the grill, and continue grilling over indirect heat until the juices run clear when a thigh is pierced, or an instant-read thermometer inserted in the thickest part of the thigh away from the bone registers 165°F, about 15 minutes longer. Let rest for 10 minutes before carving into serving pieces.

BRAISED CHICKEN WITH APPLE CIDER, TARRAGON, AND CREAM

Serves 4

Save this main course for fall, when farms are pressing their fresh apples for cider. The cider bathes the chicken as it braises, mingling with the poultry juices. To finish the dish, cream is added and the pan juices reduced to a luscious sauce with a hint of sweetness. If you like, add some carrot chunks or turnip wedges.

INGREDIENTS

1 whole chicken, 3½ to 4 pounds, cut into
   10 pieces (2 thighs, 2 drumsticks, 2 wings,
   4 breast pieces)
Kosher or sea salt and freshly ground black pepper
1 tablespoon olive oil
1 tablespoon unsalted butter
3 large shallots, minced
¾ cup chicken broth (if canned, use equal parts
   broth and water)
½ cup apple cider (unfiltered apple juice)
1 tablespoon minced fresh tarragon
⅓ cup heavy cream
1 tablespoon minced fresh Italian parsley

1. Season the chicken pieces all over with salt and pepper. Heat the olive oil in a large skillet over high heat. When the oil is smoking hot, add the chicken, skin side down, working in batches if necessary to avoid crowding. Brown the chicken well on the skin side, then turn and cook on the flesh side until the flesh is no longer pink, about 10 minutes total. Transfer the chicken to a platter.

2. When all the chicken has been browned, pour off the fat in the skillet. Return the skillet to moderately low heat and add the butter. When it melts, add the shallots and cook, stirring with a wooden spoon and scraping up the browned bits stuck to the pan bottom. When the shallots are soft, after 2 to 3 minutes, add the broth, cider, and tarragon. Bring the liquid to a simmer and return the chicken to the pan, along with any juices that have accumulated on the platter. Baste the chicken with some of the pan juices, then cover and adjust the heat to maintain a gentle simmer. Cook just until the juices run clear when the meat is pierced in the thickest part, 12 to 15 minutes for the breast pieces, about 5 minutes longer for the thighs, drumsticks, and wings. Remove the chicken pieces to a platter as they are done.

3. Add the cream to the skillet, raise the heat to high, and simmer the sauce until reduced to the consistency of thick cream. Reduce the heat to moderate, return the chicken to the skillet, and turn it in the sauce to coat it and warm it through.

4. Transfer the chicken pieces to a warmed serving platter and pour the sauce over it. Garnish with the parsley. Serve immediately.

OMELET WITH LEEKS, SPRING HERBS, AND GOAT CHEESE

Serves 1

As the former proprietor of a popular breakfast and lunch spot in California's Napa Valley, Sally Gordon has made thousands of omelets. She has closed the restaurant, sadly, but fortunately she has not lost her omelet technique. Her secret is whisking the eggs furiously until they produce a frothy foam, a step that yields an especially light result.

INGREDIENTS

3 tablespoons unsalted butter

1 cup thinly sliced leeks, white and pale green parts only

Kosher or sea salt and freshly ground black pepper

2 ounces fresh goat cheese, at room temperature

2 tablespoons minced fresh chervil

3 large eggs

1 tablespoon minced fresh chives

1 tablespoon minced fresh Italian parsley, plus more for garnish

1 tablespoon water

1 Melt 1 tablespoon of the butter in a small skillet over moderately low heat. Add the leeks, season with salt and pepper, and stir to coat with the butter. Cover and cook, stirring occasionally, until the leeks are tender but not meltingly soft, about 10 minutes.

2 In a small bowl, mash the goat cheese with the chervil until blended.

3 Crack the eggs into a bowl and add the chives, parsley, and water. Beat vigorously with a whisk until the eggs are light and very foamy.

4 Melt the remaining 2 tablespoons butter in a 10-inch non-stick skillet over moderately high heat. When the butter begins to sizzle and foam, add the eggs and spread them in an even layer with a heatproof rubber spatula. Let the eggs set for a few seconds, then use the spatula to push the firmer cooked egg at the edges toward the center of the skillet so that the uncooked portion flows onto the bare pan bottom. With the spatula, gently pat the eggs into an even layer.

5 When the eggs have almost completely set but are still a little moist on the surface, dollop the goat cheese on one-half. Spoon the leeks over the goat cheese. Fold the other half of the omelet over the filling and slide the omelet onto a warm plate. Top with a little parsley and serve immediately.

FRITTATA WITH ZUCCHINI, CHERRY TOMATOES, AND GOAT CHEESE Serves 2 to 3

You can use this recipe as a template to make frittatas with whatever your local farmers provide, such as cauliflower, sweet peppers, leeks, artichokes, Swiss chard, or fennel. Cook the vegetable first, then incorporate with the beaten eggs and seasonings. Replace the goat cheese with grated Parmigiano Reggiano or pecorino cheese, if you like. Frittatas are cooked slowly, not rapidly like an omelet, and they taste better when they have cooled a bit. In fact, any leftover frittata—cold or at room temperature—makes a delicious sandwich tucked between two slices of toast.

INGREDIENTS

2 tablespoons extra virgin olive oil

1 zucchini, about 5 ounces, ends trimmed and cut into ⅓-inch-thick slices

6 large eggs, beaten

1½ teaspoons kosher or sea salt

Freshly ground black pepper

10 cherry tomatoes, halved

2 large fresh basil leaves, torn into smaller pieces

1½ ounces fresh goat cheese

1 Preheat a broiler and position a rack 8 to 10 inches from the element.

2 Heat 1 tablespoon olive oil in a 10-inch nonstick broiler-proof skillet over moderately high heat. When the oil begins to ripple, add the zucchini. The slices should fit in a single layer. Cook, turning once, until browned on both sides. Using tongs, transfer the slices to paper towels to drain and cool. Discard the oil remaining in the skillet and wipe the skillet dry with a paper towel.

3 Return the skillet to moderately low heat and add the remaining 1 tablespoon oil. Whisk the eggs with the salt and pepper in a bowl, then stir in the sautéed zucchini. Add to the hot skillet and use a heatproof rubber spatula or fork to separate the zucchini slices so that they are evenly spaced. Cook slowly until the frittata is mostly set but still a little runny on top, 8 to 10 minutes. Scatter the cherry tomatoes and basil over the surface, poking them down into the moist egg. Dot with pinches of the goat cheese.

4 Put the skillet under the broiler element until the top is puffed, firm to the touch, and golden brown, 2 to 3 minutes. Slide the frittata out onto a cutting board or serving platter. Let rest for at least 15 minutes before cutting into wedges. The frittata is best when warm, not hot.

CREAMY EGGS WITH TOMATO AND PEPPERS, BASQUE STYLE

Serves 4 to 6

A specialty from France's Basque region, pipérade ranks among the world's tastiest egg dishes. To make it, a tradition-minded cook will sauté some onions and bell peppers until soft and sweet, then add a generous amount of chopped fresh tomato. Once the tomatoes have collapsed into a sauce, beaten eggs are added and cooked slowly, slowly until the mixture thickens into a creamy mass. Toast is a must. If you can find piment d'Espelette (see Note), the moderately spicy ground red pepper from the Basque region, your pipérade will have an authentic taste. Serve in small portions as a first course or in larger portions for supper.

INGREDIENTS

3 ounces slab bacon or pancetta, cut into slices about
  ⅓ inch thick

1 tablespoon extra virgin olive oil

1 medium yellow onion, halved and thinly sliced

2 medium bell peppers of different colors, halved,
  cored, seeded, and thinly sliced

3 cloves garlic, minced

1 teaspoon minced fresh thyme

Kosher or sea salt

1½ cups grated plum (Roma type) tomato (page xiv)

Large pinch of hot red pepper flakes

8 large eggs, lightly beaten

Piment d'Espelette (see Note), Spanish paprika, or
  freshly ground black pepper

2 tablespoons minced fresh Italian parsley

1 Cut the bacon into ½-inch pieces. Put them in a 12-inch cold skillet with the olive oil and set over moderately low heat. Cook, turning with tongs, until the pieces are crisp and nicely colored all over, 10 to 12 minutes. Using a slotted spoon, transfer to paper towels to drain.

2 Add the onion, bell peppers, garlic, and thyme to the skillet and season with salt. Cook, stirring, until the vegetables have softened, about 10 minutes. Cover, reduce the heat to low, and cook until the vegetables are fork-tender, about 5 minutes longer. Uncover, add the tomato, hot pepper flakes, and another pinch of salt. Raise the heat to moderately high. Cook, stirring almost constantly, until the tomato collapses into a sauce, about 5 minutes. Add water as needed if the mixture threatens to scorch.

3 Reduce the heat to low or moderately low. Add the eggs, then stir constantly with a heatproof rubber spatula, frequently scraping the bottom and sides of the skillet. Continue cooking slowly until the eggs begin to thicken the mixture, about 4 minutes. Stir in the bacon and continue stirring until the mixture is creamy and custardlike, 1 to 2 minutes longer. You are not trying to make scrambled eggs. Taste for salt.

4 Divide among warmed individual plates, and top each serving with some *piment d'Espelette* and a sprinkle of parsley. Serve immediately.

NOTE: *Piment d'Espelette* is available by mail order from Kalustyan's (www.kalustyans.com).

Lamb Burgers with Grilled Red Onions and Feta

Serves 6

Lamb shoulder has sufficient internal marbling to make a juicy burger. When ground, it is the lamb equivalent of ground chuck. Grill the patties, then layer them on a soft bun with tomato, smoky onions, and crumbled feta to make a burger with a Middle Eastern accent. Sumac, a brick red spice sold at Middle Eastern markets, has an invigorating lemony tang that complements grilled meat.

Ingredients

2 pounds freshly ground lamb shoulder

1 tablespoon plus 1 teaspoon dried oregano

Kosher or sea salt and freshly ground black pepper

½ teaspoon hot red pepper flakes

6 red onion slices, ½ inch thick

1 tablespoon extra virgin olive oil

⅓ pound Greek, French, Bulgarian, or Israeli feta
   cheese, at room temperature, crumbled

6 hamburger buns, split

Ground sumac (optional)

2 tomatoes, thinly sliced

Feta cheese (optional)

1 Prepare a moderate charcoal fire for indirect grilling (page xiv) or preheat a gas grill to medium (375° to 400°F), leaving one burner unlit.

2 Put the lamb in a large bowl. Add the oregano (crumbling it between your fingers as you add it), 2 teaspoons salt, and hot pepper flakes, and season with black pepper. Work the seasonings in gently, then, with moistened hands, shape the meat into 6 patties each about ⅜ inch thick. They should be a little wider than your hamburger buns, as they will shrink in diameter when cooked.

3 From opposing directions, insert 2 toothpicks horizontally into each red onion slice; the toothpicks will hold the onion layers together on the grill. Brush the onion slices on both sides with some of the olive oil and season with salt and pepper.

4 Grill the onion slices first: Place them directly over the coals or gas flame and cover the grill. Cook, turning once, until nicely colored on both sides, about 5 minutes, then move to indirect heat until they are softened but not limp, about 5 minutes longer. Keep warm while you grill the burgers.

5 Grill the burgers directly over the coals or gas flame—lid off on a charcoal grill, lid on for a gas grill. Cook until they are done to your taste, which you can best determine by touch. A rare burger feels soft, with no spring back. A medium burger will offer some resistance to the touch, but will not feel firm. A well-done burger will be firm to the touch. Cooking time depends on the heat of your fire, but a medium burger will take about 10 minutes. A couple of minutes before the burgers are done, top with the feta, dividing it evenly, and toast the bun halves on the grill, cut side down.

6 To assemble the burgers, place the bottom halves of the buns, cut side up, on individual plates. Sprinkle generously with sumac. Top with tomato slices and sprinkle with salt. Remove the toothpicks from the onion slices and place on top of the tomato. Top the onion with a burger, sprinkle with feta cheese and sumac, then cover with the top half of the bun. Serve immediately.

Harris, Minnesota

NITTY GRITTY DIRT FARM

Vast cornfields blanket the prairie around Harris, Minnesota, an hour's drive north of the Twin Cities. But on a country road off the highway, a couple of miles past the Heartbreakers Bar, a tiny vegetable farm thrives amidst this monocropped landscape.

At the Nitty Gritty Dirt Farm, Robin Raudabaugh and Gigi Nauer cultivate six acres of vegetables—more than one hundred types—during Minnesota's condensed growing season. They also raise pigs and lambs on pasture for their one-hundred-member CSA; gather honey from their own hives and maple syrup from their trees; and turn the fresh milk from their goats into yogurt and cheese. Their free-range chickens produce eggs with such astonishing orange yolks that some CSA members have asked if the eggs are all right. The couple, who are partners in business and life, struggle to make the farm break even but feel wealthy in other ways.

"On paper, we lose money every year," admits Robin, "but I think we live really well. Who eats better than we do?"

Like so many small farmers, the couple rely on incomes from off-farm jobs—Robin as a United Church of Christ minister; Gigi as a music teacher at the Homestead Picking Parlor in Richfield, near Minneapolis. In lieu of a salaried crew, they depend on young, motivated interns willing to exchange a summer's labor for a place to stay, a chance to learn, and a modest stipend.

"If I had paid labor, it would just feel like a factory to me," says Robin, who grew up on a Minnesota dairy farm.

Instead, she and Gigi view the farm as a venue for teaching and the crew as young people to nurture. Farm work stops every day for a communal lunch around the farmhouse table, prepared in turn by Robin or one of the interns. A professionally trained baker who has fed her own large family since the age of nine, Robin has the skills of a 1940s farm wife. She bakes cinnamon rolls that scent the farm kitchen, stocks the pantry with dilly beans and red cabbage sauerkraut, and puts three kinds of homemade catsup on the table.

Gigi, who has city roots, manages the office. Robin runs the farm, harvesting radishes, potatoes, and peas alongside the interns—at about four times their pace—or hopping on a tractor to disk a field. "When she gets on that thing, I'm a tractor widow," says Gigi.

Neighbors lend a hand, too, sometimes stepping in to manage crises when Robin has to be at church. Once, unable to get back to the farm in time, she talked a spunky neighbor, via cell phone, through the process of birthing a kid. She is accustomed to fielding calls at church from farm volunteers with questions like, "Can I keep the milk if the goat stepped in the bucket?"

"This farm is where my faith comes from," says Robin. "I couldn't do what I do at church without it." Every day on the farm provides life lessons and tests, fodder for the next week's sermon. To "have faith like a mustard seed" (Matthew 17:20) resonates with a farmer who has grappled with tenacious mustard weeds.

On harvest morning, the interns set up makeshift stations for washing, sorting, and bunching. One hundred portions of Swiss chard, eggplant, tomatoes,

1⅛ BUSHEL BY VOLUME

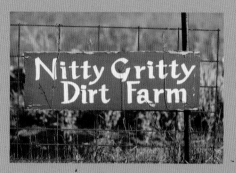

At a Glance

Mission: "We tend to be a 'staples' CSA— hearty midwestern stuff," says Gigi. "Fluted tomatoes aren't our niche."

Consciousness-raising: "When interns ask if something can be tossed, the answer is almost always no," says Robin. "You don't leave the farm in a vehicle without at least two errands."

Annual farm highlight: Summer canning workshops, when Robin and participants put up six hundred-plus quarts of tomatoes.

Summer lunch on the farm: Hamburgers on homemade sesame-seed buns with homemade catsup (page 171), dilly beans (page 22), and harvest slaw (page 50).

Favorite crops: Bull's Blood beets (for greens), Early Green cabbage, Red Express cabbage, Taxi and Orange Blossom tomato, Cascadia sugar snap pea, Ambrosia bicolor corn, Packman broccoli.

Kitchen tips: Extra zucchini, turnips, broccoli? Blanch them, cut them up, and freeze. "These become your veggies for soup," says Robin. And don't toss those radish greens. They're tender when young. Robin makes pesto with radish greens and mizuna, or cooks them with other greens and tops them with a fried egg.

red cabbage, peppers, and pattypan squash must be hosed down, trimmed up, banded, counted and re-counted. Empty cardboard boxes stand ready in the shade of the hoop house, waiting to be filled according to Robin's posted diagram: heavy stuff on the bottom, shapes juxtaposed artfully, a riot of color on top. She wants shareholders to open the box and be stirred by the beauty.

At dusk, Gigi and an intern sit down under the birch trees for a guitar lesson. In a warm, folksy alto, the teacher sings one of her own compositions, a sweet love song about life on the farm: . . . *The crickets are singing by the river. / The stars are numbered thousands in the sky. / You put your hand in mine and you shiver / at the cool prairie breezes blowing by. / Simply home . . .*

GRILLED COUNTRY PORK CHOPS WITH BOURBON-BASTED GRILLED PEACHES

Serves 4

Grilling gives peaches and other stone fruits a flavor boost, bringing their natural sugar to the fore. Use freestone peaches so that you can easily twist the halves off the pit. Baste them with butter, honey, and bourbon as they grill to give them a sheen, then serve with a juicy pork chop, brined for a full day to season it all the way through.

INGREDIENTS

BRINE

1½ quarts water

6 tablespoons kosher or sea salt

1 teaspoon coarsely cracked black pepper

Handful of thyme sprigs

2 cloves garlic, peeled and smashed with the side of a chef's knife

4 bone-in pork loin chops, about ¾ inch thick

2 tablespoons unsalted butter

2 tablespoons bourbon

2 teaspoons honey

2 large freestone peaches (such as O'Henry or Elberta), halved and pitted

1 To make the brine, in a medium saucepan, combine all the ingredients. Bring to a boil over high heat, stirring to dissolve the salt. Set aside until completely cool.

2 Put the pork chops in a container that holds them snugly in a single layer. Add the brine, which should cover them. Cover with plastic wrap. Alternatively, you can put the port and its brine in a 1-gallon heavy-duty resealable food storage bag. Refrigerate for 24 hours.

3 About 1 hour before cooking, remove the pork chops from the brine and set them on a wire cooling rack at room temperature to dry.

4 Prepare a moderate charcoal fire for indirect grilling (page xiv) or preheat a gas grill to medium (375ºF), leaving one burner unlit.

5 Combine the butter, bourbon, and honey in a small saucepan. Set over moderately low heat, stirring until the butter melts and the honey dissolves. Keep warm.

6 Pat the pork chops with paper towels to remove any remaining surface moisture. Set the chops directly over the coals or gas flame and brown on both sides, turning once, for about 3 minutes per side. Transfer to indirect heat, cover the grill, and cook until the chops offer some resistance to the touch but are still springy, not firm, about 4 minutes longer. If you are unsure of doneness, measure the internal temperature with an instant-read thermometer, inserting it horizontally into a chop; it should register about 150ºF for medium.

7 Once you have moved the pork chops to indirect heat, you can grill the peaches. Brush them all over with the butter-honey mixture and place, cut side down, directly over the coals or gas flame. Cook until they are nicely charred, then turn, baste again, and cook just until they are tender and juicy. The pork chops and peaches should be done at roughly the same time, but if not, move whichever is done first to a cooler area of the grill to wait. Serve each pork chop with a grilled peach half alongside.

GRILLED PORK TACOS, YUCATÁN STYLE, WITH PICKLED RED ONIONS

Serves 4

A brick red achiote paste, made from pounded annatto seeds, is the Yucatán's signature flavoring for grilled meat. It takes perhaps fifteen minutes to prepare your own paste, and it is well worth the effort—not only for the freshness, but also because most store-bought achiote paste contains preservatives and food coloring. For best results, grill the pork over a searing-hot fire so that it chars in spots.

INGREDIENTS

ACHIOTE PASTE

2 tablespoons annatto seed

1 teaspoon dried Mexican oregano

1 teaspoon cumin seed

1 teaspoon black peppercorns

3 whole cloves

1/8 teaspoon ground cinnamon

6 cloves garlic

1 teaspoon kosher or sea salt

2 tablespoons cider vinegar

4 slices boneless pork sirloin, 1/4 pound each

MARINADE

2 tablespoons achiote paste

1 tablespoon fresh orange juice

1 tablespoon fresh lime juice

1½ tablespoons canola oil

Kosher or sea salt

Pickled Red Onions, Yucatán Style (page 116)

Grilled Tomatillo Salsa (page 160) or store-bought tomatillo salsa

1 large or 2 small avocados, halved, pitted, peeled, and sliced lengthwise

Coarsely chopped fresh cilantro

1 dozen corn tortillas, about 6 inches in diameter, warmed

1 To make the achiote paste, put the annatto seed, oregano, cumin seed, peppercorns, cloves, and cinnamon in a spice grinder and pulverize to a powder. This will take a minute or more because the annatto seed is so hard. Using a chef's knife, mince the garlic to a paste with the salt. Sprinkle the ground spices over the garlic and continue mincing and smashing the mixture with the side of the knife until you have a smooth paste. Transfer to a bowl and stir in the vinegar. You will have about 1/3 cup paste. Set aside 2 tablespoons for the recipe; wrap the remainder in plastic wrap and refrigerate for up to 1 month.

2 Working with 1 pork slice at a time, put the slice between 2 sheets of parchment paper and pound with a meat mallet or rolling pin until it is about 1/8 inch thick. Make sure the meat is uniformly thick so it will cook evenly. Transfer to a tray or platter.

3 To make the marinade, combine all the ingredients in a small bowl and stir to blend. Spread the marinade over the meat, coating both sides evenly. Cover with plastic wrap. Alternatively, you can put the pork and its marinade in a 1-gallon heavy-duty resealable food storage bag. Refrigerate for at least 2 hours or up to 12 hours. Bring to room temperature before grilling.

4 Prepare a very hot charcoal fire or preheat a gas grill to high (450° to 500°F).

5 Season the pork on both sides with salt. Grill directly over the coals or gas flame, turning once, until the meat is no longer pink but still juicy, about 1½ minutes per side. Transfer to a cutting board and chop coarsely. Serve immediately with the pickled onions, salsa, avocado, cilantro, and tortillas.

Spicy Pork, Focaccia, and Sweet Pepper Kebabs

Serves 6

Any type of sweet pepper works in this recipe, from meaty bells and pimientos to elongated frying peppers, like Corno di Toro and Gypsy. The thin-walled frying peppers are an especially good choice because they cook through in about the same time as the pork. Bell peppers, with their thick walls, remain a little firmer when the pork is done, but they are still tasty. Brining the lean pork tenderloin helps to keep it moist.

INGREDIENTS

BRINE

1 quart lukewarm water
2½ tablespoons kosher or sea salt
6 thyme sprigs
2 large cloves garlic, sliced

1 pork tenderloin, 1 pound

YOGURT SAUCE

1½ cups plain yogurt, preferably whole milk
1 large clove garlic, finely minced
¼ cup finely chopped fresh dill
Kosher or sea salt

1 large red onion
1 large red or gold bell pepper, seeded and cut into 1-inch squares
1 large green bell pepper, seeded and cut into 1-inch squares
¼ cup extra virgin olive oil
3 cloves garlic, thickly sliced
1 tablespoon minced fresh rosemary
½ teaspoon hot red pepper flakes
¾ teaspoon kosher or sea salt
24 cubes focaccia (1-inch cubes)

1. To make the brine, put the lukewarm water and salt in a bowl and stir together until the salt dissolves and the water becomes clear. Add the thyme sprigs and garlic. Cool to room temperature. Put the pork tenderloin in a container that holds it snugly. Add the brine. It should cover the pork. Cover with plastic wrap. Alternatively, you can put the pork and its brine in a 1-gallon heavy-duty resealable food storage bag. Refrigerate for 8 to 12 hours. One hour before cooking, remove the pork from the brine and pat dry. Cut it into 24 roughly uniform chunks.

2. Prepare a moderate charcoal fire for indirect grilling (page xiv) or preheat a gas grill to medium (375°F), leaving one of the burners unlit. To make the yogurt sauce, in a bowl, whisk together the yogurt, garlic, and dill. Season to taste with salt.

3. Halve the onion through the stem end, then cut into roughly 1-inch cubes. Separate the onion layers. In a large bowl, combine the pork, onion, bell peppers, olive oil, garlic, rosemary, hot pepper flakes, and salt. Toss to coat the meat and vegetables with the seasonings. Add the focaccia and toss again.

4. Thread the focaccia, pork, onion, and peppers onto metal or wooden skewers, alternating them attractively and using all the ingredients. Put the skewers over indirect heat. Cover the grill and cook for about 4 minutes, then turn and cook until the pork feels medium-firm to the touch and the vegetables have softened slightly, 3 to 4 minutes longer. If necessary, put the skewers over direct heat for the final couple of minutes to char the ingredients lightly, but watch carefully to avoid burning the focaccia. Serve the kebabs immediately, passing the yogurt sauce separately.

Grilled Sausages with Baby Turnips and Turnip Greens

Serves 4

The best turnips for this preparation are the small white Tokyo turnips, so thin skinned that they don't need to be peeled. The more familiar purple-topped white globe turnips will need peeling unless they are very young.

Ingredients

2 to 2½ pounds turnips (about 10 golf ball–size turnips with greens attached)

¼ cup extra virgin olive oil

1 small dried red chile, broken in half

Kosher or sea salt

2 large cloves garlic, minced

4 fresh sausages (such as hot or sweet Italian), about 6 ounces each

Hot pepper vinegar, homemade (page 124) or store-bought (optional)

1 Prepare a hot charcoal fire or preheat a gas grill to high (450° to 500°F).

2 Cut the turnips away from their greens, leaving no stem attached. Remove the stems from the greens but not the ribs at the center of each leaf. You should have about 1 pound trimmed turnip greens. Peel the turnips if the skin feels thick; otherwise, leave them unpeeled. Cut the turnips in half if they are smaller than a golf ball; quarter them if they are larger.

3 Bring a large pot of salted water to a boil over high heat. Add the turnip greens and boil until they are tender, 3 to 5 minutes, depending on their size and age. Drain in a sieve or colander and immediately run under cold running water until cool. Drain again and squeeze to remove excess moisture. Chop coarsely.

4 Heat the olive oil in a large skillet over moderate heat. Add the turnips and chile, season with salt, and toss to coat with the oil. Cover and reduce the heat to moderately low. Cook until the turnips are lightly browned in spots on the cut sides and almost tender when pierced, about 5 minutes. Add the garlic and cook, uncovered, stirring, for 1 minute to release its fragrance. Add the chopped greens and cook, stirring, until they are hot throughout and coated with oil. Taste and adjust the seasoning. Keep warm while you grill the sausages.

5 Grill the sausages directly over the coals or gas flame, turning often and moving them as necessary to prevent flare-ups. They are done when the internal temperature registers 145° to 150°F on an instant-read thermometer.

6 Put the sausages on a platter and surround them with the greens and turnips, or pass the vegetables separately. Serve immediately. Offer hot pepper vinegar for the greens.

Your Urban Homestead

As an enthusiast of eating locally, you may have fantasized about harvesting your own fruits and vegetables right outside your kitchen door, or perhaps raising chickens for eggs. If so, consider joining the growing movement of urban farmers across the country who are planting gardens in the most unlikely places, including the White House. More than a half century after Victory Gardens helped a nation at war to be more self-sufficient, an estimated 40 million Americans are returning to backyards, balconies, and rooftops to grow their own food.

Whether you plant a kitchen garden, start a worm bin, acquire a laying hen or two, or simply grow herbs on a windowsill, these steps can have a positive impact on your table and your wallet. Use this resource guide to begin your research as you plan your kitchen garden or urban barnyard.

The Kitchen Garden

Like a French *potager,* a small kitchen garden can be both useful and beautiful. In addition to providing herbs that you can snip on a whim and a daily vegetable harvest, a kitchen garden can include edible flowers, cutting flowers, berries, and even fruit trees. If you only have enough space for a few pots on a deck, you can still grow a surprising number of edibles.

If you have never gardened before, start slowly with a few pots of herbs on your windowsill or deck. Identify the sunniest spot in your yard and dig a small vegetable bed, or plant some lettuces or cherry tomatoes in containers. Begin composting your kitchen scraps—trimmings and leftovers—and experience the satisfaction of knowing you are throwing nothing useful away.

The following resources can help you get started with gardening and modern homesteading:

- www.garden.org (National Gardening Association, general interest, resources, and articles)
- www.almanac.com (*The Old Farmer's Almanac,* trusted information on farming and gardening)
- www.motherearthnews.com (organic gardening, modern homesteading, and sustainable farming)
- www.homegrownevolution.com (guide to self-sufficiency and to author's book, *The Urban Homestead*)
- Bradley, Fern Marshall, and Barbara W. Willis, eds. *Rodale's All-New Encyclopedia of Organic Gardening: The Indispensable Resource for Every Gardener.* Emmaus, PA: Rodale, 1993.
- Denckla, Tanya. *The Gardener's A–Z Guide to Growing Organic Food.* rev. ed. North Adams, MA: Storey Publishing, 2004.
- Fowler, Alys. *Garden Anywhere.* San Francisco: Chronicle Books, 2009.

GET HELP, AND GET INVOLVED. If you are not up to the task on your own, you can hire a professional to create and tend your kitchen garden. Or donate your land to a gardener looking for space and receive a basket of fresh vegetables in exchange. These sites will hook you up:

- www.sharingbackyards.com (links people with unused yard space and those looking to grow food)
- www.backyardharvest.org (promotes community gleaning: harvesting produce that would otherwise go to waste and redirecting it to people in need)
- www.portlandfruit.org (organizes locals to harvest urban fruit trees in the Portland, Oregon, area; also offers workshops on fruit-tree care and food preservation)
- www.homegrown.org (discussion board for people interested in connecting to the land and growing their own food)
- www.kitchengardeners.org (international nonprofit group promotes growing your own food for self-sufficiency)
- www.urbangardenshare.org (Seattle program matching experienced gardeners to homeowners with extra garden space)
- www.seattletilth.org (inspires people to grow organic food at home; offers workshops and classes in the Seattle area)
- www.backyardharvest.wordpress.com (Twin Cities organization matching small-scale growers to people with extra garden space)
- www.yourbackyardfarmer.com (Portland, Oregon, organization that plants and maintains customized backyard vegetable gardens)
- www.detroitagriculture.org (provides resources for home gardeners in the Detroit area)
- www.silverlakefarms.com (garden design and cultivation; workshops and classes on urban farming in Los Angeles)
- www.grazetheroof.blogspot.com (San Francisco workshops on beekeeping, rooftop gardening, and other aspects of urban farming)

CREATING YOUR GARDEN

Survey your surroundings with an eye to carving out growing space. Could you tuck a few tomatoes in that strip on the side of the house? Could you build or buy window boxes to grow a few favorite go-to greens? Don't forget the front yard. It's not the conventional location for a vegetable

garden, but many people are ripping up their thirsty front lawns and replacing them with crops they can eat. Recommended for beginners:

- Bartley, Jennifer. *Designing the New Garden: An American Potager Kitchen Handbook.* Portland, OR: Timber Press, Inc., 2006.
- Thompson, Sylvia. *The Kitchen Garden.* New York: Bantam, 1995.
- Smith, Edward C. *The Vegetable Gardener's Bible.* North Adams, MA: Storey Publishing, 2000.

MAKE A PLAN. You will need at least six hours of direct sun to grow vegetables. After you select your location, map out a plan. For container growing, you will need pots in a variety of sizes and depths. Lettuces and fast-growing crops like radishes and arugula are relatively shallow rooted. Plants with larger root systems, such as Swiss chard, need deeper, wider pots. Note that unglazed pots dry out more quickly than glazed containers. Get creative: you can grow edibles in halved wine barrels, stacked old tires, or any container that can hold dirt and provide drainage.

If you don't have a yard, consider planting on your rooftop:

- www.goodgreennyc.com (New York City designer of edible rooftop gardens)
- www.greenroofgrowers.blogspot.com (Chicago resource for rooftop gardeners)
- www.baylocalize.org (San Francisco Bay Area rooftop-gardening resource)

REAP THE REWARDS OF COMPOST. Compost is nature's way of recycling. It transforms biodegradable coffee grounds, tea leaves, eggshells, food trimmings, spent flowers, undyed paper, and yard waste into a crumbly brown soil amendment. To a roughly equal mix of high-carbon "brown" material (such as dried leaves) and high-nitrogen "green" material (such as vegetable peelings), add water, turn frequently, and watch the pile break down into a rich, dark, crumbly humus that is gold for gardeners. Buy self-contained composting bins, make your own, or simply mark off an area in your garden to start a pile. If properly maintained, it won't be smelly. Make sure it is near a water source, and avoid adding meat, dairy products, diseased plants, or anything grown with chemicals.

If you don't have room for a compost pile outdoors, try vermicomposting indoors. This process relies on worms to make compost out of kitchen scraps and paper products, and it's not messy at all. Buy or make a worm bin, line it with moistened bedding such as newspaper, add the worms and some kitchen scraps, and cover with a little soil. The worms eat the scraps and produce their own waste, known as worm castings, a prized soil amendment that is especially good for topping off container plants. For more information:

- www.sonomavalleyworms.com (mail-order red worms)
- www.wormpoop.com (worm composting and materials)
- www.ciwmb.ca.gov/Organics/HomeCompost/#BinPile (composting techniques and composting shopping guide)

USE GOOD SOIL FOR A HEALTHY GARDEN. Before planting, dig in several inches of organic matter, such as compost or aged manure, to improve your soil. For pots and raised beds, use high-quality organic potting soil and amend with compost or worm castings for healthy growth. For organic fertilizer and soil conditioner:

- www.dirtworks.net
- www.harmonyfarm.com
- www.waltsorganic.com

PLANT THE BASICS. Salad greens and herbs are easy to grow. Plant looseleaf lettuces, parsley, and radishes in pots after the last frost for almost instant gratification. Add variety and more challenging plants in successive years. If you must grow tomatoes right off, consider a cherry tomato such as Sun Gold, which grows well in pots. Other edibles that do well in containers include chives, basil, strawberries, and Swiss chard.

For gardening supplies, buy locally or find organic starts online:

- www.groworganic.com (Peaceful Valley Farm & Garden Supply)
- www.homeharvest.com (Home Harvest Garden Supply)

START FROM SEED OR TRANSPLANT. Purchase your starts from a reputable garden center or catalog. For plants with a long growing season, such as tomatoes and peppers, start seeds indoors in early spring and transplant seedlings after the last frost date. Sow beets, beans, cucumbers, lettuces, and nasturtiums directly in the earth when it warms up. Transplant seedlings in the late afternoon so starts have the cool evening hours to adjust. Give plants a good soak after tucking them in.

For seeds:

- www.reneesgarden.com
- www.seedsofchange.com
- www.kitchengardenseeds.com
- www.johnnyseeds.com
- www.fedcoseeds.com
- www.rareseeds.com
- www.wildgardenseed.com

PLANT A FRUIT TREE. If your climate allows, consider planting a lemon tree. The trees grow quickly, do well in pots, and it's pure heaven to pluck a fresh lemon when you need it. For small spaces, look for dwarf varieties. Plant in wine barrels on your deck or in a sunny part of your courtyard. Bush berries, such as blackberries and raspberries, also do well in pots and some can be trained up trellises. For a wealth of information on the planting and care of backyard fruit trees, see www.davewilson.com, the site of Central California's nearly three-quarter-century-old Dave Wilson Nursery.

DON'T FORGET TO WATER. Most vegetables and annual herbs, such as basil and parsley, need regular water. Never let them dry out completely. Perennial herbs, such as thyme and rosemary, prefer to be on the dry side. If growing in pots, you may need to water daily during heat spells; otherwise, container plants may need watering two to three times a week. To eliminate hand watering, install drip irrigation, a water-wise solution for containers and larger gardens. In hot-weather areas, mulching with straw or wood chips can also help retain moisture. See www.earthbox.com to find self-contained gardening systems for small-space gardening.

PUT UP SEASONAL PRODUCE TO ENJOY LATER. Freeze, can, or pickle excess fruits and vegetables, choosing ones that are blemish free and not overly ripe. Read contemporary books on home preserving that offer a new look at an old art. Three easy ways to get started:

1. Arrange berries and other fruits in a single layer on baking sheets and freeze, then drop them into resealable plastic bags and return to the freezer. Pit stone fruits prior to freezing; blanch vegetables briefly before freezing to denature the enzymes that cause flavor loss. Preserve the taste of summer by making a large batch of tomato-basil sauce and freezing it in plastic bags or small containers.

Plant Flowers with Your Produce

Flowers add color and beauty to your kitchen garden and allow for homegrown floral arrangements. They also attract beneficial insects and bees, which do the essential work of pollinating your fruits and vegetables. Choose edible flowers, like cascading nasturtiums, multicolored pansies, and blue borage, and tuck them next to your vegetables. Add their edible petals to salads. Cosmos and sunflowers are easy to grow from seed, thrive almost anywhere, and are bee friendly.

2. To dry herbs, tie up a bundle and hang upside down in a dry, dark room. Or dry in a very low oven for a couple of hours. Remove the stems and store the leaves in airtight containers in a cool, dry cupboard. Make your own herb salt by combining your favorite dried herbs, gently crushed, with sea salt.

3. Making jam is one of the joys of summer and easier than you think. All you need is fruit, sugar, lemon juice, a heavy-bottomed pot, and canning jars. Avoid commercial pectin, which makes jam too stiff, and use the seeds and pith of lemon instead, or combine a low-pectin fruit, such as blackberries, with a fruit naturally loaded with pectin, such as apples.

To learn more about preserving food safely or to find enthusiastic canners near you:

- Hertzberg, Ruth, Beatrice Vaughan, and Janet Greene. *Putting Food By.* Brattleboro, VT: Stephen Greene Press, 1975.
- Kingry, Judi, and Lauren Devine, eds. *Ball Complete Book of Home Preserving.* Toronto: Robert Rose, 2006.
- www.cansacrossamerica.wordpress.com (a nationwide collective of home cooks dedicated to home preserving and sharing resources)

An Urban Barnyard

Around the country, people long to produce more of their own food, including meat, eggs, milk, and honey. If you have the room and the inclination, consider an urban barnyard of chickens, bees, rabbits, or goats.

Chickens are the easiest next step after produce. For fresh eggs with the most deeply colored yolks you have ever seen, add a few laying hens to your yard, something many cities allow. Chickens pair well with gardens, as they like leftover greens, fruit and vegetable scraps, slugs, and insects. Their waste is high in nitrogen and excellent for your compost pile. Children enjoy chickens, too, giving youngsters a connection to their food they'll never forget.

Get a few female chicks to start. They cost anywhere from three to five dollars each, and hatcheries ship them in cardboard boxes. Don't bother with roosters, which are illegal in most neighborhoods and not necessary for eggs anyway. Choose chicks bred for egg production, such as White Leghorns and Golden Comets, or those that make docile and playful pets, such as Australorps, Silkies, Cochins, and Brahmas. Three hens produce an average of two eggs per day, but check the breed for egg production, as some are better layers than others. Eggs come in different colors, depending on the breed. Araucanas and Ameraucanas lay varying shades of blue. For more guidance:

- Damerow, Gail, *Storey's Guide to Raising Chickens: Care/Feeding/Facilities.* North Adams, MA: Storey Publishing, 1995.
- Luttman, Rick, and Gail Luttman. *Chickens in Your Backyard: A Beginner's Guide.* Emmaus, PA: Rodale Books, 1976.
- www.atlantachickenwhisperer.blogspot.com (national radio show about backyard poultry)
- www.urbanchickens.org (promotes backyard chickens in urban residential landscapes)
- www.chickendiapers.com (for indoor chicken raising)
- www.mypetchickens.com/FarmsHatcheries.aspx (farms and hatcheries that sell chickens and chicks)
- www.mccurrayhatchery.com (hatchery selling mail-order chickens, poultry, rabbits, and supplies)

Ready to expand to bees, rabbits, or goats? Check city ordinances to make sure they're allowed in your backyard.

To read:

- Damerow, Gail. *Barnyard in Your Backyard: A Beginner's Guide to Raising Chickens, Ducks, Geese, Rabbits, Goats, Sheep, and Cows.* North Adams, MA: Storey Publishing, 2002.

Bees can be a challenge, but the rewards are sweet. While some major cities allow beekeeping, many urban areas have laws against it because of swarms. Honeybees are not aggressive, however, and most stings come from wasps. There's a movement to overturn these laws so urban farmers can enjoy their honey and pollination. Resources to read:

- www.honeybee.com/beeinfo.htm (information on keeping honeybees)
- www.outdoorplace.org/beekeeping/citybees.htm (setting up for urban beekeeping)
- Flottum, Kim. *The Backyard Beekeeper: An Absolute Beginner's Guide to Keeping Bees in Your Yard and Garden.* Beverly, MA: Quarry Books, 2005.

Rabbits are the easiest live animals to keep for meat. They need a cage, pellet food, fresh produce, and hay for digestion. When their weight reaches about 4½ pounds, rabbits are ready for stews and braises.

- www.wikihow.com/Raise-Rabbits-for-Food (instructions on raising rabbits for food)
- www.thefarm.org/charities/i4at/lib2/rabbits.htm (rabbit breeding, body language, and feed)

Goats are herd animals that enjoy the company of other goats, so purchase at least two. Nigerian Dwarfs are particularly popular. Enjoy their milk, try making cheese and butter, and prepare their meat in stews and curries. See www.goats4h.com, where the California 4-H Club dispenses information.

Before starting any of these projects, make sure you have the time, space, resources, and persistence to succeed. You can count on some unforeseen challenges, but they only make your harvest sweeter.

Tips for Storing Produce

Few fruits and vegetables improve in storage. Most will have the best flavor and texture, and the most nutrition, if used as quickly as possible. (Firm fruits that require some time to soften at room temperature, such as pears, are an obvious exception.) These guidelines call out some of the most perishable produce, but even the more sturdy items, such as beets and rutabagas, don't appreciate a long stay in the fridge.

When you get the produce home, remove any bands or ties. Discard any wilted or yellowing leaves or decaying parts. Do not wash produce until you are ready to use it, unless recommended below.

Most produce (but definitely not all) keeps best in a cold, humid environment. That's the logic behind the refrigerator crisper, a confined space that retains more humidity than the main refrigerator compartment. But moisture also promotes mold and decay, so make sure your vegetables and fruits can "breathe" by piercing the storage bag or leaving it open.

Vegetables

Artichokes: Refrigerate in a sealed plastic bag with a few drops of water to keep them moist.

Asparagus: Refrigerate in an open plastic bag. To rehydrate limp asparagus, trim the ends and stand in an inch of water in a container in the refrigerator for an hour.

Avocados: Leave firm avocados at room temperature until they give to gentle pressure; eat within a day or two. Avoid refrigerating, which compromises their flavor.

Beans (green, haricot vert, romano, yard long, yellow wax): Put in a paper bag inside an open plastic bag, then refrigerate.

Beans (fava): Refrigerate in an open plastic bag but use as quickly as possible.

Beans (cranberry, lima, crowder peas, black-eyed peas, and other fresh shelling types): Shell and cook as soon as possible; they mildew quickly. If necessary, refrigerate shelled beans in a lidded plastic container.

Beets: Remove the greens, if attached. Refrigerate greens and beets separately—greens in a sealed bag, beets in an open bag.

Broccoli: Refrigerate in an open plastic bag.

Broccoli rabe: Refrigerate in an open plastic bag but use within a day or two.

Brussels sprouts: If the sprouts are still on the stalk, loosely wrap the stalk in plastic film and refrigerate. Refrigerate loose sprouts in an open plastic bag.

Cabbage: Refrigerate in an open plastic bag.

Carrots: Remove greens, if attached; they pull moisture from the carrots. Refrigerate in a sealed plastic bag.

Cauliflower: Refrigerate in an open plastic bag, but use quickly for best flavor.

Celery root: Wrap in a damp paper towel and refrigerate in the vegetable crisper.

Corn: Refrigerate, still in the husk, in an open plastic bag; cook as soon as possible.

Cucumbers: Dampness promotes decay. Store in a lidded plastic container with a paper towel on the bottom and top.

Eggplants: If using within a day or two, store at cool room temperature; otherwise, refrigerate in an open plastic bag.

Fennel: Refrigerate in an open plastic bag with stalks attached.

Garlic: Store in a basket or paper bag in a cool, dark, dry place, away from the heat of the stove.

Greens for cooking (chard, collards, kale, mustard greens, turnip greens): Refrigerate in a sealed plastic bag, preferably a heavy-duty storage bag. Or protect from drying with two plastic bags, one covering the stems and another covering the leafy tops.

Greens for salad (arugula, baby greens, escarole, leaf lettuces): Wash and dry thoroughly in a salad spinner. Spread the leaves on a length of paper toweling. Roll loosely, place the roll inside an open plastic bag, and refrigerate.

Herbs: For tender herbs, such as basil, chervil, cilantro, dill, mint, and tarragon, snip the ends and place in water, like a bouquet of flowers, changing the water daily. Keep basil and tarragon at room temperature. For other tender herbs, invert a plastic bag over the leafy tops and refrigerate.

For woodier herbs, such as marjoram, oregano, rosemary, sage, and thyme, refrigerate in a paper bag.

Jerusalem artichokes: Refrigerate in a sealed plastic bag.

Kohlrabi: Remove leaves, if attached, and refrigerate bulbs in an open plastic bag.

Leeks: Refrigerate in an open plastic bag.

Okra: Refrigerate in a paper bag but use quickly; okra does not store well.

Onions, shallots, spring onions, and green onions: Put onions and shallots in a mesh bag and hang in a cool, dry place with good air circulation. Store spring onions and green onions in an open plastic bag in the refrigerator crisper.

Parsnips: Refrigerate in an open plastic bag.

Peas (English, snow, sugar snap): Refrigerate in an open plastic bag but cook as soon as possible.

Peppers, sweet and hot: Refrigerate in an open plastic bag.

Potatoes: Store in a paper bag in a cool, dark, well-ventilated place. Use new potatoes quickly.

Radicchio: Refrigerate in an open plastic bag.

Radishes: Remove all or most of the leaves, which draw moisture from the radishes. If you want to leave some greens on for display, be sure to remove any decaying ones. Refrigerate the roots in an open plastic bag. Crisp in ice water for an hour or two before serving.

Rutabagas: Store in a cool, dark, humid place such as a cellar. Alternatively, refrigerate in an open plastic bag.

Spinach: Refrigerate in a sealed plastic bag and use quickly.

Squash blossoms: Use the day of purchase, if possible. If you must store them, arrange them in a single layer in a paper towel–lined plastic container, cover, and refrigerate.

Squashes, summer types: Refrigerate in an open plastic bag.

Squashes, winter types: Store whole squashes in a cool, dark, well-ventilated place, preferably at 50° to 55°F. Refrigerate cut portions in a sealed plastic bag.

Sweet potatoes: Store in a cool, dark, well-ventilated place; do not refrigerate.

Tomatillos: Store in a paper bag in the refrigerator.

Tomatoes: Store at cool room temperate; never refrigerate.

Turnips: Remove greens, if attached. Refrigerate greens in a sealed plastic bag and roots in an open plastic bag.

FRUITS

Most fruits taste best at room temperature. If you do refrigerate them to slow their ripening, bring them to room temperature before eating.

Apples: Keep apples you will eat within a few days at room temperature. Refrigerate in an open plastic bag for longer keeping.

Asian pears: Refrigerate in an open plastic bag.

Apricots: Keep at room temperature until they soften slightly. If fully ripe, refrigerate in an open plastic bag if you don't plan to eat them within a day or two.

Berries: Avoid storing berries; try to buy just what you need. Keep dry to prevent decay. To refrigerate, arrange in a single layer on a paper towel in a lidded container.

Cherries: Refrigerate in an open plastic bag.

Citrus: Store in a cool place, such as a cellar, or refrigerate loose in the crisper.

Figs: Keep figs you expect to eat within a couple of days at cool room temperature. Refrigerate the remainder in a paper bag, or arrange in a single layer on a paper towel in a lidded container.

Grapes: Refrigerate in an open plastic bag.

Melons: If melons feel a little too firm to eat, leave at room temperature until they give slightly at the stem end, then refrigerate loose in the crisper.

Peaches and nectarines: Keep peaches and nectarines you expect to eat within the next two to three days at cool room temperature. Refrigerate the remainder in an open plastic bag, but bring to room temperature before eating, allowing an extra day or two for fruits that are still firm to soften.

Pears: Store firm pears at room temperature until they give to gentle pressure near the stem. Then use immediately or refrigerate in an open plastic bag for a day or two.

Persimmons: Store Hachiya persimmons at room temperature until they are as soft as jelly, then refrigerate on a plate or tray. Keep firm Fuyu persimmons at room temperature, or refrigerate in an open plastic bag to prevent further softening.

Plums: If too firm to eat, leave plums at room temperature until they soften slightly, then refrigerate in an open plastic bag.

Pomegranates: Keep at room temperature, or refrigerate in an open plastic bag if you prefer them chilled.

Rhubarb: Refrigerate in an open plastic bag.

The Farms

Amy's Garden
13630 Sandy Point Road
Charles City, VA 23030
Phone: 804-829-5655
www.amysorganicgardenVA.com

Dancing Roots Farm
29820 East Woodard Road
Troutdale, OR 97060
Phone: 503-695-3445
www.dancingrootsfarm.com

DeLaney Community Farm
170 South Chambers Road
Aurora, CO 80017
Phone: 303-292-9900
www.dug.org

Full Belly Farm
P.O. Box 251
Guinda, CA 95637
Phone: 530-796-2214
www.fullbellyfarm.com

Genesis Growers
8373 East 3000 S Road
St. Anne, IL 60964
Phone: 815-953-1512
www.genesis-growers.com

Green Gate Farms
8310 Canoga Avenue
Austin, TX 78724
Phone: 512-949-9831
www.greengatefarms.net

Golden Earthworm Organic Farm
652 Peconic Bay Boulevard
Jamesport, NY 11947
Phone: 631-722-3302
www.goldenearthworm.com

Morning Song Farm
2120 Rainbow Glen Road
Rainbow, CA 92028
Phone: 949-310-4870
www.morningsongfarm.com

Nitty Gritty Dirt Farm
10386 Sunrise Road
Harris MN 55032
Phone: 651-226-1186
www.nittygrittydirtfarm.blogspot.com

Red Fire Farm
7 Carver Street
Granby, MA 01033
Phone: 413-467-7645
www.redfirefarm.com

ACKNOWLEDGMENTS

I would like to gratefully acknowledge the hospitality of all the farmers who welcomed us onto their farms and into their homes at the busiest time of their year. For sharing their stories, dreams, and farming expertise, sincere thanks to Donna Buono of Morning Song Farm; Erin Flynn and Skip Connett of Green Gate Farms; Vicki Westerhoff of Genesis Growers; Shari Sirkin and Bryan Dickerson of Dancing Roots Farm; Robin Raudabaugh and Gigi Nauer of Nitty Gritty Dirt Farm; Judith Redmond, Dru Rivers, Paul Muller, and Andrew Brait of Full Belly Farm; Michael Buchenau, Heather DeLong, Abbie Harris, and Deb Schaffer of DeLaney Community Farm; Amy Hicks and George Ferguson of Amy's Garden; Ryan Voiland and Sarah Ingraham of Red Fire Farm; and Maggie Wood, Matthew Kurek, and James Russo of Golden Earthworm Farm.

For help with recipe testing, I am deeply indebted to Claudia Sansone. A more willing and helpful assistant I could not have imagined. Thanks also to chefs Annie Baker and Sally Gordon and to food writer John Carroll for recipe contributions and advice.

For producing such a beautiful book, I am grateful to the talented design team: photographer Sara Remington, who managed to capture the soul of each farm; food stylist Kim Kissing; prop stylist Kerrie Sherrell Walsh; and designer Jenny Barry.

My thanks to Sharon Silva for her expert copyediting; to Jean Lucas and Kirsty Melville of Andrews McMeel for making this book such an enjoyable collaboration; and to Doralece Dullaghan and Sur La Table for inviting me to participate in this rewarding adventure. Finally, I am indebted to my agent, Carole Bidnick, for her dependably wise counsel, and to my husband, Doug Fletcher, for cheerfully going along for the ride.

—Janet Fletcher

Having the opportunity to have the ten farmers profiled in this book share part of their life with us was a privilege and an inspiration and reinforces the importance of the sacrifice that these passionate and hardworking folks are making to each one of us every day. Their contribution in giving us delicious, healthy food grown in a sustainable manner is a treasure. It's clear that the major compensation for their toil is the joy they receive from producing amazing products. Sur La Table cannot thank enough Gigi, Robin, Skip, Erin, Ryan, Sarah, Amy, George, Maggie, Matt, James, Heather, Deb, Michael, Abbie, Donna, Dru, Paul, Andrew, Judith, Vicki, Shari, and Bryan for sharing their stories and farms with us. Thanks to Guillermo Payet and Erin Barnett from LocalHarvest.org for connecting us to the farmers.

We are honored to have Alice Waters set the tone for the book in the foreword. She consistently serves as an inspiration through her steadfast support of the locavore movement not just through her words but her deeds.

There was no better writer to bring this story to life and create the recipes inspired by the farmers than Janet Fletcher. Her award-winning credentials speak for themselves and her knowledge of the subject is unquestioned. Sara Remington's impeccable eye for catching people and produce at the right moment creates a synergy with Janet's words that leaves you awestruck. Kim Kissling, Sarah Fairhurst, Kerrie Walsh, Lori Ehlers, and Stacy Ventura were a well-oiled machine working with Sara to make every shot jump off the page. Jenny Barry brought it all together into an amazing package with the dedicated team of Jean Lucas and Kirsty Melville from Andrews McMeel. Thanks also to Sharon Silva for her skillful job of copyediting, Janis Donnaud for being there when we needed help, and the folks at Haberman for telling the story from coast to coast.

The team at Sur La Table: Jacob Maurer, Linda Nangle, Kimberley McBain, Sarah Chadwick, Robb Ginter, Jason King, Kate Dering, Nathan Slusser, Dave Bauer and Morgan McQuade were invaluable. We especially want to thank Deb Pankrat, Audrey Borreani and the staff at the Berkeley store and the Weber-Stephen Products Company for providing the grill to test the grilling recipes.

To Doug Fletcher and Bill Dullaghan for good cheer along the way and to Dianne Jacob for her research for Your Urban Homestead.

Together these folks planted and nurtured the seeds that have grown into this fresh and inspiring book. We hope it encourages you daily to delight in the flavors of *Eating Local*.

—Sur La Table

Recipe Index by Category

Index